Introspection

Introspection

Exploring the Racialized Politics and Conception of Ideal-Blackness Within African American Culture

CORY J. MAY

PICKWICK *Publications* • Eugene, Oregon

INTROSPECTION
Exploring the Racialized Politics and Conception of Ideal-Blackness Within African American Culture

Pickwick Publications
An Imprint of Wipf and Stock Publishers
199 W. 8th Ave., Suite 3
Eugene, OR 97401

www.wipfandstock.com

PAPERBACK ISBN: 979-8-3852-5536-8
HARDCOVER ISBN: 979-8-3852-5537-5
EBOOK ISBN: 979-8-3852-5538-2

Cataloguing-in-Publication data:

Names: May, Cory J., author.

Title: Introspection : exploring the racialized politics and conception of ideal-blackness within African American culture / Cory J. May.

Description: Eugene, OR : Pickwick Publications, 2026 | Includes bibliographical references.

Identifiers: ISBN 979-8-3852-5536-8 (paperback) | ISBN 979-8-3852-5537-5 (hardcover) | ISBN 979-8-3852-5538-2 (ebook)

Subjects: LCSH: African Americans—Intellectual life. | African Americans—Race identity. | Black people—Intellectual life | Racism—Religious aspects—Christianity. | Black theology.

Classification: BT734.2 .M29 2026 (paperback) | BT734.2 (ebook)

VERSION NUMBER 04/27/26

I am inspired by various African Americans throughout
our history who sacrificed themselves to acquire knowledge
and truth, bettering themselves and those around them.

Contents

Preface | ix

Introduction: The Spirit of Inquiry and the Spirit of Truth | 1

1 The Taint of Racialized Nationalism: And the Need for Genuine Spiritual Awe | 21

2 A Conservative Evangelical Critique: Black Power and the Theology of James Cone | 56

3 The Afrocentric-Liberationist School of Black Religiosity | 95

4 Racialized Politics Within African American Colonial Literature | 121

5 The Politics Within Politics: The Ambiguity of Racialized Politics and Relations | 150

6 The Fragmentation of Colonial Whiteness: Antislavery Reform and Antislavery Christianity During the Seventeenth Century | 180

7 The Fragmentation of Colonial Whiteness: Antislavery Reform and Antislavery Christianity During the Seventeenth Century, Part 2 | 205

Conclusion: Continual Introspection and a Precursor to the Gospel According to Jupiter Hammon | 227

Bibliography | 233

Preface

As iron sharpens iron, so one person sharpens another.

PROVERBS 27:17

MOST OF THE RESEARCH in this discourse is revisions of my doctoral dissertation. I encourage you to view this project as the reasoning and motivation that grounded my first book, *An Introduction to Colonial African American Evangelical Christianity: Colonial Identities, Sense of Belonging, and Shared Space*. Looking back, I felt it was more important to first present my interpretations of key influential colonial African American evangelical Christians than to display my critique of contemporary African American studies. It is here you will see the details of why I believe we, as African Americans, in a general sense, have been symbolically self-imprisoned by hyper-fixations of race, Whiteness, constructs of an Ideal-Blackness, and complementary conceptions of liberation.

The research in this book and the material excluded have shaped my emphasis on principles of dehumanization, hyper-politicizations, racialized binary reasoning, racialized nationalism, and how they all relate to principles of deception. I'm convinced our fascination, if not obsession, with these elements has distorted our sense of Christian faith, theology, and spirituality. By no means am I saying we should stop discussing these issues and realities. I am merely questioning the extent of our discussions and how they affect our identities, our sense of belonging, and how we share space with the human-Other. For Christians, I am questioning who and what defines our existence, religious faith, and spirituality in this world: Christ or our Blackness vis-à-vis race?

My aim is not to attack or discredit any of the scholars I discuss and disagree with throughout this project. I only aim to engage them in the spirit of inquiry and the Spirit of Truth. We, as African Americans, must have more open engagement with one another, unafraid to publicly express our disagreements, so we can invite more people to participate through our research. I have felt for years that African American scholarship has enshrined itself in ways that represent regression, not progress. For example, we have ignored important historical figures and events, simply because they don't fit our current racialized sociopolitical agenda. This results in symbolically dehumanizing the person or community we reject, and surprisingly sometimes those we openly elevate, by focusing on racialized sociopolitical issues, not the person for who they truly were. We reinterpret and reimagine them into someone different, exerting a form of symbolic control over their identities that we would never want someone exhibiting over us. Yet, I do mean this in the general sense, as there are African American scholars who bless us with impressive scholarship, excellent work that informs and challenges people worldwide.

Introduction

The Spirit of Inquiry and the Spirit of Truth

Jesus answered, "I am the way and the truth and the life. No one comes to the Father except through me."

John 14:6

Instead, speaking the truth in love, we will grow to become in every respect the mature body of Him who is the head, that is, Christ.

Ephesians 4:15

HUMANIZING TRUTH AND DEHUMANIZING UNTRUTH

Truth will always transform the human-Self in ways untruth cannot, especially within the realities of positive affirmation, psychological stability, and spiritual emancipation. To think otherwise is simply an expression of either an unacknowledged submission to untruth or an acknowledged endorsement of a concealed lie. The former is a case of untruth accomplishing its goal, to deceive the human-Self in ways it's oblivious to its bondage. The latter is representative of the human-Self deceived into thinking it's free, and again, assuming a level of authority it truly doesn't have. Loyalty to untruth, whether we acknowledge or are oblivious to it, is never greater than the existential state of the human-Self who sincerely desires the Truth. We have a moral and divine responsibility to seek the truth, as it assists in shaping us and how we engage the sociopolitical and religiocultural worlds. Furthermore, we must assess how our spirituality is deeply influenced by the knowledge we receive, whether it's factual or not.

We should always question and scrutinize everything in life and life itself as we earnestly seek truth, regardless of one's racial, religious, and sociopolitical allegiance. This becomes a simple principle for some, and maybe an unwarranted action for others who are overwhelmed with reality and thrust themselves into escapism. I'm not advocating the forms of questioning presented through Western anti-religious skepticism or its Christian hyper-fundamentalist counterpart. Rather, it is the forms of questioning that scrutinize the motives of the human-Self and human-Other, when it comes to how we relate to one another through the realms of *self-sacrifice* and *self-emptying*, *justice* and *love*, and *politics* and *spirituality*, all of which are grounded within truth. As Christians, all of these elements are grounded with Christ, not our Blackness or conceptions of American nationalism.

In this discussion, I'm emphasizing the construction and implementation of transformative secular and religiopolitical beliefs, both inside and outside the church and academy. Transformative beliefs as radical ideologies and dogmas naturally derive from our perception and concrete understanding of the past and present. These radical ideologies and dogmas can dramatically change the way we see the world and choose to exist in it, relating to the human-Other. When we abide by truth and seek to be its embodiment, we not only remain humane but are taken on a journey, not in isolation, but in a community with others who are becoming better than who they currently are. Truth brings us to proper intellectualism and genuine spirituality. Counter to this are those who are dehumanized by the distortions of untruth. What develops isn't progress but regression.

The human-Self becomes a caricature or a mannequin that bears semblance to its once healthy state, but never to those who embody truth. In this discussion, a *caricature* is an exaggerated mimicking by an internally fragmented person who is increasingly losing a healthy sense of oneself, or has already completely lost it. The acting itself is to primarily convince oneself of one's supposed stability, in part through a convincing portrayal of authenticity and normality to the human-Other. A *mannequin* is someone who is empathetically devoid, or emotionally empty within their spirit, and psychologically detached from the human-Other. These theories are applicable to race—examples being Black caricatures and Black mannequins. Civil Rights legend Martin Luther King

Jr. (1929–68) provides a view which I believe partially represents what I'm discussing:

> The hardhearted person never truly loves. He engages in a crass utilitarianism that values other people mainly according to their usefulness to him. He never experiences the beauty of friendship, because he is too cold to feel affection for another and is too self-centered to share another's joy and sorrow. He is an isolated island. No outpouring of love links him with the mainland of humanity.
>
> The hardhearted person lacks the capacity for genuine compassion. He is unmoved by the pains and afflictions of his brothers. He passes unfortunate men every day, but he never really sees them. He gives dollars to a worthwhile charity, but he gives not to his spirit.
>
> The hardhearted individual never sees people as people, but rather as mere objects or as impersonal cogs in an ever-turning wheel. In the vast wheel of industry, he sees men as hands. In the massive wheel of big city life, he sees men as digits in a multitude. In the deadly wheel of army life, he sees men as numbers in a regiment. He depersonalizes life.[1]

Truth humanizes us, brings us to healthier states of self-awareness, ethical/moral astuteness, and increasing intelligence, and strengthens our faith in YHWH.[2] Regarding race, I assert there isn't any genuine Black solidarity and healthy Black consciousness in and through untruth and romanticism from reimagining our history and present identities. Likewise, within Christianity, we cannot have a healthy relationship with YHWH nor an accurate understanding of him through heresies. King describes an individual who is apathetic and indifferent to the human-Other. They gradually relinquish aspects of their humanity through detaching themselves from the human-Other, and in some cases oppress them. I refer to this as self-dehumanization through the dehumanization of the human-Other. Now, imagine these types of individuals occupying positions of authority within the academic, sociopolitical, and religious institutions of our communities.

In today's context, it's obvious the enemy, if we can label some as such, is not only outside our communities, but also within them. It is relational. I

1. King, *Strength to Love*, 6.

2. I will employ the name YHWH (Yahweh) for God throughout this project. I have grown dissatisfied with the generic term that various people apply to any conception of a higher power. My emphasis is solely on God as Trinity within Judaic Christianity.

use the term *enemy* in a broad and loose sense, and the term *within* with a double-meaning. The enemy represents those individuals within our communities, as well as our inner selves in their divided nature, for we can sometimes fight against ourselves within the depths of our souls and consciousness. We can interpret an enemy as one who intentionally and unintentionally positions themselves against another. Again, this is relational. For example, historically, within the colonial conception of race, Whiteness was positioned as an antithesis to Blackness. They both had binary oppositional identities within the secular and pseudo-Christian world. This is relational, not individualistic—individualistic in the sense that someone mistakenly believes they can construct their identity completely independent of others. Only YHWH can do this.

The Jamaican sociopolitical activist Marcus Garvey (1887–1940) consistently focused on similar concepts related to racial solidarity and betrayal. In one particular writing, *Lack of Co-Operation in the Negro Race*, he states,

> It is so hard, so difficult to find men who will stick to a purpose, who will maintain a principle for the worth of that principle, for the good of that purpose, and if there is a race that needs such men in the world today, God almighty knows it is the race of which I am a member.
>
> The greatest stumbling block in the way of progress in the race has invariably come from within the race itself. The monkey wrench of destruction as thrown into the cog of Negro Progress, is not thrown so much by the outsider as by the very fellow who is in our fold, and who should be the first to grease the wheel of progress rather than seeking to impede it.
>
> But notwithstanding the lack of sympathetic co-operation, I have one consolation—That I cannot get away from the race, and so long as I am in the race and since I have sense and judgment enough to know what affects the race affects me, it is my duty to help the race to clear itself of those things that affect us in common.[3]

Garvey emphasized that there was always a need for morally grounded and dependable leaders. Yet, in his honesty, he tended to discuss the lack of qualified people to be true Black leaders. This also extended to Black society, in the sense that it appeared most Black people weren't committed to achieving true emancipation. I want us to reflect on

3. Garvey, *Philosophy and Opinions*, 49.

those within our community who pose as the faithful and self-sacrificial. They don't believe in the community, nor its belief systems. They are only there for their own self-interest, which is antithetical to the interests of the community. Thus, their presence and activity always represent cloaked regression, not visible progression. For Christians, this view is familiar, as it is reflected in the New Testament. For example, the apostle Paul in Rom 16:17–18 states, "I appeal to you, brothers, to watch out for those who cause divisions and create obstacles contrary to the doctrine that you have been taught; avoid them. For such persons do not serve our Lord Christ, but their own appetites, and by smooth talk and flattery they deceive the hearts of the naïve."

Many African Americans would assert that our racial identities are still being positioned as the antithesis of one another, especially within contemporary American socio-politics. Yet, for some evangelical African American Christians, this binary oppositional identity is not present within Christ and genuine Christianity. Yet, in returning to a previous point, there are questions that I cannot escape from, as they may seem simplistic on the surface, but may uncover issues we haven't previously examined enough: Has our fascination, if not obsession, with race, blinded us to the true Black enemies within our communities who, at least visually, appear to be united with us? Has the desire to reimagine themselves into a Black existence that does not, nor will ever, exist completely distorted the efforts of these particular African Americans? Does this also affect how we construct and teach African American (Black) studies to the world?

The obvious answer for some people is a resounding *yes*. Since colonialism, there have always been people who violated the reality and perception of racial solidarity by betraying one's trust. This has occurred within both colonial Anglo and African American societies. During colonialism, it was principally a matter of life or death, as many slave rebellions and individual attempts of escaping for freedom were stopped by a Black betrayer. I often wonder how many African Americans were manipulated unknowingly into betraying their comrades. Likewise, there were Anglo-Americans who violated the principles of White supremacy by aligning themselves with Africans and Indians. These thoughts and questions persist as I reflect on America's current landscape. I find myself scrutinizing American conceptions of freedom, equality, and equity as we are subject to their increase today, compared to that of colonial America and the Civil Rights movement. We can also include the academy relating to African American (Black) studies and the dominant scholarship presented. With these increases come more racial dialogue and literature. Yet is this from our doing as African Americans? Or is it partially from those we deem the enemy, White society? Is there a hidden darker agenda undergirding the sustaining of *divisive* American racial discourse, particularly in its cloaked obsessive forms?

I'm referring to an aspect of White society from the standpoint of people and institutions who provide various liberties to certain African Americans and withhold those same liberties from other African Americans. Again, I'm not speaking about the entirety of White society. I'm only questioning how we are often forced to think in oppositional relationships: Black vs. White, Democrat vs. Republican, etc. Connected to this is, for me at least, the reality that our enemies are sometimes those we don't deem as such. In this vein of thought, suppose the liberties provided to specific African Americans was in the intent to cause further fragmentation and instability within Blackness, not to help enlighten and transform American society, through true equality and reconciliation. For example, a White institution may graft African Americans within its structure, who are either so conservative or timid that they do not discuss racial or culturally specific things that truly matter to African Americans. Instead, they embrace *tokenism* in the name of racial enlightenment, intellectualism, or gospel universality, as they too conceal their distorted agendas and consciousness. I view this as simple racial collusion.

Martin Luther King Jr. provides more insight into corrupted African American leadership. King describes someone who undergoes a process of manipulation and assimilation to Whiteness that coincides with relinquishing all healthy attachments to their Black communities. The frightening aspect is there are some assimilated African Americans who are oblivious to what is occurring to them, because they are clothed in Black garments. They view themselves on the side of righteousness, progress, and YHWH even though they are indifferent to the dehumanization of their *former* people. King explains,

> Negro leaders suffer from this interplay of solidarity and divisiveness, being either exalted excessively or grossly abused. Some of these leaders suffer from an aloofness and absence of faith in their people. The white establishment is skilled in flattering and cultivating emerging leaders. It presses its own image on them and finally, from imitation of manners, dress and style of living, a deeper strain of corruption develops. This kind of Negro leader acquires the white man's contempt for the ordinary

> Negro. He is often more at home with the middle-class white than he is among his own people. His language changes, his location changes, his income changes, and ultimately he changes from the representative of the Negro to the white man into the white man's representative to the Negro. The tragedy is that too often he does not recognize what has happened to him.[4]

It isn't simply the image of Whiteness that is implanted within the Black caricature and Black mannequin. Rather, it's the image of a passive and cloaked form of White supremacy. Nevertheless, a second group of African Americans are so antithetical to Whiteness that one assumes their presence within White structures was their doing, not a consequence of cruelty and manipulation from skewed Anglo-Americans. This becomes a political landmine for a third category of African Americans who seek silo within a hyper-conservative and liberal context, as they may find themselves fighting Whiteness and Blackness. For example, this third category of African Americans will have to deal with being the minority of the minority, as they seek to resolve the disagreements within Blackness, regarding its ideologies and theologies. Yet, they will also need to fight the ignorance and indifference of fragmented Whiteness. What I'm suggesting lies beyond disagreements between Black liberals and Black conservatives. It calls for each group to assess whether there are cloaked Black caricatures and Black mannequins within their community, whose main goal is to satisfy their self-interest. In this context, fulfilling one's self-interest is to feign Black solidarity when Black disunity is more beneficial.

In returning to the issue of tokenism, we must accept that tokens exist in almost every part of life. They are in the sociopolitical and religiocultural worlds. There are different types of tokens, like those of Black caricatures and Black mannequins. They aren't easy to detect, and the ones that are, are unapologetically seeking to obtain their self-interests and assimilate into Whiteness. I'm more concerned with the ambiguous and concealed individuals within our society. Some individuals may have had good intentions, but from circumstances beyond their control are forced to a fork in the road: self-sacrifice for the betterment of oneself and the community or satisfy their self-interest at the expense of the community's needs. Another group of tokens don't see themselves as such. They truly believe they are on the side of Black solidarity and liberation. Yet, they are puppeteered according to the needs of those who are socio-politically

4. King, *Testament of Hope*, 307.

powerful and desire racial disunity. Again, King provides further insight into this issue, regarding his experiences during the Civil Rights movement. He states,

> Those who argue in favor of tokenism point out that we must begin somewhere; that it is unwise to spurn any breakthrough, no matter how limited. This position has a certain validity, and the Negro freedom movement has more often than not attained broad victories which had small beginnings. There is a critical distinction, however, between a modest start and tokenism. The tokenism Negroes condemn is recognizable because it is an end in itself. Its purpose is not to begin a process, but instead to end the process of protest and pressure. It is a hypocritical gesture, not a constructive first step.[5]

King brings us to an important observation. One that can only be received through a heightened self-awareness, and desire for the truth. Tokenism is an end of itself, in the minds of those with a fragmented White and Black consciousness. The ignorant and naïve will view tokens as the representatives of "equality in opportunity, but inferior in capability." At least in a general sense, as there will always be the perception of the 1 percent of Blacks who rise above their people, demonstrating some level of adequate competitiveness with White society.

WHITE TOKENS, CARICATURES, AND MANNEQUINS

Conceptions of White tokenism, caricature, and mannequins differ from those within Blackness. Sociopolitical positioning and power determine the differences. There is a disturbing sense of loyalty, the relinquishing of the human will, that White supremacists typically demonstrate. Loyalty is always to a skewed cause, a sense of purpose, a duty to preserve the existence and power of Whiteness. Eurocentric patriotic White nationalist Christianity is another beneficiary and conduit for White loyalty. Consequently, this coincides with the compulsion and impulse to subdue the non-White existence through interrogation and physical restraint, when they deem it necessary.

> When that tape comes out tomorrow; it's going to be horrific,
> but I want each and every one of you to protest in peace.
> I don't want us burning up our cities, tearing up the streets,

5. King, *Why We Can't Wait*, 23.

> because that's not what my son stood for.
> If you guys are here for me and Tyre,
> then, you will protest peacefully.[6]

These were the words spoken by Mrs. RowVaughn Wells, the grieving mother of Mr. Tyre Nichols, at an evening vigil in his name. On January 7, 2023, five Black police officers viciously assaulted the twenty-nine year old Mr. Nichols, an innocent Black man, within a middle-class neighborhood in Memphis, Tennessee. He eventually died three days later from this brutal attack. A police officer's body camera and an aerial recording captured this demonic event. The barbaric nature of how these Black police officers beat Mr. Nichols was beyond savagery, usurping the tragic events of Mr. Rodney Glen King's beating by White Los Angeles police officers on March 3, 1991. Mr. Nichols's beating was gruesome to the extent that his head dramatically contorted in various ways from the severe blows from a police officer who repeatedly hit him in the face. At another point, an officer runs toward Mr. Nichols and the group of police officers who were assaulting him. However, rather than stopping the irrational violence, without hesitation, he fiercely kicked Mr. Nichols, gingerly walking off after the act. Mr. Nichols spent some of his last minutes alive in excruciating pain, pleading for his mother as police officers and a paramedic denied him medical attention.

The death of Mr. Nichols and his mother's words strike at the heart of America's *obsession* with and enslavement to conceptions of race, racism, White supremacy, Black pride, and the forms of exaggerated identity politics within our contemporary context. Mrs. Wells demonstrates sound reasoning, grounded ethics, discernment, and responsibility by requesting that all protesting in the name of justice for Mr. Nichols, and her desire to aid this process, be accomplished through *peace*. Justice and peace are seamlessly intertwined and cannot be separated. I argue that connected to these two principles are forgiveness, redemption, and reconciliation.

Another tragic element of Mr. Nichols's story is the lack of genuine and righteous Black outrage from five Black police officers killing him. I employ the word *lack* by comparing the general reaction from Black America toward Mr. Nichols's death to other Black women, children, and

6. Norman, "Tyre Nichols' Mother Urges Peaceful Protest"; Finton, "3 Memphis Fire Department Personnel"; Heyward, "Mostly Peaceful Protest"; Rojas and Jaglois, "Five Officers Charged"; Sainz, "5 Memphis Police Officers."

men who died from the actions of White police officers.[7] I emphasize the words *genuine* and *righteous* to indicate the relatively pure motives of individuals, groups, and organizations who truly seek justice, healing, redemption, and reconciliation from this tragedy. Nevertheless, a reasonable and morally grounded mind will inevitably confront a series of questions: Where were the thousands upon thousands of hyper-liberal Black identity politics protestors expressing their anger about this tragedy and calling for justice? How many Black Lives Matter representatives protested nationwide, urging police reform, and confronting the atrocity created by five *Black* police officers?[8] How do members of the LGBTQIA+ community feel about this tragedy? Has the lack of sexual and gender discourse minimized the outcry from its universal community?[9]

Again, my focus is on the *limited* involvement of the most vocal individuals and groups in our current sociopolitical and religious protest era. The absence of a *heightened* demonstration of Black outrage against these Black Memphis police officers senselessly killing an innocent Black man demonstrates the lack of morality, justice, and commitment to Christ, not only within the Black community but within America.

On a deeper level, this tragedy demonstrates the degree to which some African Americans have lapsed from our conservative evangelical tradition of gospel-centered social justice and practical notions of Western American democracy.[10] In its stead has developed a superficial *theatrical façade* of Black protest and solidarity, concerned solely with presenting the imagery of an assertive, militant, and romanticized form of Blackness. I also must mention the rise of *racially enlightened* Anglo-Americans who take a timid or passive role to those representatives of hyper-liberal Black protest. Connected to these deceiving visible expressions is the concealment of a utopian sociopolitical secularized representation of the kingdom of God, cloaking the inner desire of its inhabitants to acquire wealth and power.

7. Iati et al., "Nearly 250 Women"; Ater, "In Memoriam: I Can't Breathe."

8. Goodman and Sherman, "Memphis BLM Activist."

9. Aceto and Tracy, "LGBTQ Activists Protest Police Killing."

10. There are typically two dominant Christian sociopolitical traditions within colonial America: conservative evangelicalism and classical/moderate-liberal nationalism. The former is represented by Mrs. Zilpha Elaw (1790–1873), Mrs. Julia A. J. Foote (1823–1900), and Mrs. Jarena Lee (1783–1864). The latter is representative of Henry Highland Garnet (1815–82), Prince Hall (1783–1897), and Gabriel Prosser (1775–1800). See W. Andrews, *Sisters of the Spirit*; Garnet, *Address to the Slaves*; Garnet, *Memorial Discourse*; and Moses, *Classical Black Nationalism*; Moses, *Golden Age*.

As it should be, we have become accustomed to moments of sharp sensitivity and a heightened moral outrage against White police officers killing innocent Black people. The heightened awareness is complemented by an equally harsh critique of White societal complicity to these events, representing White societal silence regarding the guiltiness of *some* White police officers. Yet, with tragic irony, perhaps those silent Black people within the context of Mr. Nichols's death can now empathize with their White counterparts who stand silently when White authority figures oppress and kill innocent Black people. For example, Black societal silence is present in the context of Black-on-Black gang violence. Silence amid awareness of injustice is a sign of self-contradiction and hypocrisy. In this context, a secular moral societal sin expresses itself within the scriptural context of Jas 4:17, "So for one who knows the right thing to do and does not do it, for him it is sin."

Some Anglo-Americans are not innocent observers in Mr. Nichols's story. We witness some people, albeit slightly, intentionally distorting this event within conservative mainstream media. They indirectly ridicule and dehumanize the Black community through Mr. Nichols's death to the extent of using Black conservative political representatives. These individuals employ a conservative form of Blackness, as tokens, caricatures, and mannequins against their liberal counterpart in the guise of color blindness and moral aptitude. For example, Jason Whitlock, a sports analyst and Fox News commentator, is a conservative African American who blamed the death of Mr. Nichols on single-parent African American women. Whitlock stated that African American men raised solely by their mothers embody a rebelliousness toward authority, and this rebelliousness is connected to Mr. Nichols's death.[11]

Additionally, comical irony did not evade former Fox News analyst Tucker Carlson. He rightly and with eerie calculation discusses the immorality and irrationality of Mr. Nichols's death. Carlson also demonstrated faith in the justice system to punish the former police officers. However, things quickly lapsed into America's predictable us versus them political rhetoric. He applauds Mrs. Wells for calling for peaceful protest but shifts most of his attention to the irrational rhetoric and actions of Antifa. Carlson warns about left-wing propaganda creating unnecessary negative attention to the tragedy that could incite riots and unproductive

11. Whitlock, "Tyre Nichols Tragedy."

protests nationwide. Yet, he apparently cannot see how his words could provoke adverse reactions within the far-right communities.[12]

Another example is viewed on Fox News' "The Five." The five members debated the inappropriateness of releasing the video of Mr. Nichols's death on Friday evening rather than a Monday morning. They believed there was a legitimate fear that people could riot if the public saw the video during that period. The panel, like Carlson, rejected the notion that their focus on the potential negative consequences of this tragedy created the illusion of its plausibility, which could generate paranoia within their constituents.[13] We must ask ourselves, are they genuinely empathetic and seeking solutions to this dehumanizing issue? Or are they merely engaging in the *entertainment* of sociopolitical theatrics? Are they, in various ways, representative of White tokens, caricatures, and mannequins?

The views of some conservative White media outlets are complemented by the questionable racialized politics of some liberal Black politicians who capitalized on this tragedy, creating the image of Black solidarity and legitimate attempts to acquire justice. My cynicism points to the Reverend Al Sharpton, attorney Ben Crump, and possibly former vice president Kamala Harris. These three individuals attended Mr. Nichols's funeral. Nevertheless, through a Christian theological perspective, informed by racialized politics, how can we make sense of Mr. Nichols's death by five *Black* police officers? Can we interpret this event, and others like it, as representative of Black nihilism? Furthermore, what is the evangelical church's response to this and similar tragedies?

Yet, from an African American evangelical perspective, the negation, dismissal, and ignorance of spiritual laws do not affect those laws' influence upon humanity. This principle includes the purpose of humanity's existence and how we fulfill our destiny. Both depend on a relationship with a superior reality (God) and our worship of that existence. The starting point for my discourse begins scripturally with the purpose of humanity's existence, fulfillment of its destiny, and suppression of our universal sinful nature. From here, we turn to the exposed and concealed expressions of quasi-deification and skewed worship within the secularized world.

Conceptions of White tokenism, caricature, and mannequins differ from those within Blackness. Sociopolitical positioning and power determine the differences. There is a disturbing sense of loyalty, the

12. Fox News, "Tucker."

13. Fox News, "Five."

relinquishing of the human will, that White supremacists typically demonstrate. Loyalty is always to a skewed cause, sense of purpose, a duty to preserve the existence and power of Whiteness. Patriotic White Christian nationalism, authoritarian Christian fundamentalism, and White sociopolitical evangelicalism are beneficiaries and conduits for White loyalty. Consequently, this coincides with the compulsion and impulse to subdue the non-White existence through interrogation and physical restraint, when they deem it necessary.

We have an example of this through the tragic death of twenty-five-year-old Mr. Ahmaud Arbery on February 23, 2020, by two White men. The father and son chased Mr. Arbery through their neighborhood as he was running away to avoid conflict with them. Ultimately, Mr. Arbery was killed with a shotgun as he was cornered by the assailants' vehicles and forced to defend himself. The two men accused Mr. Arbery of stealing from the houses in their neighborhood without concrete evidence. They merely suspected Mr. Arbery because he was a Black man running through a White neighborhood. For them, there was no legitimate reason for him to be there. Hence, they assumed Mr. Arbery was the person responsible for the crimes.[14]

Their convoluted reasoning expressed itself further in the unjustified belief that they wielded the authority to stop Mr. Arbery, question him without his consent, and chase after him when he refused to cooperate. A court of law determined that racism was the cause that motivated their altercation with Mr. Arbery. Another White male associated with the father and son was also convicted of murder and federal hate crimes. One of the confusing elements of their trial was the difficulty in understanding what they believed was sound reasoning for repeatedly chasing Mr. Arbery. The three men assumed a level of power and righteousness that endowed them with the imaginary ability to assert their will upon Mr. Arbery. From this context, can we safely speculate that there are similarities between Mr. Arbery's and Mr. Nichols's deaths? Does the race of their killers matter? Did Mr. Nichols's killers possess the illusion of superiority closely connected with their identities as police officers? Could they have self-justified their actions through a skewed conception of righteousness and an identity representing the law (quasi-deification)?

Perhaps Mr. Nichols's Black killers developed supremacist reasoning from deluded notions of a *Black ideal* connected to a theoretical

14. Justice News, "Federal Judge Sentences Three Men"; Fausset, "What We Know"; Hanna and Caldwell, "Jury Finds Ahmaud Arbery's Killers."

virtue placed upon their profession as police officers. Societal injustice typically involves a person or group's attempt to assert itself upon the human-Other. The initial act of self-assertion through oppressive ways inevitably meets an oppositional form of self-assertion by the human-Other, in its attempts to emancipate itself.

THE WAR WITHIN OURSELVES

Like most African Americans, I'm typically forced to scrutinize my Blackness relating to Whiteness and other realities of racialized Otherness. I state this as a normalized good, as every person and group can only gain a heightened self-awareness in relation to the human-Other. We cannot mature, maximize our full potential, and embody our purpose on this earth in isolation. Yet, I would be a liar if I didn't state that I also scrutinize my Blackness relating to other forms of Blackness, whether hyper-conservative or hyper-liberal. It is the latter that I will focus on for the entirety of this project, but not completely detached from the former. As the former has its own sets of issues, types of fragmentations that I will reserve engaging in another discussion.

Since colonial slavery in America, there has always been tension between different forms of Blackness. To some extent, conflict has shaped and defined aspects of Blackness in America, whether that be culturally, politically, or religiously. Conflict is always attached to examination of the human-Other and self-examination. Self-examination and heightened self-awareness as *Introspection*, at least for this discussion, encompass the realities of knowledge, belief, and dogma as they too relate to truth, facts, and reality as reality truly is.

From a Black evangelical perspective, introspection is something YHWH created for us to practice to the extent it becomes instinctual. It's something we do naturally, but must be disciplined, refined, and matured if we are to grow emotionally, psychologically, and spiritually. In certain ways, the biblical narrative always encourages introspection, primarily through examination of our motives, desires, and who/what we love. Yet, we would be naïve not to acknowledge self-examination relating to our identity, sense of belonging, and how we share spaces with the human-Other. We could also deceive ourselves by dismissing introspection concerning our true purpose in life and the divine *responsibility* we cannot avoid. Genuine introspection is central to understanding, practicing, and embodying true Christian spirituality. I would even go so far as to include reaching our full potential as Black people in this world. Naturally, this influences how we participate in the sociopolitical world. Introspection is foundational in our search for the knowledge that creates and is birthed from the truth, as both should ideally define our sacred beliefs, ideologies, and dogma of the religious and sociopolitical worlds. As an evangelical Christian, I believe YHWH is the Infinite Truth and all finite truth is grounded upon him.

Introspection is a fitting tittle for this project as it expresses two important things. First, it characterizes part of my journey within the academy, which is also representative of other African Americans. This journey, at least in part, concerns the nature of genuine Christian spirituality, Black religiosity in America, Afrocentric-Liberationist discourses, and the dominant African American discourses that have shaped the trajectory of African American academics. Second, introspection is what I hope to elicit within African American culture concerning how we truly define our existence, live in authenticity, and present ourselves to the world. This project also describes, as best as possible, some of the research that caused me to reflect on the scholarship that aided or frustrated the development of African American studies, as it has influenced parts of the world.

In chapter 1, "The Taint of Racialized Nationalism: And the Need for Genuine Spiritual Awe," I begin by presenting a brief theory of authentic Christian spirituality as it relates to our identities, sense of purpose, and responsibility as YHWH's image bearers. My concern is that we are gradually losing our genuine sense of religious awe in YHWH, and this is noticeable within African American studies. Generally speaking, some concepts of spirituality appear ambiguous in terms of concrete beliefs/dogma, as if overwhelmed by principles of relativism. Connected to this is the obvious focus, almost entirely on conceptions of liberation, itself sometimes spiritualized in an ambiguous way. I then progress to examining interpretations of Black religion by various African Americans scholars. For me, Black religion becomes an ambiguous construct, often used to displace orthodox/evangelical dogma within African American Christianity through Afrocentric beliefs and racialized sociopolitical agendas.

Chapter 2 is titled "A Conservative Evangelical Critique: Black Power and the Theology of James Cone." This chapter provides a brief historical overview of some principles and activism of *secular* Black Power. We will see some of the basic beliefs and categories that Cone synthesizes with

Christianity to create Black liberation theology. For me, Cone's theology will always be a Black Power theology. Some scholars either minimize or blatantly ignore this important issue. We must always read Cone through an adequate to mature understanding of Black Power and Black Nationalism within the Civil Rights movement. Otherwise, we will decontextualize his theology into something other than what it really is. I've been exposed to various students and scholars alike who employ Cone's theology as a starting point for understanding Black theology in America, as if anyone prior to him hasn't produced anything of merit. This comes at the expense of ignoring various conservative evangelical African American Christians from colonialism to the present. Cone appears to articulate particular forms of Blackness, an Ideal-Blackness, and liberation that people embrace during times of heightened White supremacist activity in America. I've also been surprised to discover people worldwide who aren't aware of Cone and his contribution to global Christianity. I affirm his theology must be engaged as he occupies a strong presence within African American Christianity.

"The Afrocentric-Liberationist School of Black Religiosity" is chapter 3 of this project. I continue my discussion of some influential African American scholars who contributed to what I refer to as the Afrocentric-Liberationist school of African American scholarship. I will discuss the work of Curtis J. Evans, Kelley Brown Douglas, St. Clair Drake, Henry H. Mitchell, Gayraud Wilmore, and Dwight N. Hopkins. The Afrocentric-Liberationist consists of two dominant approaches to Black scholarship. It isn't an attempt to construct an exhaustive list. I will provide examples of scholars and their research who have been influenced by essentialist/racialized binary reasoning, racialized nationalism, and an Ideal-Blackness. The Afrocentric element naturally seeks to uncover, teach, and embody our traditional African heritage that was established on American soil during colonialism. Afrocentric scholars focus on demonstrating the preservation of traditional African culture and religion which shaped African American culture. The Liberationist element embraces the scholarship of the Afrocentric scholars but doesn't place a strong emphasis on Africa, opting to strengthen American Blackness as the new construct from the fusion of diverse African nations. Scholarship from these two approaches have minimized and negated the orthodox evangelical presence within African American scholarship.

Up to this point, we see a progression of my reasoning. Black nationalist and Black Power advocates advanced beliefs/dogma of the Civil

Rights movement that were eventually reconfigured into hermeneutics and methodologies within the academy. Black harbingers like Cone influenced subsequent generations of scholars who have shaped the current trajectory of African American studies. It's difficult to assess the concrete presence of conservative African American scholars.

Chapter 4 is titled "Racialized Politics Within African American Colonial Literature." It completes my critique of some contemporary African American scholars, relating to the transference of essentialist/racialized binary reasoning, racialized nationalism, and the Ideal-Blackness. It's important to note that many Black scholars don't self-identify with or openly promote these forms of reasoning. Rather, I suggest they have been deeply influenced by various scholars who did, as the hermeneutics/methodologies derived from Black Nationalism and Black Power are implanted within their scholarship. This chapter focuses partially on the education of colonial African Americans as it relates to their partial dependence upon *redeemed Whiteness*. Redeemed Whiteness are those people, secular and religious, who didn't submit to the spirit of White supremacy. Although the White minority within Whiteness, these Anglo-Americans and Europeans educated both slave and emancipated people, influenced by selfish to pure reasons. The approach I'm employing is to confront and question interpretations that portray every relationship between African and Anglo-Americans as one of conflict. For example, some scholars portray uneducated/illiterate colonial slaves as symbolically held in bondage to their White amanuensis. Educated/literate slaves and emancipated Blacks were free to articulate their story apart from White dominance. Consequently, educated African Americans are established by some contemporary scholars as representative of an Ideal-Blackness. I conclude the chapter by discussing the narrative of Olaudah Equiano. Equiano was an influential educated African abolitionist whom scholars have elevated to a higher position in African American literature, based upon his narrative's sophistication. Yet, some recent scholars have questioned aspects of Equiano's narrative relating to his birthplace and how he viewed/trusted Anglo-Americans and the British.

"The Politics Within Politics: The Ambiguity of Racialized Politics and Relations" is chapter 5. Politics is never a one-dimensional reality. Regardless of whether we are studying a historical context or figure, there always appear to be various layers and potential layers within what we view as the political world. This seems to be true when studying the self-interests and the methods to acquire them, by Anglo-Americans and Europeans during the transatlantic slave trade, and the development of the American British colonies. First, I will explore the first initial interaction between the Portuguese and West African nations. I want to emphasize the chaos we can contribute to when we obsess over our self-interest at the expense of the human-Other. In this context, it's the relationship between European global imperialism and African local imperialism. Secondly, I will articulate an example of Whiteness turning upon itself, through the politics of White individualized self-interest taking precedence over universal White solidarity. There is an illusion of racial solidarity within certain contexts. The colony of Virginia in the sixteenth century regarding its headright law and some early seventeenth-century African American emancipated people is an ambiguous case study to examine.

Chapter 6, "The Fragmentation of Colonial Whiteness: Antislavery Reform and Antislavery Christianity During the Seventeenth Century," explores the inner conflict within Whiteness, generated from the dehumanization of Barbadian slaves. I will discuss the Quakers, through the missionary efforts of George Fox's (1624–91) early involvement in what I view as the latter seventeenth-century Anglo-European antislavery Christianity. Secondarily, I will connect Fox with the antislavery discourses of the English Puritan Richard Baxter (1615–91) and the Irish Quaker William Edmondson (1627–1712). I interpret Fox as a reluctant and passive activist, as his intent wasn't to stop slavery but to initiate slavery reform that was intentional in evangelizing the slaves. I also view Fox's efforts as representing a small ripple in the ocean of progress, that gained momentum from the late seventeenth century to the early eighteenth century in America, assisting in the numerous conversions of African American slaves during the Great Awakenings.

Chapter 7, "The Fragmentation of Colonial Whiteness: Antislavery-Reform and Antislavery Christianity During the Seventeenth Century, Part 2," continues the discourse established in chapter 6. The primary focus of chapter 6 was the missionary efforts of George Fox and his conflict with the proslavery Anglican/Quakers of Barbados. In chapter 7, I focus on the antislavery discourses of the Anglican minister Morgan Godwyn (1640–ca. 1690), the Germantown Protest of 1688, and the Scottish missionary, Presbyterian turned Quaker, George Keith (1638–1716). Collectively, chapters 6 and 7 are employed as examples of necessary historical events and figures who should be discussed within African American studies, not in the intent of placating Whiteness. Rather, it is in the Spirit of Truth, if we are to discuss the people YHWH used to gradually deconstruct the institution of colonial slavery, and proslavery Anglo-Christianity, and the subsequent rise and empowerment of African American evangelical Christianity.

INDIVIDUAL AND COMMUNAL INVITATIONS

For some people, commonsense grounded reasoning is reinterpreted in their minds as genius level thinking. I don't presume to be a genius, but someone who at least desires the truth, and for it to be presented to me through basic common sense. Common sense is the foundation for all complex reasoning. Yet, it's difficult for me to ignore what I perceive to be contradictions, inconsistencies, and irrationality when it comes to aspects of knowledge, beliefs, and dogma as depicted within African American culture/studies. This is the case especially when these defy basic common sense but are clothed in the garments of intellectualism. For me, people today proudly claim to be intellectuals inside and outside of the academy. This isn't the issue. I am questioning the type of intellectualism that claims an authority that it shouldn't and truly doesn't wield: cloaked pseudo-intellectualism. The more troubling part is those of us who believe certain forms of pseudo-intellectualism as representing concrete truth, a truth that transforms lives and brings about sociopolitical and religious emancipation, eventually end up becoming the embodiments of Black disunity.

The methods to acquire true emancipation and emancipation itself can be distorted into vices when sinfully appropriated. The sinful appropriation, at least in part, comes through the total degradation of the human-Self and the human-Other. Any emancipation that is used to oppress the human-Other isn't emancipation at all. It is concealed bondage via self-confinement. Untruth is the pillar of self-confinement, as genuine truth, no matter how we feel about it, always brings emancipation. The dark reality is that some of us do not truly desire emancipation as emancipation truly is within reality, the greater reality that is infinitely beyond our control. Thus, we construct concepts of Ideal-Blackness that seek to confine ourselves in racial fantasy.

To some extent, the church and the academy appear to exist in subtle tension with each other over this issue. It is clear that there is a presence of anti-intellectualism within the church. There are Christians who believe you will forfeit your salvation by attending a university for higher education. This is especially the case if it's a divinity school within a secular institution. Thus, for these people true faith in Christ Jesus requires a simple, childlike mind of sorts. For them, the more intelligent we become in the pursuit of knowledge, the more this equates to a higher focus on the human-Self, not YHWH, which may lead to self-worship. Yet, we would be naïve to assume there isn't a binary opposite stereotype within the academy of preachy Christians devoid of intellectual depth. For there are certain academics/intellectuals who view portions of the church as somewhat backward in its simplicity. This is a simplicity in appearance that masks intentional laziness, intellectual insecurity, and forms of ineptness, especially within the call to preach to the world. I often ask myself where I stand between these two communities. I'm also forced to scrutinize the contours of the communities nestled between these two communities.

It isn't a sin to question and doubt, as long as it's in the realm of sincerity and the desire for truth. These are important aspects of introspection. I encourage my readers to engage my views in the spirit of inquiry and the Spirit of Truth. We cannot be afraid to invite one another to participate in our journeys. Nor should we be intimidated to join other people's journeys. The positive development of Blackness must be grounded in sincerity and truth, as both are situated within reality as reality truly is—not from the imagination of a Black consciousness that is skewed by oppression and lacks the self-awareness to acknowledge it hasn't received what it claims to wield and embody.

1

The Taint of Racialized Nationalism

And the Need for Genuine Spiritual Awe

God is spirit, and those who worship Him must worship in spirit and truth.

JOHN 4:24

Now the Lord is the Spirit, and where the Spirit of the Lord is, *there* is freedom.

2 CORINTHIANS 3:17

A THEORY OF AUTHENTIC CHRISTIAN SPIRITUALITY: IDENTITY, PURPOSE, AND RESPONSIBILITY

FOR THE SAKE OF this conversation, I will speak as a Christian who acknowledges the realities of spiritual practices outside of Judean Christianity.[1] Naturally, this presupposes the belief in a spiritual world with

1. I want to emphasize that the Bible acknowledges the existence of various spiritual practices. Conjuring, divination, and sorcery are viewed as detestable in the mind of YHWH (Deut 18:10–12; Lev 19:31; and Isa 8:19). A popular story regarding divination is read in 1 Sam 28. King Saul sought the aid of the deceased prophet Samuel through a medium. The context of this event took place during a war between Israel and the Philistines. For whatever reasons, it is assumed that YHWH permitted it. Saul, being a hypocrite, violated not only YHWH's law but his decree upon the land, as he previously prohibited divination and expelled its practitioners from the land. The Lord forbade divination, as its successful results appear to be well known. In this chapter I am emphasizing the spiritual openness of the individual and community, not endorsing the practice of divination.

distinct laws, a spiritual world more real than our physical world. Let us suppose YHWH speaks to everyone according to his salvific will and love for humanity. We must not forget the apostle Paul's words in 1 Tim 2:3–4, "This is good and acceptable in the sight of God our Savior, who wants all people to be saved and to come to the knowledge of the truth." I cannot accept the skewed belief that YHWH simply ignores everyone until we sincerely desire to accept Jesus as the Christ. Universal grace and love are given to all. A heretic I may sound and a heretic I may be . . . on this issue.

Being spiritual and genuine worship of YHWH are not synonymous. These are distinct realities that do overlap. There are many Christians today, and especially throughout history, who claim to be spiritual but appear devoid of authentic worship of YHWH. True worship is more than singing unto the Lord. Nor is worship expressed physically through obsessive attention and activity in the sociopolitical arena. Worship involves prayer, immersion in the word of God, and love for God and the human-Other. Worship is the totality of our existence. My dogmatic claim is this: As humans we are worshiping beings and have a core spiritual *identity* connected to our divine *purpose*, that carries with it certain unavoidable *responsibilities*.

Generally, to be spiritual involves a variety of things, one of which is to have faith through the assistance of sound reasoning, believing in those things unseen.[2] The lack of visibility does not equate to the absence of sensing and feeling those things of the spiritual world. The physical world would be a chaotic place if reality was determined by our knowledge and what can be solely verified through our finite senses. Again, from an African American evangelical perspective, *Christian* spirituality is grounded upon the reality of YHWH as the "really-real." It involves embracing the gospel narrative in a transformative way through salvation, love of Christ, and a self-sacrificial existence. Divine revelation is crucial as we are not spiritual alone but in community, first with our Triune God, and secondly with the body of Christ. It does not manifest vis-à-vis socio-politics. Yet, true Christian spirituality is connected to the physical world, first through the prioritization of the salvific message to be accepted and then presented to the world; secondly, to the sociopolitical world that we cannot detach ourselves from. These are core elements of African American evangelical Christianity and conceptions of social

2. Hebrews 11:1, "Now faith is confidence in what we hope for and assurance about what we do not see."

justice. However, we must not be naïve to assume everyone has agreed to this view.

I'm convinced spirituality and to be spiritual are rather ambiguous today. They have been imprisoned by relativism/subjectivism that are slavishly used to minimize and disregard the qualitative and quantitative differences of religions. Sound reasoning and inner fulfillment are also ignored to advance the ideologies and worldviews of those who have skewed agendas against Christianity.

As Christians, our created purpose, identity, and responsibility derive from YHWH, and he alone determines their *ideal* according to his will. These are important elements to real Christian spirituality and genuine spiritual awe of YHWH. It is worth adding that we worship YHWH in spirit and truth (John 4:24), the grounding for true Christian spirituality and awe of YHWH. Theologically, there is the necessity to primarily view this through a biblical Christological lens, relating to salvation and the continual forming of our existence into the *imago Christi*.[3] However, we cannot be naïve to assume YHWH hasn't provided humanity with the ability to disagree and reject his will, deciding to define one's existence apart from him. In so doing, we commit the sins of Lucifer and Adam. In this context, we must ask ourselves a few questions: What becomes of Christian spirituality and awe of YHWH when we seek to redefine and recreate our identity, purpose, responsibility? How is our contextualized Judean Christianity affected when we submit it to our notions of racialized nationalism?

In the hearts of humanity, our identity, purpose, and responsibility have both a righteous and unrighteous side. These sides represent categories of purity from the Divine, over and against the corruption of the human-Self. The human-Self as the rebellious self-determined seek an existential purpose apart from YHWH, where there is a danger of the self-determined collapsing within themselves. We can embody a complex yet skewed identity that represents these two categories or poles of a spectrum,

3. Romans 8:29, "For those whom He foreknew, He also predestined to become conformed to the image of His Son, so that He would be the firstborn among many brothers and sisters." 2 Corinthians 3:18, "But we all, with unveiled faces, looking as in a mirror at the glory of the Lord, are being transformed into the same image from glory to glory, just as from the Lord, the Spirit." These verses relate to Col 1:15, "He is the image of the invisible God, the firstborn of all creation." Hebrews 1:3, "And He is the radiance of His glory and the exact representation of His nature, and upholds all things by the word of His power. When He had made purification of sins, He sat down at the right hand of the majesty on high."

which not only exist in tension but contradict one another in terms of their relationship. Connected to this is the reality that humanity exists in a state of *intended ignorance*, an ignorance that is established by YHWH for his specific purposes. We are ignorant of a complete understanding of our existence and the overall purpose for creation itself as it relates to perfect clarity of our consciousness. In part, this establishes and is established by the creation of religious faith as existing within the Judean Christian tradition. Yet, intended ignorance is temporary as we have the capacity for maturation and of self-determination through righteous means, which are products of YHWH's will. Thus, we are created in divine accountability and responsibility unto YHWH, despite sin and the dark reality of self-deception in which we choose to immerse ourselves.

The relationship between our central human identity, purpose, and responsibility isn't a foreign concept to Judean Christianity. Heinrich Emil Brunner (1889–1966), an influential Swiss theologian, articulates his concept of human responsibility that is dependent upon the purpose of our existence and the full awareness of it relating to our relationship with YHWH. For Brunner, our responsibility appears to reside in the fabric of our being, and to deny our responsibility is to deny our humanity. As I interpret Brunner, he implies there is an important and complex psychological and social dimension of our being that is deeply affected by how we understand, embody, and be responsible through love of YHWH. Brunner states,

> In the Christian doctrine of man we are concerned with the true knowledge of responsible existence. One who has understood the nature of responsibility has understood the nature of man. Responsibility is not an attribute, it is the "substance" of human existence. It contains everything: freedom and bondage, the independence of the individual and our relation to one another and the fact of community, our relation to God, to our fellow-creatures and to the world, that which distinguishes man from all other creatures, and that which binds him to all other creatures. Thus even the knowledge of responsibility is that which makes every human being a real human being—although otherwise he may be and think or believe, what he wills—thus it is an absolutely universal human element. Yet responsibility is at the same time that which no man rightly knows, unless he holds the Christian faith.[4]

4. Brunner, *Man in Revolt*, 50–51.

The very foundation of how we exist as Christians, and live as spiritual beings in this physical world, is created and matured by our love for Christ and the human-Other. Connected to this is our care for the earth and the animal kingdom. It is here I repeat a previous dogmatic assertion: true Christian spirituality must begin with an accurate and truthful understanding of YHWH, that leads to acceptance of Christ Jesus as Lord and Savior. Brunner also asserts, "The boundary of the knowledge of responsibility coincides with the boundary of human existence; if a human being had lost all sense of responsibility, he would have ceased to be a human being."[5] Ceasing to be human is not a physiological transformation into something ontologically grotesque. Rather, as I interpret Brunner, it is a moral and spiritual self-debasement into an existence of apathy and indifference to the human-Other. All of which begins when people seek to redefine and recreate themselves in and of themselves. Brunner makes another point worth mentioning:

> Responsibility is existence in the Word of God as an existence which is derived from and destined for the Word of God. If any human being were ever to respond to God in harmony with His Word, and upon the basis of His Word, in believing love, he would be truly human. He would know what human existence means, and he alone would express and represent this knowledge in his life.[6]

Naturally, Brunner is framing his theological anthropology through the Judean Christian narrative. The assumption is that all humans are made in the *imago Dei*, and that we are created *for* YHWH. Thus, our central identity and the maximizing of our human potential are grounded within him. Life is a movement toward the salvific decision to either accept or reject Jesus. We can either embrace our ideal glorified existence as a new creation in the eschaton, or decide to be an existence detached from YHWH with an eternal void, unknowingly unfulfilled through godless self-determination. Naivety must be stripped from any mind that believes the issues Brunner presents are irrelevant or minimized within African American evangelicalism.

Alexander Crummell (1819–98) was a pioneering evangelist, Episcopalian priest, and theologian. Crummell articulates human purpose, identity, and responsibility as grounded in and matured only through

5. Brunner, *Man in Revolt*, 51.

6. Brunner, *Man in Revolt*, 53.

our salvation in Christ Jesus. He expounds upon this belief through an exposition of Luke 9:62, "But Jesus said to him, 'No one, after putting his hand to the plow and looking back, is fit for the kingdom of God.'" Crummell's central thesis is that humanity has the primary responsibility to obtain salvation, and from this, everyone must live dedicated to Christ in eternal love and service. There is no wavering or a double mind from the Christian. They are not to serve Christ and their fleshly pleasures. The imagery we receive from Crummell is that of someone who is seeking to be deceptively lukewarm. Crummell asserts,

> For first he has his own soul to save and by this I mean that, with the gift of divine aid, God has also thrown personal responsibility upon every man to achieve his own salvation. "Work out your own salvation, etc." We are not saved passively, in a state of effortless inertia. We, ourselves, have got to ward our own spirits from the power of Satan to shield them from the poison of sin. And this is an arduous work: *not* the light easy effort which many suppose it to be.[7]

Crummell believes self-discipline and reception of YHWH's discipline in our lives is not an easy task to employ and accept. He implies that there is the inner presence of arrogance and self-deception in those Christians who oversimplify the Christian life. They construct distorted beliefs to justify disobedience to God's word, and the perception of their spiritual maturity, that makes YHWH a non-necessity in their life: "With false views of the character of God, with profound ignorance of their own nature and their depravity; they deem themselves capable of meeting all the moral responsibilities of life; of answering all the demands of the divine law; by the force of their intrinsic merit of securing the blessedness of the righteous."[8] Crummell isn't ignorant of the religiopolitical responsibilities of Christians in the world. Existence presupposes a spiritual identity, divine purpose, and inherent responsibility as true Christianity endows the Christian with earthly sociopolitical duties:

> Let me be understood. I do not mean that Christianity divorces any of us disciples from our earthly relations and duties. I have no faith in that sort of piety which is so divine and unearthly, that it can't attend to the concerns and responsibilities of life. Christianity makes no such requirement on us. But this is what I say—if you are a Christian man,—if religion is the most important concern

7. Crummell, *Destiny and Race*, 98.

8. Crummell, *Destiny and Race*, 98.

> that can come home to the business and bosoms of men,—if it is the grandest object of thought that can be entertained by the human mind; treat it as such. Make it, in all things the highest. Be sincere. Do not belie your profession. Prove your manhood. Quit you like men. Vindicate the holy name by which you were called. Main[tain] your integrity, through Christianity, against all odds. Let God be the *first* in the whole category of thought.[9]

As I interpret Crummell, it is not a matter of either or. We are not forced to choose spiritual issues and consequently disregard the sociopolitical world. It is a matter of *prioritization*, establishing what is the grounding for our *central* identities, purpose, and responsibilities that empower those that are secondary. Christ is first, and from our first love comes a new, transcendent existence composed of our core spiritual identity, purpose, and responsibilities.

In returning to a previous point, intended ignorance does not hinder humanity from discovering its ultimate purpose, identity, and responsibility from YHWH. The illusion of achieving complete control of ourselves, defining our purpose for existing, and being responsible solely to ourselves, is just that, a deceptive illusion that breaks down the human will. This is a central element of the cycle of dehumanization. These elements are always present in how we perceive, construct, and embody our notions of spirituality (religion) and nationalism (politics). From this reasoning, I'm haunted by certain questions: How is African American Christian spirituality affected when submitted to sociopolitical agendas and ideologies? Do African American religiosity and conceptions of spirituality undergo transformations?

It seems an acceptable norm, at least for some individuals, to dismiss foundational aspects of Christianity, replacing them with contemporary politically minded people, ideologies, and conceptions of their imagination. This newer set of methodologies and hermeneutics, albeit secular and Christian-influenced in some capacity, are used to create new conceptions of Black Christianity and spirituality. This is also applicable to contemporary amalgamations of Christian nationalism and White Christian patriotism.[10] Advocates from these camps appear to *primarily* view things through a lens of race and accompanying sociopolitical views. These overwhelm a direct reading of the gospel of Christ, or the entire biblical testimony that embraces unity within diversity, reconciliation, and self-sacrifice.

9. Crummell, *Destiny and Race*, 102–3.

10. Austin, *American Christian Nationalism*.

From a conservative evangelical perspective, it is an issue of *prioritizing*, not mutual exclusivity. If there is some merit to what I am stating, then certain hyper-liberal Black sociopolitical ideologies, academic Black theology, and Black religiosity in America have done an efficient job of severing traditional aspects of African American spirituality, Christianity, and theology from their orthodox system of beliefs. This is consequential when anyone overemphasizes racial uniqueness, racial solidarity, and some humanistic purpose in a way that merely inverts the oppressive systems and agents that are being fought against. Perhaps severance is too strong of a word. Dislodge, displace, minimize, or conceal may be more appropriate. Again, these beliefs are also applicable to segments of Anglo-American Christianity which appear to have confused American imperialism with Christian evangelism and church (military) planting.

Restating a dogmatic point: From a biblical worldview the Christian faith is not racialized, hyper-politicized apart from genuine spirituality, or designed for some elite class of humans. The Christian faith is a universal faith, an inclusive faith of distinct spirituality that connects people from different nations, social classes, and periods in time. The minimizing and absence of these elements, the Bible, and the essence of Christianity as the centering sources of our Christian faith grossly distort our understanding of Christianity and deeply affect our Christian lifestyles and faith in Christ. It impairs us and leaves a severe void. A void that is desperately sought to be filled by the individual through racialized politics, counterintuitive principles of relativism, hedonism, and emotionally driven ambiguous religiosity. Thus, we witness and experience the distortion of our sense of purpose, identity, and responsibility through what I view as Western postmodernity confusion.

As an extension of my faith, I affirm the Paraclete connects us through his will. Without him, the human mind and heart wander in a nomadic search for love, acceptance, peace, stability, and a lasting community. For me, this undoubtedly thrusts many African Americans into conceptions of divisive racial ideologies and godless modes of discriminatory Blackness. The Paraclete also participates in the community of people, Christian and non-Christian, as they embody authentic spirituality and religious awe. One is situated within the body of Christ, and the other is positioned in *salvific accountability*, forward moving to a *salvific decision*. It may sound heretical to some, but I advocate a form of genuine communication and fellowship between the two groups, with the Trinity at the center. I frame my perspective in a particular way that emphasizes the basic principles of natural theology and a personal belief that YHWH perpetually speaks to every human on this earth.[11] How and to what extent is beyond my comprehension. I only affirm that religious disagreements should not result in the dehumanization of one another. To do so is a contradiction to the essence of the gospel narrative. I also reason from what I consider *African American evangelical realism*.[12] I define this as a religious, political, and theological disposition within the Christian tradition, as embodied by specific African Americans who perceived the spiritual world as a self-evident reality, partially concealed through various secular and areligious sociopolitical and religiocultural systems.

For the sake of this discussion, the experiences of fellowship between the two groups can be bracketed within conceptions of evangelism. However, I would suggest that they are mostly not confined to evangelism. I am merely emphasizing the organic, genuine communication between Christians and non-Christians that may *appear* as guided by religious self-interest, but is manifested in purer or genuine interest in the human-Other.

Genuine Christianity advocates recognizing all humans as created in the *imago Dei*. This is what makes us unique and deeply connected with one another within YHWH. However, only believers are formed into the *imago Christi*, which is the ultimate goal of YHWH that does not infringe upon the individual's free will. I am not rejecting the importance of Christian evangelism, just placing it within what I view as its proper contexts. It is an issue of prioritization relating to honoring the individual's humanity and existence as the *imago Dei* and aspects of YHWH that he has *concealed* within the human-Other. The revelation of God from within the human agent cannot be taken, but given, and it is only given when we seek to love the person without an agenda. This particular revelation and experience in the Divinity are offered when we do not seek them. It is a reward for achieving some form of self-emptying and self-sacrifice for the human-Other. Examples of what I am theorizing are observed within the testimony of Bishop Polycarp of Smyrna (69–155 CE).

11. Brunner, "Nature and Grace."

12. The scholarship of Martin Luther King Jr. (1929–68) and Reinhold Niebuhr (1892–1971) has shaped my views of Christian realism and how I articulate it within African American Christianity. Their scholarship also influences my interpretation of Black Nationalism, Black Power, and Black theology vis-à-vis James Cone. See King, "Malcolm X," 265–69; and "Black Power," 314–32; King, "Black Power," 23–69; R. Niebuhr, *Christian Realism*; Lovin, *Reinhold Niebuhr*.

POLYCARP'S CARE FOR THE HUMAN-OTHER

The early church, within the first two centuries, was plagued with dehumanizing persecution, which often ended in the death of Christians. Martyrdom was common, especially involving church leaders. St. Polycarp was one of them.[13] He was roughly eighty-six years old when he found himself pursued by the Roman state. His eventual execution was the goal, the death of a traitor to be made a spectacle for the nation's entertainment. Evidently Polycarp must have become weary from evading arrest at such a frail age. During the last moments of his deserved freedom, he is recorded as refusing to flee, opting to embrace his divine destiny:

> They found him lying down in the upper room of a certain little house, from which he might have escaped into another place; but he refused, saying, "The will of God be done." Matthew 6:10; Acts 21:14. So when he heard that they had come, he went down and spoke with them. And as those that were present marvelled at his age and constancy, some of them said. "Was so much effort made to capture such a venerable man?" Immediately then, in that very hour, he ordered that something to eat and drink should be set before them, as much as indeed as they cared for, while he besought them to allow him an hour to pray without disturbance.[14]

Polycarp exhibited the mind and character of Christ during his impending death. For me, Polycarp embodied the *fruit of the Spirit*, and they guided his thoughts and behavior toward his capturers. Polycarp was not bitter or angry; nor did he desire physical harm to those who were simply following their orders. Yet, he was oddly concerned with their humanity. I imagine his capturers had a distorted view of Polycarp, shaped by the Roman religiopolitical system that demanded supreme loyalty to the emperor. They, like us today, aren't immune to being manipulated by our representative governments. Polycarp did not use this time to attack the Roman political system or the culture. He simply sanctified the time and space for the care of the human-Other. He demonstrated a distinct Christian spirituality that was not concerned with social status, ethnicity, gender, or sexual disposition. Polycarp fellowshiped with his capturers, respecting their humanity as YHWH's image bearers and potential

13. D'Ambrosio, "Martyrdom of Polycarp," 29–37; Aquilina, "Martyrdom of Polycarp," 68–73, 19, 26, 29, 32, 41, 42, 55, 57, 62, 63, 102, 241, 328, 337; Haykin, *Rediscovering the Church Fathers*, 38, 39, 163; Liftin, *Getting to Know the Church Fathers*, 30, 34, 65, 67, 68, 88, 111.

14. Unknown, *Martyrdom of Polycarp*.

family members in the body of Christ. I imagine Polycarp was awarded a vision of seeing YHWH within the human-Other.

Polycarp's only request was to be allowed solitude with the Lord. Polycarp enjoyed two long hours of intimacy with YHWH, possibly being prepared for his irrational and dramatic death. It is impossible to know the thoughts, feelings, and emotions he experienced. Perhaps he recollected the kind and wise words of his former friend St. Ignatius of Antioch (ca. 30–ca. 100 CE).[15] Ignatius was martyred, but before passing into the next life, he encouraged the Christian church to withstand their persecution and dedicate the entirety of their existence to worshiping Christ. Ignatius was extremely influential. Many Christians traveled to fellowship with him as he was being escorted to Rome to be killed. Polycarp was one of these Christians. I often wonder just how much Ignatius functioned as a vital example of faith, confidence, and love to Polycarp as a Christian embracing glorifying Christ in their death.

In returning to the issue of the conflict between the idolatry of Blackness and the essence of Christianity, we must explore some intriguing questions: Which is the source that grounds and helps define reality, YHWH, Blackness, or a concealed Whiteness in Black *flesh*? Who or what governs our conception of Black spirituality?

A SEARCHING CONSCIOUSNESS: THE STATE OF BLACK SPIRITUALITY AND RELIGIOSITY

Within the worldview of Judean Christianity, there is an obvious connection between our relationship with YHWH, our spiritual faith, and how we truly embody our genuine spirituality. Genuine *Christian* spirituality is dependent upon salvific faith in the Divinity as Trinity, and the One as Son who sacrificed himself, as the ultimate act of love for the opportunity to be in union with us. The current union of the indwelling of the One as Paraclete within us is a foreshadowing of our complete union with the Divinity as Trinity within the eschaton. It is here where I must restate a previous point: There is no sincere spiritual awe of the Divinity without salvific faith or the *searching* faith that leads to it, which I call the *faith of accountability* or *salvific accountability*. For some Christians, this may be a controversial or heretical statement. I am not advocating salvation apart from accepting Christ as our Lord and Savior. The

15. Haykin, *Rediscovering the Church Fathers*, 31–48, 29, 66.

sincerity or genuineness of salvific and searching faith have a space of overlapping, a space where two distinct communities can communicate with one another in the presence of the Divinity. This is the space where authentic spiritual awe is born. It is also a space where mature Christian faith is grounded and receptive of the human-Other outside of the body of Christ.

Genuine Christian spirituality takes seriously the reality that YHWH exists beyond human self-awareness, and he, as Trinity, does not require permission to be nor to act. YHWH freely *intrudes* upon the human existence according to his will. We accept this as fact according to faith and personal experience. The biblical testimony, both Old and New, portrays YHWH as desiring intimacy with humanity. This special union is synergistic, a genuine consequence and manifestation of the reciprocal love for one another. Yet, these are intentional demonstrations of tension between the self-disclosure of God and the reality of his intentional *hiddenness*.

I will return to the importance of this divine concealment at a later point. As of now, I only want to emphasize a theory of the essence of genuine Christian spirituality and how it is contextualized according to specific and universal ways. The authenticity of Christian spirituality and religious awe, at least for me, is clearly seen in the lives of many colonial African American Christian slaves and emancipated people. This current discussion on genuine spirituality and religious awe is a necessary step, before moving forward to my critique of the ambiguity of Black religiosity in America.

For many Christians, divine revelation is believed to perpetually occur in the lives of countless people worldwide. Connected to this is our desire to include YHWH in every righteous aspect of our lives. There is an *intentional* and *participatory* aspect of genuine Christian spirituality. Yet, our spiritual faith, faith to believe YHWH exists, and our genuine desire to know him, cannot exist apart from human reasoning grounded upon common sense. Faith and reasoning via common sense are the conduits for a specific spiritual self-awareness that opens us to our divine responsibility. Within this context, genuine spiritual awe in YHWH is crystallized within our lives or total being.[16] It is an intricate part of our

16. I make the dogmatic theological assertion that God speaks to everyone, but how we interpret his voice varies depending upon an inexhaustive set of factors. Part of my belief, at least academically, is influenced by Rudolf Otto's (1869–1937) theories of the "Numinous" and "Mysterium Tremendum." As I interpret him, Otto articulates a relatively universal experience and achievement whereby an individual obtains a heightened sense of spiritual self-awareness within the genuine moment of sensing and

syncretistic relationship with him. We must also accept the representative triune relationship between the human-Self, YHWH, and the human-Other.[17] The human-Self is created for YHWH, but he also created us to secondarily live for the human-Other, and in this reality is the collective spiritual awe of the community.[18]

I am not suggesting that we live in a way that negates our well-being to live in an intentional pseudo-self-sacrificial world. I am not advocating the permissibility of some concealed forms of oppression, slavery, or questionable religious pacifism that sit idly by in the presence of the former. The human-Self must be focused on YHWH to maximize its full potential, to achieve a higher understanding of its well-being, and to properly love the human-Other apart from its self-interest.

What I am doing is advocating that the neglect and rejection of YHWH and sincere spiritual faith will drastically affect our notion of spirituality and how we perceive the human-Other, especially if they are enemies or perceived as such. My fear is that this is one of the great sins of contemporary African American Christianity, and by extension African American religiosity. As I see it, an aspect of academic Black religiosity, being primarily socio-politically driven, has always expressed some disdain for various evangelical Christians and the Black Church that prioritize the spiritual over the political. This has been, at least in my eyes, an overstated position to hold by any African American educated in the origin and development of African American Christianity from colonialism to the present. Again, I am emphasizing the *prioritization* of the spiritual essence of Christianity, which is worship-centered, and this centering informs the ethical/moral dimensions of political participation. I am not suggesting a spiritual focus that rejects political involvement, making itself completely inept.

Colonial evangelical African American Christianity presented some of the most balanced and influential people who articulated a biblical faith in Christ, Christian ethics, and evangelical political theology.[19]

---

feeling the authentic presence of God, as something "Wholly-Other." Eliade (1907–86) builds upon Otto's theories in his work *The Sacred and the Profane*. See Otto, *Idea of the Holy*.

17. R. Niebuhr, *Self and the Dramas of History*.

18. An emphasis is placed on the two New Testament commandments (Matt 22:37; Mark 12:30; and Luke 10:27).

19. I interpret the conservative evangelical tradition of African American Christianity as a collection of biblically centered contextual expressions of scriptural reading/reasoning, church traditions, creeds, and church doctrines that collectively define

There were influential figures who did not neglect the essence of Christianity at the expense of establishing a quasi-religious sociopolitical ideology of race. These individuals, at least from an evangelical view, understood their life and calling stemmed from Christ, and he encouraged participation within the political sphere. We see this most notably from individuals like David Walker (1786–1830), Hosea Easton (1798–1837), Alexander Crummell (1819–98), and Francis J. Grimke (1850–1937).[20]

It is still somewhat of a mystery seeking to understand why these individuals are absent from the literature and public discourse of some politically minded Black people. Perhaps these representatives of our colonial heritage are not deemed worthy to assist in the contextualisms of our contemporary Black theologies, biblical studies, and ethics. If this is not the case, maybe the sin lies upon the shoulders of our Black educators for not keeping their voices within the halls of prestigious universities, local churches, social media, and public discourses. Christians like Walker, Crummell, and Grimke cannot be erased from American history, even if they have been in the minds of some *enlightened* African Americans.

Christianity. Representatives of conservative African American Christianity are Jupiter Hammon (1711–1806), John Marrant (1755–91), and Lemuel Haynes (1755–1833). John Marrant was one of the first nationally recognized African American preachers and evangelists. In 1786, Marrant published a narrative describing his early life, Christian conversion, and ministerial experience. Marrant also published a sermon in 1789, and a lengthy journal detailing the specifics of his ministry in 1790. Lemuel Haynes was a popular Christian minister who fought against and wrote extensively about slavery. Jupiter Hammon is the first African American to publish a poem in America. Collectively, there are over seven published works by Hammon.

Jupiter Hammon's work consists of "Evening Thought. Salvation by Christ, with Penitential Cries" (1770); "Address to Miss Phillis Wheatly, Ethiopian Poetess" (1778); "Essay on Ten Virgins" (1779); "Poem for Children on Death" (1782); "Dialogue Entitled the King Master and the Dutiful Servant" (1782), which was published as part of a prose titled *An Evening Improvement. Shewing, the Necessity of beholding the Lamb of God* (1782); "Winter Piece: Being a Serious Exhortation" (1782); "Address to the Negroes of the State of New York" (1786); and "Essay on Slavery, with Justification to Divine Providence" (1786).

Lemuel Haynes's work includes "Character and Work of a Spiritual Watchman Described" (1792); "Important Concerns of Ministers and the People of Their Charge" (1797); "Universal Salvation: A Very Eminent Doctrine" (1805); and "Sufferings, Support, and Reverend of Faithful Ministers, Illustrated" (1820).

John Marrant's published works are "Narrative of the Lord's wonderful Dealings with John Marrant" (1785); "Sermon Preached on the 24th Day of June 1789, Being the Festival of St. John the Baptist" (1789); "Journal of the Rev. John Marrant, from August the 18th, 1785, to the 16th of March, 1790" (1790); "Funeral Sermon Preached by the Desire of the Deceased, John Lock" (1790).

20. Walker, *Walker's Appeal.*

They were the influential voices within grassroots colonial America, contributing to not only African American Christianity but also European American Christianity. It is irrational to disregard them, pushing them to the outer boundaries of our consciousness to select specific colonial voices that represent a distinct contemporary illusion of Ideal-Blackness. I fear this is the case for some of us.

Generally, colonial evangelical African American Christians preserved the importance of sharing their relationship with YHWH with the public, the transparency of their genuine Christian faith, and a biblically rooted conception of spirituality. These elements were central to their understanding of Christianity. These Christians developed a sense of justice that was not devoid of redemption and reconciliation.

JARENA LEE: WHITE ANTAGONISM AND POTENTIAL REDEMPTION

Christians typically remind the world of how powerful God's love is and how it completely transforms human life. This tends to overshadow the reality of our free will and responsibility to choose to follow Christ, embodying the two New Testament commandments. Consequently, from this misappropriation, some Christians often superficially construct Western views of love and transformation. They sometimes do not require any substantial self-sacrifice from the Christian in question. The Christian can cling to their skewed beliefs of discord, hate, elitism, and racial superiority without experiencing any guilt or spiritual conviction from the Paraclete. This is a clear sign not of his absence or laziness, but of the Christians' calloused heart and willful ignorance.

A striking testimony of obedience to YHWH, perseverance, and genuine spiritual transformation can be gleaned from the narrative of Mrs. Jarena Lee (1783–1864).[21] Lee was the first woman preacher of the African American Episcopal Church (AME), founded by Mr. Richard Allen (1760–1831).[22] On one occasion, Lee was holding a ministerial service at her uncle's home, who was also a Methodist. At this point, she was a traveling preacher, and it was common for her to attract people of different races, holding varied curiosities and intentions for hearing her

21. Lee, *Brand Plucked from the Fire*; W. Andrews, *Classic African American Women's Narratives*; W. Andrews, *Sisters of the Spirit*.

22. Allen, *Life, Experience*.

preach. We shouldn't be surprised at the possibility of extreme skeptics, misogynists, and racial supremacists occupying seats within YHWH's sacred space during her services. We are introduced to an elderly Anglo-American man who apparently felt inclined to see whether Lee was truly called by God or was simply another religious circus act. Lee recounts her interesting experience with this man:

> At the first meeting which I held at my uncle's house, there was, with others who had come from curiosity to hear the coloured woman preacher, an old man, who was a deist, and who said he did not believe the coloured people had any souls—he was sure they had none. He took a seat very near where I was standing, and boldly tried to look me out of countenance.[23]

It is interesting that Lee felt the old man's religious and racial beliefs were important to mention. Race and religion often make venomous bedfellows within the human heart, influencing the human-Self to vomit vitriolic rhetoric. For Lee, the old man had skewed beliefs about YHWH and Black people. He did not believe God had any care and activity in the world, but had enough to create Black people as a separate species of human without a soul.[24] We could argue that his ignorance possibly

23. W. Andrews, *Sisters of the Spirit*, 46.

24. Human ignorance is a universal reality. It becomes demonic when submitted to sin vis-à-vis compulsions to establish an individual/group's illusory superiority over the human-Other. It is likely impossible to determine within human history the first and initial cases of multiple creation narratives per human diversity. These views grafted within Christianity are often referred to as polygenism (polygenesis). Polygenism became a pseudo-theological monstrosity employed by colonial White supremacy to establish Europeans above the non-European. An example is viewed in Theophrastus von Hohenheim (1493–1541) known as Paracelsus, the Swiss physician, alchemist, philosopher, and lay theologian. In 1520, Paracelsus posed what is known as Co-Adamism, the belief of different groups of men created alongside Adam, displaced within different parts of the earth.

In 1655, Isaac La Peyrere (1596–1676), a French lawyer, theologian, and writer, endorsed Pre-Adamism. This view posited the Gentiles and Jews had two creation accounts articulated in Gen 1 and 2. Peyrere states, in *Theological Systeme upon That Presupposition, That Men Were Before Adam*: "It is worth our taking notice, that the men of the first creation, (who, according to my supposition, are Gentiles,) as also the whole world, were created *by the word*. The first Chapter of *Genesis* hath this expresly; which is the Chapter of the creation. *And God said, Let us make man according to our own Image.* He said, *Let us make.* And by his word he made him. But not by his word, but of wrought clay, the Lord made *Adam, Gen.* Chap. 2. Which Chapter peculiarly handles the creation of *Adam*, and the framing of the Jews in *Adam*. Whose Historie *Moses* being about to write, began it from the dust of *Adam*; the first father of the Jews, as is usual amongst all Historiographers who write the Historie of their Nation, to begin from the first Authors of them." These are merely two examples of influential Europeans

stemmed from the level of distancing, or disconnect from YHWH and the Black-Other. God and Blackness were not detached existences in his mind. They were identified with one another, as entities that warranted apathy and indifference. However, even this theory would imply a level of hypocrisy or contradiction within the old man, because Lee would not have seen him at her service, if he was truly indifferent to Black people and YHWH.

We are left to wonder about the convincing evidence the old man had that defined his confidence in the irrational belief of a soulless human. Aside from this, the intent of the old man was clear. He wanted to make himself known to Lee, to demonstrate the duality of his belief that functioned as the binary opposite to her genuine faith in YHWH and call to preach. The conflict established itself between male and female, White and Black, areligious and religious. However, Lee was undeterred, as throughout her life she endured many ordeals. For example, she had various conflicts with Satan concerning suicidal ideation and fighting to legitimize her call to preach within the organized church. Lee was accustomed to the immorality and negativity of certain people and continually learned to cling to Christ to overcome them. It wasn't Lee's responsibility to correct or save the old man. She was there to preach the gospel of Christ: "But I laboured on in the best manner I was able, looking to God all the while, though it seemed to me I had but little liberty, yet there went an arrow from the bent bow of the gospel, and fastened in his till then obdurate heart."[25] The old man came to battle who he thought was a weak enemy, but was overcome not by Lee, but by the overwhelming presence of YHWH via divine revelation through Lee's preaching within that particular context:

> After I had done speaking, he went out, and called the people around him, said that my preaching might seem a small thing, yet he believed I had the worth of souls at heart. This language was different from what it was a little time before, as he now seemed to admit that coloured people had souls, whose good I had in view, his remark must have been without meaning. He now came into the house, and in the most friendly manner

who advocated the distorted pseudo-theological creation narratives per ethnic/racial diversity. The study of this topic is beyond the scope of the chapter and overall project. See La Peyrere, *Theological System*, 13; Gossett, *Race*, 3–31; Jordan, *White over Black*, 3–98; West, *Prophesy Deliverance*, 54.

25. W. Andrews, *Sisters of the Spirit*, 46.

> shook hands with me, saying, he hoped God had spared him to some good purpose.[26]

We witness the transformation of this old man. The assumption holds that someone or a group of people were possibly called beforehand, ministering to him, attempting to plant the seeds of faith within his spirit. Lee was simply the vessel YHWH used to water those seeds, observing the growth elicited by the enlightenment of the Paraclete. God used his Black child, who had not only a soul but the indwelling Paraclete who strengthened her during an important moment within her ministry. The old man left Lee through expressing hope, hope in the reception of salvation. He became a living testimony for YHWH through pronouncing his presence in and around Lee, endorsing what he sensed to be her good heart. Lee provides us with more information about the old man and the deeper significance of his transformation:

> This man was a great slave holder, and had been very cruel; thinking nothing of knocking down a slave with a fence stake, or whatever might come to hand. From this time it was said of him that he become greatly altered in his ways for the better. At that time he was about seventy years old, his head as white as snow; but whether he became a converted man or not, I never heard.[27]

Lee displayed no animosity or hate to this man. She exemplified a love for Christ that opened the door and invited all participants to meet YHWH. Her demeanor toward the old man was guided by love. Lee did not embrace a spiritual elitist theology that rejected the possibility of salvation for this then-current slave trader, whose reputation for cruelty and violence was well known. Lee had a lasting impact on this slave trader, as a week later, "Here again I saw the aged slaveholder, who notwithstanding his age, walked about three miles to hear me."[28] A roughly seventy-year-old White slave master walked nearly three miles to hear a dedicated Black Christian woman preach the gospel. We can only imagine how YHWH worked within him to create the change that Lee was able to witness.

Lee's experiences with the old White slave trader are examples of the spiritual context from which authentic faith in YHWH engages a form of salvific accountability or faith of accountability. YHWH, as the hidden

26. W. Andrews, *Sisters of the Spirit*, 46–47.

27. W. Andrews, *Sisters of the Spirit*, 47.

28. W. Andrews, *Sisters of the Spirit*, 47.

God, is present but unable to be fully acknowledged, as the agents within the contexts are focused on obtaining what they desire. For some, it is answers, and for others, it is simply being obedient to whom they are indebted. We must honor and preserve these genuine spiritual experiences apart from the coopting of skewed sociopolitical agendas or superficial religious agendas constructed from sociopolitical intentions.

Representatives of colonial evangelical African American Christianity took seriously the tension between seeking emancipation from their oppressors and seeking their salvation. Contemporary African American Christians should see the value in studying our colonial evangelical history, in relation to the entirety of Christian history, especially from the church fathers/mothers to the series of reformations within the colonial era. We will see a common bond that stretches throughout our humanity and love for Christ. Our contemporary faith and theologies would be strengthened. The absence of these elements produces an underdeveloped Black academic theology and faith that staggers to construct itself from the limitations of the theologian and their self-interest. In this context, glory goes to the human-Self, not YHWH. Is there value in discerning whether there are different traditions within African American Christianity? If so, how can we trace the development of these traditions and the positive and negative issues that accompany them? Where and whom can we use as starting points for our discussions?

A GROUNDED CONSCIOUSNESS: DIVINE CONNECTION, SPIRITUAL UNION, AND RELIGIOUS AWE

We must preserve the fact that, within colonial African American Christianity, the dominant contextualism has been conservative and embodied the spirit of evangelicalism. This involves not minimizing, rejecting, or reinterpreting the Christians within this tradition and their genuine dogmatic faith into concealed sociopolitical tools for liberation. The hidden God had revealed himself by intruding upon the lives of countless enslaved African American Christians and the emancipated class. It was YHWH, not Whiteness or systemic oppression, that established the meaningful constellations of experiences of many colonial African American Christians. Divine revelation and the genuine salvific faith of African American Christians were both transcendent and concealed, from those colonial European Americans who represented the anti-gospel of proslavery European American Christianity, at whose center resided the racialized nationalistic White Christ. These elements and realities were continually present from colonialism to the Civil Rights movement. Through faith and a commitment to biblical justice, genuine African American Christians and the Black Church established themselves as influential theopolitical agents of YHWH.

My concern is that the dominant *interpretations* of African American slaves derive from *Afrocentric* and *Liberationist* methodologies that are loosely determined by twentieth- and twenty-first-century, concealed and overt, hyper-liberal African American politics. As I interpret things, the *substance* of the colonial evangelical tradition of African American Christianity has been underrepresented within African American religious scholarship. It has been overshadowed by some Black scholars' fascination, obsession, and fetish with Whiteness, a *liberated* Blackness, and conceptions of nationalistic racialized politics. In this, I'm afraid there appears to be a conflict among African Americans, a conflict *within* Blackness, that exposes itself between conservative evangelical and hyper-liberal Liberationist traditions of African American Christianity and theology. This conflict is typically concealed through discourse articulating a form of Black solidarity that transcends religious differences, not united by the biblical Christ, but by an ideal Blackness in opposition to corrupt Whiteness.

We exist in an era of seemingly unacknowledged *fragmented Blackness*, a fragmentation that Whiteness does not sustain. It is Blackness. My attempt is not to theorize a starting point for this internal fragmentation. I desire to locate a moment in American history where conflict between Black people had *exacerbated* the already established issue, and whether the outcome of this conflict set African American Christianity and theology on a trajectory that has created devastating unintentional consequences. When did increased conflict among African Americans arise? What was the meta-context from which it originated and continued for some time? Who were the willing and unwilling participants?

My starting point of exacerbation is the Civil Rights movement. As I mentioned earlier, it involves Martin Luther King Jr., the Black Church, Black Nationalism, and Black Power. Connected to them is the rise and reign of James Cone and Black liberation theology. I have always viewed Conian theology as Black Power theology. This may be an obvious point for anyone who is familiar with Cone. I agree. However, my emphasis is rather on the hermeneutics, themes, and structures of Cone's theology that he inherited from Black Power (Black Nationalism), which he always embraced and never renounced. Cone is a product of the Civil Rights movement. From his testimony, Martin Luther King Jr. and, more so, Malcolm X were the primary influences on Cone's racialized political theology. Arguably, from roughly 1969 to his death in 2018, Cone has been considered, at least in some people's minds, the greatest Black theologian that America has produced. His theology, or what I consider the Conian School of Theology, has dominated the Black theological academy.

We must ask ourselves whether there exists some negative consequence that stems from Cone's polarizing theology in the academy. I believe his theology pollinated the hermeneutics and themes he inherited from the hyper-liberal sociopolitical ideologies: racialized binary reasoning, irredeemable Whiteness, minimizing of Christian spiritual emphasis, excessive critique of the Black Church, and waning relationship with the institution. Connected to this is the consequential minimizing, negating, and undermining of adequate scholarship on the colonial evangelical tradition of African American theology. This is clear when we simply look at the landscape of literature within academic Black theology and Black religion. To some extent, the saving grace has been various research from African American historians and literary scholars, most of whom appear to be women who have maintained a strong focus on colonial African American religiosity.[29]

I make a distinction between the theology of the evangelical African American Church with Conian theology. I do acknowledge that there is some overlap and integration to a certain extent. Aspects of Conian theology are indeed present within the Black Church in America, but to what extent is unclear to me. Yet, I do not see it having a dominant presence. Likewise, African American evangelical theology has a minor presence within the academy. I suspect it is drastically overshadowed and displaced.

Aspects of academic Black theology have successfully established themselves as an antithesis to the supremacist side of White America, its contextualized Christianity, theologies, and the White Christ who represents them. I do not disagree with this stance, as I, too, take one. However, Black theology has, intentionally and unintentionally, also created division with conservative evangelical African American Christianity by

29. Berry, *From Bondage to Liberation*; Cooper, *Word, Like Fire*; Davis et al., *New Cavalcade*; Hanch, *Storied Witness*; Moody, *Sentimental Confessions*; Peterson, *Doers of the Word*; Waters, *Maria W. Stewart*; Warner, *Saving Women*.

approaching theology through the lens of hyper-racialized nationalism. I am also concerned about how this bears upon conceptions of the essence of African American spirituality and our religious awe. My fear is that genuine spirituality and religious awe in the Divinity have been sacrificed at the altar of sociopolitical Black solidarity. However, before providing a fuller discussion of Cone, we must deal with my concerns regarding Black religion in America. Again, my issue is that Black religion has been primarily influenced by certain Afrocentric and Liberationist sociopolitical ideologies, that initially influenced Conian theology. What is Black religion? Are there specific religions that primarily define it? Is Black religion truly a constellation or family of religious beliefs at all? Is it merely Black sociopolitical ideologies that create a spiritual identity crisis within its staunch proponents?

THE AMBIGUITY OF BLACK RELIGION

It is common for people to merge two or more religious/spiritual beliefs to achieve those things that define their self-interest. One is the establishment of unity between two or more groups who have historically been at odds with one another. In a general sense, this is a noble attempt at peace, justice, and reconciliation. It is also common to witness the substance or essence of a religion displaced from the center of its advocate's public life, pushed to the outer boundaries of their existence to achieve said goals. This causes me to advocate for a newer constellation of dialogues between Black evangelicals and members of the Black religious tradition devoid of hyper-politicization. However, I have been haunted by the ambiguity of Black religion, which at times appears to be more sociopolitical than religious.

Black religion is a rather broad and ambiguous concept. Pioneering African American scholar C. Eric Lincoln (1924–2000) wisely stated, "Neither scholars nor practitioners are in precise agreement over what 'Black religion' is, or, for that matter, whether it in fact exists. What is usually demanded as a minimum by the skeptics is evidence that 'Black religion' is sufficiently distinct from other forms to warrant a distinguishing terminology."[30] Lincoln eventually defined his view of the term,

> Black Religion is a conscious effort on the part of Black people to find spiritual and ethical value in their understanding of history. Their history. This is neither parochialism nor racism. Rather,

30. Lincoln, *Black Experience*, 1.

> it is the realization that even as God is above history, He acts in history, and that somewhere in the flux, at some time the individual is confronted with the question of what God's acts mean. He must also find satisfactory answers regarding his proper response to God and how that response should be translated in terms of personal and social behavior based on his understanding of what characterizes God, i.e., what spectrum of values and what kind of behavior he supposes God to approve of Himself and for man. Out of his understanding of God, in the context of his own experience, man gropes for meaning and relevance. Assurance and reconciliation. This is religion. When the context of that groping is conditioned by the peculiar, anomalous context of the black experience in America, it is black religion.[31]

Lincoln, as I interpret him, makes it clear that God is real and actively engaging humanity. God is real, as in the *really-real*, the ultimate being/existence from which ethics/morality and ultimate human purpose derive. God as the really-real is the grounding for genuine Black spirituality, which transcends human-made pseudo-religiosity. God is not an abstract concept, social construction, or fictitious cultural, moral, political, or racial object to manipulate the masses. For me, to construct a god from the categories just mentioned is the grounding for superficial unity, vague concepts of spirituality, and forms of quasi-deification.

Regarding the reality of God, Lincoln's view stands in opposition to various humanistic conceptions of religion endorsed by some African American scholars. Yet, honesty compels us to admit that religion is influenced by the human context, but more importantly, that God intrudes upon the human experience. We cannot begin to understand Divine revelation apart from the human experience, but human experience, at least from an evangelical viewpoint, should not govern theology or how we define religion. As a starting point for understanding God and religion, human history is significant for Lincoln. We, as humans, are historical beings. We cannot escape history and its influence upon us. Human history itself is not devoid of sociopolitical and religiocultural issues. In this context, we must ask ourselves: How do we make sense of vague conceptions of God that permeate an ambiguous view of religion? What becomes of religion when concepts of spirituality are nothing more than psychological methods to alleviate discomfort, anxiety, unhappiness, and a sense of emptiness? Does our sense of religious awe reveal itself as an

31. Lincoln, *Black Religion*, 2.

illusion, a deceptive form of emotionalism originating from concealed sociopolitical agendas?

Moving beyond Lincoln, Black religion appears to be employed by some Black scholars to establish and strengthen a racialized political agenda. The agenda is inundated with opposing White supremacy and secondarily crystallized by an illusory conception of Black solidarity against Whiteness. The sin, ignorance, and immorality of Whiteness magnify the desire for, demonstration of, and exaggeration of Black solidarity.

We witness this in the various works of Black scholars within Black theology in America and African American religiosity. For example, as I see it, specific intellectual, sociopolitical, and religious conflicts within Blackness during the Civil Rights movement (1954–68) unfortunately drifted into American higher education, mistakenly promoting some scholarship over others. In this context, the scholarship of the dominant Black teachers represented the sociopolitical philosophy and theology of Black Nationalism and Black Power, which manifested as the dominant hermeneutics, methodologies, and academic discourses. In returning to the issue of ambiguity, African American scholar Gayraud Wilmore (1921–2020) provides a view of Black religion, influenced by Clifford Geertz (1926–2006). Wilmore states,

> By black religion reference is made to a system of symbols deeply embedded in the culture of people of African descent. This symbol system, formed in slavery from Christian instruction and remnants of African religions has been preserved in the historic black Christian churches. The system acts to establish powerful psychosomatic moods and motivations in believers by evoking conceptions of a normally hostile world that blacks generally relate to white oppression, and in which both provisional accommodation and protest are found to be so necessary for survival and liberation, with the help of mystical or divine powers, that the psychosomatic moods and motivations seem uniquely appropriate for overcoming present distress and for guaranteeing a future and happy existence in a world to come.[32]

Wilmore emphasizes a variety of commonly accepted principles. First, he mentions the healthy and natural relationship between culture and religion. Many African Americans, myself included, advocate traditional African cultures during colonialism as the foundation for the developing African American culture. Our culture could not exist without

32. Wilmore, *Pragmatic Spirituality*, 281n7; see also 18–19.

colonial African cultures. However, the details of this relationship and the development of African American culture with the waning of traditional African cultures are highly disputed.[33] I believe it is an issue we can never settle. Yet, a likely more controversial discussion is how much African and African American culture influenced the development of Anglo-American culture.

Wilmore also broadly references the religious syncretism of African and African American Christians. The extent of religious syncretism, as far as I am concerned, is never explained in detail by most African American scholars beyond ring shouts, drums, rhythm, and broad religious categories.[34] For Wilmore, Whiteness is a central influence in shaping African American Christianity. Whiteness as the oppressive-Otherness is a clear designation, but specific structures of Black religious syncretism remain vague. Black survival from White oppression is a necessary element of Black religion that appears to stand above and beyond the individual's authentic experience of recognizing God as God is, the really-real.

I am establishing a starting point for my theory of the *hyper-politicization* of race and how it affects our interpretation of culture, politics, and religion. Racialized politics can be interpreted as an influential aspect of how some Black religionists define and practice their spirituality. We can intentionally and unintentionally naturalize the supernatural and secularize our perception of spirituality. The consequence is unacknowledged internal theological tension and contradiction. We must entertain this possibility and similar ideological trajectories if they reach fruition. We must consider what becomes of authentic spirituality and the unique spiritual awe we experience in the presence of the Divinity once racialized politics become a quasi-religious disposition. In part, the nature of spirituality becomes privatized and absent from any meaningful mass influence in the public sphere, especially relating to politics. Authentic spirituality is subsequently relegated to religious institutions, and then said institutions undergo critiques, scrutiny, and attacks for not being sufficiently politically involved.[35]

I interpret Wilmore as a Christian and recognize his attempt to establish a balance between expressing an authentic *Afrocentric* or Black

33. See Herskovits, *Myth of the Negro Past*; Frazier and Lincoln, *Negro Church*.

34. Albert J. Raboteau provides the most grounded and scholarly interpretation of colonial African and African-American religious syncretism. See Raboteau, *Fire in the Bones*; *Canaan Land*; and *Slave Religion*.

35. See Warnock, *Divided Mind*.

Christian faith, as it relates to being socio-politically enlightened.[36] I am not questioning his salvation or acceptance of Christ Jesus as his Lord and Savior. However, I am scrutinizing the relationship between his historiography and political theology. Wilmore is not alone. I situated him within a particular school of thought.[37] Another influential Black scholar employs Black religion primarily within the American context while maintaining aspects of Black sociopolitical enlightenment. Black theologian J. Deotis Roberts (1927–2022) suggests,

> "Black religion" refers to Afro-American religion. It is African and it is American in a vital sense. It is African because its historical roots are there, and it is American because it has developed now for several centuries within the American environment. It is my contention that it has remained African in temperament in spite of the tragic history of blacks in this country. All the repressions of slavery and all the indignities of discrimination have not eradicated the essentially African flavor of the Black religious experience.[38]

Roberts, like other Black scholars, makes it a point to emphasize the preservation of ancient African cultural heritage and religiosity transferred to African American culture and religiosity. I tentatively agree with this principle in a general way. My point of departure with Roberts, Wilmore, and people with similar views is how they primarily employ racialized politics against Whiteness, articulating Whiteness as the central, or relatively equal, influence with the Divinity in shaping Black religion and African American Christianity. Their collective view ignores the history of Christian political theology and how different cultures, ethnicities, and nations contextualized traditional Christianity with their then–present-day politics. We have testimonies of various Christians who maintained a traditional theological disposition, reaffirming fundamental Christian doctrine, but did not employ their oppressive-Other as a governing hermeneutic/methodology.

Historically, the Christian church has experienced countless acts of persecution which led to many deaths. It's more common to hear about persecution from those outside the church, but there have been many brothers and sisters as enemies from within. Yet, when we focus on the

36. See Wilmore, *Pragmatic Spirituality*; Wilmore, *Black Religion*; J. Wright, "Doing Black Theology."

37. See Hopkins, *Introducing Black Theology*; Ware, *Methodologies of Black Theology*.

38. Roberts, *Black Religion, Black Theology*, 62.

theologies birthed during certain periods, those deemed the oppressor aren't established as governing hermeneutics within the theologies of the oppressed. For example, within the ancient church, Rome, with the litany of oppressive emperors, was never the primary object, subject, or theme in the crystallizing of basic Christian doctrine and Christian theology. The Reformations witnessed the irrationality of Catholics and Protestants warring with one another. English Catholic priest and theologian John Wycliffe (ca. 1328–84), Czech theologian/philosopher John Huss (ca. 1370–1415), and Czech theologian/philosopher Jerome of Prague (1379–1416) were some of the reformers who died from their opposition to the pope's corruption. The pope was never used as a governing hermeneutic that influenced Reformation theology. Returning to my previous point, authentic Black spiritual awe in the presence of the Divinity, as Wilmore and Roberts articulate it, often appears as a *reactionary reality* to White oppression. Black spiritual awe appears dependent upon Whiteness rather than existing solely from Divine revelation intruding upon human life. I employ Black spiritual awe in a general sense, understanding that the concept is contextualized worldwide in various ways. Humans also cannot dictate how God engages them. Black religion as African American religiosity can be rearticulated racially and sociopolitically through a general paradigm. African American scholar Eddie S. Glaude Jr. (1968–) provides us with another example. He remarks,

> In short, African American religious life is as rich and as complicated as the religious life of other groups in the United States, but African American religion emerges in the encounter between faith, in all its complexity, and white supremacy. My approach assumes that the political and social context in the United States is a necessary though not sufficient condition of any study of something called African American religion. If the phrase "African American religion" is to have any descriptive usefulness at all, it must signify something *more* than African Americans who are religious.[39]

Religious expression does not manifest in a void. It does so within an individual's and community's specific and general context. I agree with Glaude Jr. that the American context influences the nature of African American religiosity. Yet, we must scrutinize the boundaries and limitations of our central context. Connected to this is determining whether

39. Glaude, *Religion*, 6.

we fit within an established tradition or seek to establish something new and distinctively different. I also argue these former aspects have limited to no value if they are detached from the reality of the Divinity. If so, religion collapses into a distorted anthropology and superficial philosophy. Glaude Jr. further states, "This something more does not have to be an idea of religion, which stands apart from social and historical forces that impinge on the lives of African Americans. Nor does it refer to a definitive kind of experience that is itself religious or a religious consciousness as distinct from other forms of consciousness."[40] I interpret Glaude Jr. as expanding traditionally specific terms to create avenues of religious and sociopolitical pluralism. I agree with him in employing this reasoning regarding democracy, living in harmony with everyone and valuing diversity. My main issue is the relationship between democracy and authentic religion as defined by genuine religious people devoid of hyper-politicization. It is how we intentionally and unintentionally employ principles of democracy and racial ideology as governing hermeneutics to interpret our Christianity. I fear that God becomes a privatized concept and has limited to no participation in the political process, except by providing some psychological and emotional support via political disposition. Yet, it is always problematic and confusing when certain Black people seek to secularize religion to the extent that religion ceases to be religion. Hypocrisy and self-contradiction are surely lurking around those Black people who would have issues with Whites who wanted to redefine their Blackness. They cling to their orthodox racial beliefs more than biblical Christian principles.

Nevertheless, African American scholars have employed the term *Black religion* in generalized ways for decades. Ultimately, the term's overuse has aided in minimizing the *spiritual substance* of African and African diasporic religious systems for a heightened Black religiopolitical agenda. One example is showing Black religion as equal to White religion and demonstrating its compatibility with Christianity. It is naturally employed from multiple local contexts scattered worldwide and collectively united to form a global emphasis. I argue that Black religion, at least in the Western world, is merely a civil religion. It is the relationship between religiocultural syncretism and generalized sociopolitical principles from Black Nationalism and Black Power vis-à-vis Afrocentric Western American democracy. Yet, I also highlight the broad, inclusive, and consuming

40. Glaude, *Religion*, 7.

categories of Afrocentric racialized nationalism and a generalized inclusive racialized category of Blackness. To further complicate matters, if my interpretation has merit, Black religion, if taken seriously as a religious disposition, blurs the lines between *true* religious worship and national loyalty. It produces concealed religiopolitical systems of religious confusion and theological conflict.[41]

I am not refuting the legitimacy of studying Black religion as a broad discipline. Nor am I seeking to delegitimize Afrocentric readings and embodiments of Christianity. I sincerely value them. We need both. However, I am questioning their limitations and whether some practitioners have become distracted and preoccupied with Whiteness, creating unnecessary conflict with traditional Christianity. In this discussion, I only dogmatically advocate that we need to keep the integrity of religious experience as an authentic reality and not reinterpret it as a relativistic philosophical concept with limited moral and sociopolitical importance. With this, I do give a genuine nod to Wilmore, who provides a polished view of his Afrocentric pragmatic spirituality that takes seriously the reality of the Divinity:

> I call Africentric spirituality *pragmatic* because it is not particularly interested in mystical experiences, speculative theologizing, or idealization of what it means to exist in the eternal presence of the Supreme Being who mainly deals with us in the nonmaterial, spiritual realm. To speak of the *pragmatic* character of this spirituality is to emphasize its interest in practical or human considerations and consequences—but not to the extent that all transcendence is summarily wiped out and religion thereby reduced to an especially moralistic kind of human engineering or an impersonalistic instrumentalism that seeks to calculate the program all human relationships. Quite the opposite! The pragmatic character of this spirituality is rooted in its human direction and goal, its propensity for loving service to others as an emulation of God's love of humankind that is manifested primarily in the biblical picture of Jesus' earthly ministry to "the least" of his sisters and brothers.[42]

41. I am influenced by the scholarship of ethicist and theologian H. Richard Niebuhr (1894–1962) and principles within Contextual theology. See H. Niebuhr, *Christ and Culture*; H. Niebuhr, *Radical Monotheism*; Schreiter, *Constructing Local Theologies*; and Bevans, *Models of Contextual Theology*.

42. Wilmore, *Pragmatic Spirituality*, 4–5; see also 1–12.

In this context, Wilmore creates tension between his perception of spirituality that excessively focuses on meditation, philosophical speculation, and an escapist fascination with the Divinity against a grounded spirituality primarily focused on the present sociopolitical reality. I am concerned that Wilmore and others project a small escapist spirituality that exists into a more significant presence than it truly has. The form of spirituality he rebukes is typically identified within Eurocentric Christianity, and portions of the African American Church, making it impotent against White supremacy. I appreciate Wilmore's scholarship, as challenging as it is, and see the value in his school of thought. I only question its internal harmony, relationship with Scripture, methodology, and the core principles of his contextualized theology of racialized politics, concerning the preservation of a genuine experience of spiritual awe. The danger of Wilmore's view, *if* taken to the extreme, is the waning of real spirituality within the Christian tradition, which stems from the individual seeking to redefine their relationship with God, as the ultimate Divinity.

My concern is also that the hyper-conflation of racialized politics against White society places our racial identity on par with or above our religious/spiritual identity. As I see it, this secular epistemological maneuver becomes an interpretative issue within Christian theology. The racial sociopolitical identity/worldview is employed consciously and subconsciously as a set of hermeneutics and methodologies to contextualize Christianity. Thus, Black religiosity, to some extent, is reinterpreted and cloaked in racialized patriotism that conceals itself under the veneer of politically conscious religiosity. Consequently, authentic human spiritual self-awareness and experience of God, as God is, begins to wane until the connection is severed. Acknowledging the spiritual world as the *truly real*, a transcendent reality, is a central element from our colonial Black religious tradition. I ask the question, have African American theologians adequately articulated this principle or merely reinterpreted it through secular political ideologies?

For example, conceptions of idolatry, as defined within Judean Christianity, do not necessarily exist within Black religion because of its religious syncretistic nature. The concept of idolatry is typically replaced with forms of patriotic racialized *treason* through racial assimilation and integration into White culture. The line between religious syncretism and proper contextual expressions within Judean Christianity is blurred or, for some, blatantly rejected/ignored. I contend that these forms of hermeneutics, methodologies, and historiographies have saturated themselves within Black academia and culture, casting a veil upon the consciousness of some Black people worldwide. The consequence is that some people may not see clearly nor comprehend the healthy relationship between the two sets of religious categories, apart from polarizing racialized politics.

To articulate my concerns further, I will employ some of Reinhold Niebuhr's views regarding the relationship between American Christianity and secularism. He provides a distinct lens to view the consequence of racialized politics' hyper-politicization and the waning of authentic spiritual awe.

INTERNAL CONTRADICTIONS AND INCONSISTENCIES: THE CONSEQUENCE OF MAKING POLITICS A QUASI-RELIGION

An aspect of what I am suggesting can be gleaned from Niebuhr's views of the quasi-religious elements of American secularism and how it affects some Christians. I interpret him as questioning the essence of Christianity once it is stripped of its authentic spiritual awe through hyper-politicization. I also believe his views apply to what I view as the universal essence of human spirituality, as an actual force that is a part of our humanity. Regarding the union between American religiosity and secularism, Niebuhr says, "For in our nation secular and religious viewpoints tend to verge into a kind of vague and sometimes sentimental religion of democracy, with no strong anti-religious or anti-secular fanaticism."[43] Niebuhr theorizes that American secularism expresses itself in two ways: theoretical and practical. For him, theoretical secularism "dismisses ultimate questions about the meaning of existence, partly because it believes that science has answered these questions and partly because it regards the questions as unanswerable or uninteresting."[44] Niebuhr defines practical secularism as expressing "itself in the pursuit of the immediate goals of life."[45] Again, I am emphasizing Niebuhr's views on secularism's religious or quasi-religious elements. Referencing secularism, he further states, "It was religious in the sense that it provided a sense of the ultimate meaning of existence. Its God was 'history' or 'reason' or 'progress' through reason or the advance of the scientific method, or through the application of the

43. R. Niebuhr, *Secular America*, 16.

44. R. Niebuhr, *Secular America*, 2.

45. R. Niebuhr, *Secular America*, 2.

methods of science to problems of history."[46] If Niebuhr's views have merit, I suggest aspects of racialized nationalism and hyper-politicized Black religiosity, with their openness to religious syncretism, create conflict with traditional spiritually centered Black religiosity, as they aggressively prioritize the present immediate sociopolitical issues above and beyond what is traditionally deemed "spiritual," or "spiritual issues."

The consequence is a form of Black civil religion that continuously distances itself from a traditional expression of religious experience and religious awe in the presence of the absolute Divinity. Black religion, as a Western democratic religiopolitical concept, opposes the distinctiveness of Christian and universal spirituality and its historical engagement with secular politics. Thus, taken to the extreme, African American Christianity and Black religiosity exist only in appearance, as the *veneer* of authentic spirituality is visible, concealing the absence of God-Self within the individual and their involvement in politics. In theory, this may connect to the increasing presence of secularism within African American culture. Some individuals may lose interest in religion, specifically Christianity, not because they are concretely irrelevant and do not express an authentic experience with the absolute Divinity. Instead, some individuals drift away because they are overexposed to sociopolitical issues and particular religious dispositions that elevate their self-interest above God. They gradually lose their unique sense and experience of religious awe in the presence of the absolute Divinity. Religious evangelism is reinterpreted as political campaigning, the spirit of Western democracy replaces the Spirit of God, and our favorite quasi-messianic presidential candidate replaces Christ Jesus. Yet, how is the African American Church affected? Is there a healthy balance of authentic religious awe within the church and its influence on American politics? Does the church deserve the scrutiny it has received from certain African American scholars?

I want to emphasize Niebuhr's view of the *veneer* of Christianity and how it deceives and confuses people into assuming it is or represents the true *essence* of Christianity. Likewise, theoretically, I would imagine similar ideologies, hermeneutics, and quasi-religious political reasoning of racialized nationalism deeply affect authentic spiritual Black religious expression worldwide. I suspect the true essence of certain African religiosity is suffocated by Black sociopolitical reasoning that experiences an

46. R. Niebuhr, *Secular America*, 16.

identity crisis, similar to what I perceive within Black America. Yet, this critical issue requires further discussion at another time.

We must entertain the possibility that Whiteness has become a governing hermeneutic within the scholarship of some African Americans. I view this racialized hermeneutic as consequential from opposing White supremacist or Eurocentric Christianity within the American context. Again, I am not advocating submission and assimilation to Whiteness. However, I merely take issue with the unacknowledged construction and employment of racialized binary reasoning within African American scholarship and how the righteous aim to defeat White supremacist ideology, and everything it entails, becomes a consuming enticement that draws some Black people away from traditional Christianity, Christian theology, and the evangelical African American Church.

YHWH AND WHITENESS: THE DISPLACEMENT OF TRADITIONAL CHRISTOLOGY FOR THE CENTERING OF "WHITE-OLOGY"

From an evangelical viewpoint, Christ Jesus (Christology) is the center, the governing hermeneutic within Christian theology. A biblically sound Christology is necessary for any authentic Christian faith and to articulate said faith intellectually outside and within the academy. Furthermore, Christian theology is consistent and harmonious, as each category represents a lived, spiritually transformative, and *believed* factually transcendent reality that strengthens one another. For example, the incarnation of Christ Jesus does not mean anything apart from the virgin birth, and both are meaningless *if* detached from a sincere belief in the deity of Jesus, whom everyone must concede had historically existed. My point is not to argue the legitimacy of Christianity. Instead, it is to articulate an aspect of Christian *spirituality*. Christian doctrine *represents* reality and the transcendent reality, not a fictitious inner world without any grounding within reality.

Biblically, we see the initiation of this belief by the apostle Paul in 1 Cor 15:13 and 1 Thess 4:14. We have a concrete example of authentic Christian faith and spirituality that helped shape and nurture the spiritual convictions of the church fathers and subsequent generations to our contemporary period. True Christian spirituality, created from real people and events, is Judaic in cultural origin but *universal* in divine purpose.

Christian spirituality takes seriously the reality of Christ Jesus, as depicted within the biblical testimony. There is an authentic generational spirituality today that mirrors the collective faith of the first-century Christian church. This generational spiritual faith rejects the hyper-racialized politicization of our contemporary period.

I am not stating Christians should not engage or participate in politics or issues of race. It is sheer ignorance and intellectual laziness not to acknowledge the relational history between Christianity and politics and issues of ethnic and racial conflict. However, these are not relationships that began during the colonial era with the Europeans, the transatlantic slave trade, and the social construction of race. I am questioning the overemphasis on racialized politics and structures of Black identity concerning the oppressiveness of Whiteness by some of our most influential African American scholars: James Cone, Gayraud Wilmore, J. Deotis Roberts, and at least the initial work of J. Kameron Carter and Willie James Jennings.[47]

This observation relates to the absence of African American Christian theologians who have established themselves within the tradition of Christian theologians who established necessary interpretations of essential Christian doctrine and advanced specific theological claims. Comprehending God as God-Self through Divine revelation is the appropriate starting point for experiencing a genuine sense of religious awe and, from said starting point, seeking an enlightened understanding of who we are and everything this entails. God as God-Self determines the contours of our human identities, contexts, and sociopolitical activities.

African Christianity is rooted in the era of Jesus' earthly ministry, and an African presence participated in his sacrifice on the cross.[48] African Christianity has birthed some of the most influential church fathers, theologians, and Christians in recorded history.[49] Yet, we must ask our-

47. Affirming fundamental Christian doctrine as established within Christian history does not appear to be an essential task to some contemporary Black theologians. Instead, to some extent, it is deconstructing Whiteness and has established a new liberating Blackness that stems from God in some capacity. See Cone, *Black Theology and Black Power*; Cone, *Black Theology of Liberation*; Cone, *God of the Oppressed*; Cone, *Cross and the Lynching Tree*; Carter, *Race*; and Jennings, *Christian Imagination*.

48. For example, we have Simon of Cyrene, the African cross-bearer of Jesus (Mark 15:21), and the Ethiopian Eunuch of Acts 8.

49. Clement of Alexandria (?–ca. AD 215), Tertullian of Tunisia (AD 160–?), Origen of Alexandria (ca. AD 185–ca. 253), Athanasius of Alexandria (?–AD 373), Augustine of Hippo (AD 354–AD 430), Aurelius of Carthage (?–ca. AD 430), and Cyprian of Carthage (?–AD 258).

selves whether the early Christian church of antiquity hyper-politicized their ethnicity and nationalism to construct their contextualized Christianity and theologies. Did they conflate the reality of oppression by the human-Other, whether Roman, German, or French, to function as a binary oppositional reality from which to create their identities and perceptions of God? Why haven't many contemporary African American Christian theologians established their scholarship within the testimony of the Gospels, proceeding to the church fathers, and situating the origins of African American Christianity within the body of Christ as expressed throughout Christian history?

As a social construct, Whiteness undergoes a transformation in the minds and scholarship of certain Black people entrenched within the hyper-politicization of race. Whiteness becomes a philosophical concept, a religiopolitical quasi-entity, the representation of human immorality, and an unnecessary determinant of Black self-awareness, self-identification, and counter-religious expressions from which to define ourselves. I argue that Whiteness has replaced or at least competed with the concept and reality of God as the necessary center of discourse. Theologically, the *center of discourse* provides the interpretive lens and point of departure from which to analyze everything else. The centering of discourse within traditional Christian theology is Jesus Christ (Christology). I contend that Whiteness (White-ology) within Black academic religiosity has received undue attention to the extent it has become the primary center of discourse within Black academia in America.

In principle, this also applies to aspects of African American culture and politics. This is a consequence of persistently secularizing African American Christianity and Black religiosity vis-à-vis racialized nationalism, which has become preoccupied, and arguably obsessed with suppressing and eradicating the influence of Whiteness in the world. Again, I am not denying the existence of White supremacy. Nor am I irrationally arguing we should stop exposing and seeking to eviscerate White supremacy. Instead, I am questioning whether Whiteness and White supremacy are synonymous in the minds of certain Black people. I am examining whether these people have an adequate or realistic perception of reality as reality is.

2

A Conservative Evangelical Critique

Black Power and the Theology of James Cone

THE RISE OF SECULAR BLACK POWER

SECULAR BLACK POWER POSITIONED itself in binary opposition to White America and opposed the conservative Civil Rights movement, which King and the African American Church represented. I interpret Black Power's oppositional stance as an example of essentialist and racialized binary reasoning within the social construction of a *new* Blackness. The interest, desire, passion, and obsession of certain African Americans to redefine themselves led to employing principles within Black Power, and by extension Black Nationalism, to contribute to the elusive notion of an Ideal-Blackness.

For roughly twelve years the Civil Rights movement was led by King through the conservative African American Church. No other sociopolitical alternatives had qualitatively competed with the conservative African American freedom movement through King's leadership. Although Malcolm X, the Nation of Islam, and other militant/radical groups such as the Black Panther Party had established an influential following, they never mobilized African Americans to the extent of King.[1] However, there

1. For cursory readings of Black Nationalism, the Black Panther Party, the Nation of Islam, Malcolm X, Pan-Africanism, and other groups, see Haley and Malcolm X, *Autobiography of Malcolm X*; Malcolm X, *By Any Means Necessary*; Robinson, *Black Nationalism*; Moses, *Classical Black Nationalism*; Muhammad, *History of the Nation of Islam*; Van Deburg, *Modern Black Nationalism*; Seale and Shames, *Power to the People*;

was a young Black activist who once worked alongside King and, upon his departure, contributed to the development of Black Power. Stokely Carmichael (1941–98) participated in and eventually became an influential leader within the Civil Rights movement through the Congress of Racial Equity (CORE) in 1961. He was also involved in the Student Nonviolent Coordinating Committee (SNCC) from 1964 to 1967.[2] Eventually, Carmichael became disillusioned with the conservative ideologies of King and the Civil Rights movement. In the summer of 1966, during a march for freedom in Mississippi, Carmichael aggressively chanted the words "Black Power!" as King was speaking. Afterward, King pleaded that Carmichael and other supporters refrain from using the phrase and replace it with the slogan "Freedom Now." However, King's request was quickly dismissed.[3]

AN IDENTITY AS THE ANTITHESIS

The Civil Rights movement crafted an identity and a collective voice that was influenced by Christianity, the African American Church, and King's leadership. However, there were people who obviously disagreed with King and did not identify with Christianity. This incited attempts to create alternative *identities*, collective *voices*, and sociopolitical ideologies that produced the results they craved. Generally, staunch Black Power advocates rarely identified with King. Their secular sociopolitical beliefs also created a natural distance from the core beliefs of Christianity and, consequently, the evangelical African American Church. Carmichael presents a statement of what I am referring to,

> One of the tragedies of the struggle against racism is that up to this point there has been no national organization which could speak to the growing militancy of young black people in the urban ghettos and the black-belt South. There has been only a "civil rights" movement, whose tone of voice was adapted to an audience of middle-class whites. It served as a sort of buffer zone between that audience and angry young blacks. It claimed

---

Pinkney, *Red, Black, and Green.*

2. For an examination of Stokely Carmichael's political thinking, see McCormack, "Stokely Carmichael and Pan-Africanism," 386–409.

3. Carson and Shepard, *Call to Conscience*, 91; King, *Where Do We Go from Here?*, 33–34; Fairclough, *Martin Luther King, Jr.*, 104, 115–18, 128–33, 137; C. King, *My Life with Martin Luther*, 291; Ansbro, *Martin Luther King, Jr.*, 212–18.

> to speak for the needs of a community, but it did not speak in the tone of that community.[4]

Carmichael presented a sharp critique regarding the conservative element of the Civil Rights movement. Interestingly, he dedicates attention to the tone, behavior, or character of the collective-Selves who create a movement. For Carmichael, they don't represent the Black community as he viewed it but conformed or assimilated to the interest of White America. For him, the conservative Civil Rights movement was appeasing White America through some willful submissiveness. The conservative evangelical Blacks did not entirely serve the interest of enlightened Blacks, who were the angry young Blacks. Carmichael and others believed the radical Black youth were ignored by the older conservative Blacks and, consequently, were not properly represented without a collective identity. This manifested through the absence of the angry young Black community's voice and their rejection of social norms that viewed anger as a sign of weakness, barbarism, and a lack of sophistication. In this context, we should understand why some Black Power advocates rejected the docility, passiveness, and weakness they accused King of teaching. We see the beginning of African American culture dividing into binary opposites, as the militant youth positioned themselves in opposition to their conservative elders. Carmichael explained further,

> The advocates of Black Power reject the old slogans and meaningless rhetoric of previous years in the Civil Rights struggle. The language of yesterday is indeed irrelevant: progress, nonviolence, integration, fear of "white backlash," coalition. Let us look at the rhetoric and see why these terms must be set aside or redefined.[5]

Carmichael dismisses roughly thirteen years of the Civil Rights movement. He articulates its general goals as superficial concessions to White America. We also witness a common theme within Black Power: the call for *newness* and *redefinition*. However, it is in the context of separation from Whiteness. Moreover, a continual portrait of binary

4. Carmichael and Hamilton, *Black Power*, 64; see also Carmichael, "Power and Racism," 61.

5. Carmichael and Hamilton, *Black Power*, 64. Carmichael also commented, "We had to work for power, because this country does not function by morality, love, and nonviolence, but by power." Carmichael, "Power and Racism," 62.

opposition is established through disagreements with the ideologies and practices of the conservative community of the Civil Rights movement.

We must look at the obvious disagreements that crystallized between these two groups. For some, this will be common knowledge, and for others, this brief discussion may be enlightening. Nevertheless, I am emphasizing critical reflection on the consequences of these two groups' disagreements through the lens of racialized binary reasoning. Racialized binary reasoning is more than simple disagreements. This reasoning views the world through a mythic *Manichean* struggle where two or more groups perpetually oppose each other through an either/or and us/them paradigm. I argue that Black Power established a duality of binary opposition occurring simultaneously *against* Whiteness and *within* Blackness. However, to understand what this entails, we must first ask, "What is Black Power?" This is a question I am primarily interested in as determined by the first generation within the Civil Rights movement.

BLACK POWER: WHAT IS IT?

The concept of Black Power is extremely ambiguous, yet Black Power advocate Joseph R. Washington Jr. insists this is a positive attribute: "Black Power is for many people a paradox surrounded by an enigma containing a mystery. Black Power raises more questions than answers, but this is more indicative of strength than weakness."[6] Washington maintains that "the confusion of meanings surrounding Black Power is instructive. Black Power means many things to many people; therefore it is many things."[7] Washington's interpretation is elusive. His views point to the consuming nature of Black Power as it confiscates the most basic and universal beliefs. Generally, Black Power represents to him Black people using their freedom to establish a *new* Black consciousness, and Black self-determination that recreates a Black identity *independent* of Whiteness.[8] However, I argue that the ideology and movement never developed beyond these broad themes.

6. J. R. Washington, *Subreption*, ix.

7. J. R. Washington, *Subreption*, x. Washington defines Black Power in many ways. For example, he states, "Black Power cannot be definitively defined because it is the multifaceted emergence of a whole people with all their varied experiences and achievements into a nearly common consciousness of a single destiny." J. R. Washington, *Subreption*, 63; see also 20, 111, 118.

8. MacDonald, "Black Power," 547–54; Van Horne, "Concept of Black Power," 365–89; J. Smith, "I Learned to Feel Black," 217; Poussaint, "Negro American," 100–101.

Carmichael defines Black Power as "a call for black people in this country to unite, to recognize their heritage, to build a sense of community. It is a call for black people to begin to define their own goals, to lead their own organizations and to support those organizations."[9] Carmichael insists that these goals were never established prior to Black Power. Evidently, in his view, African Americans had embodied a limited form of collective agency. He further elaborates on Black Power, stating, "Black people must come together and do things for themselves. They must achieve self-identity and self-determination in order to have their daily needs met," and "Black Power therefore calls for black people to consolidate behind their own, so that they can bargain from a position of strength."[10] Carmichael implies that Black unity, self-identity, and self-determination are achieved solely through racial segregation. LeRoi Jones echoes a similar belief, citing "Black Power is the power first to be Black" and "a program of Consciousness. The consciousness to Act."[11] Jones further explains, "Black Power must mean a black people with a past clear back to the beginning of the planet, channelling the roaring energies of black to revive black power."[12] Beyond the broad calls of racial unification, self-consciousness, and self-determination there was a strong emphasis on *redefining* Blackness within specific oppositional paradigms.

REDEFINING BLACKNESS

Black Power advocates describe a world created and defined by Whiteness. *Blackness*, by the extension of slavery through European colonial imperialism, is also partially created by Whiteness. For Black Power advocates, this justifies redefining Blackness independently from Whiteness. Carmichael claims,

> Our basic need is to reclaim our history and our identity from what must be called cultural terrorism, from the depredation of self-justifying white guilt. We shall have to struggle for the right to create our own terms through which to define ourselves and our relationship to the society, and to have these terms recognized.[13]

9. Carmichael and Hamilton, *Black Power*, 58.
10. Carmichael and Hamilton, *Black Power*, 60, 61.
11. L. Jones, "Civil Rites," 122, 125.
12. L. Jones, "Civil Rites," 123.
13. Carmichael and Hamilton, *Black Power*, 49.

Carmichael's approach to redefining Blackness stems from an assumption that a set of purely Black sources, hermeneutics, and methodologies exist that are not *tainted* by Whiteness. He also insinuates that this is a temporary process. However, I interpret this as a perpetual struggle, because this process is burdened with the responsibility of redefining an entire race and culture within a void. Within a pluralistic society, every culture has a relative influence upon other groups. Thus, Whiteness will influence Blackness, and vice versa. Moreover, Carmichael's thinking entertains the possibility of racial and cultural purity: a refined Blackness that exists in and of itself.

The call to redefine racial identity and to reclaim a mythic conception of Black history alludes to the continent of Africa as a source to achieve these goals. Some scholars refer to this as *Pan-Africanism*. Regarding sociopolitical unity, Carmichael suggests this direction: "The extent to which black Americans can and do 'trace their roots' to Africa, to that extent will they be able to be more effective on the political scene."[14] Thus, through Africa, African Americans have the potential to establish adequate sociopolitical unity and power to achieve their liberation. This is also a significant theory among Black nationalists and Afrocentric people. However, Carmichael is not alone; Washington makes a similar claim: "Black people must change this society through reorientation to their African heritage because in the long run time is on the side of black people throughout the world; they are the real source, inspiration, commitment, identity, and models."[15] As African Americans, Black Power advocates assume they are not influenced or *tainted* by Whiteness. There is the perception that they are enlightened and have escaped such challenges, and this creates a distance not only from Whiteness, but also with unenlightened Blacks. Black Power advocates falsely assume that their binary opposition *against* Whiteness does not have a relative equivalent *within* Blackness. Redefining Blackness apart from Whiteness becomes a central pillar in the construction of the mythic Ideal-Blackness. Attempts to redefine Blackness developed in various ways, one of which was centered on opposing King and the conservative element of the Civil Rights movement on the issue of integration.

14. Carmichael and Hamilton, *Black Power*, 59.

15. J. R. Washington, *Subreption*, 94; see also Davis and Brown, "Antipathy of Black Nationalism," 241.

INTEGRATION

Black Power advocates argued that Blackness is preserved and recreated by avoiding sociocultural integration into middle-class America. For them, middle-class America was defined by and represents the corrupted nature of Whiteness. Carmichael insists that "'Integration' is another current example of a word which has been defined according to the way white Americans see it."[16] He also implied that King's attempts to advance racial integration were naïve: "We must face the fact that, in the past, what we have called the movement has not really questioned the middle-class values and institutions of this country. If anything, it has accepted those values and institutions without fully realizing their racist nature."[17] Washington suggests,

> Some hold the objective to be integration beyond desegregation. By integration is meant the social process of interaction and effective communication between blacks and whites whereby there is a sharing of societal life. Integration in this sense means developing a style of life compatible with the white middle class in terms of education, occupation, income, housing, and basic values.[18]

The racialized binary reasoning of some Black Power advocates prohibited them from conceiving Blackness as a stable existence that influences Whiteness. This developed from their interpretation of Blackness as existing in a state of survival, self-preservation, and redefining itself *against* Whiteness.

Black Power advocates described integration into middle-class America as a process whereby Whiteness controls, deconstructs, and redefines Black humanity through sociocultural *assimilation*. For Carmichael, "'Integration' also means that black people must give up their identity, deny their heritage."[19] Blackness cannot coexist alongside Whiteness, because Whiteness consumes Blackness, and Blackness loses its unique identity. A compromise does not exist for Carmichael, as he describes a

16. Carmichael and Hamilton, *Black Power*, 51.

17. Carmichael and Hamilton, *Black Power*, 55.

18. J. R. Washington, *Subreption*, 7–8. African Americans have struggled to practice the four modes of multicultural relationships: assimilation, accommodation, integration, and segregation. African American philosopher Cornel West reinterprets these categories into the assimilationist, exceptionalist, humanist, and traditionalist. West, "Four Traditions of Response," 69–91.

19. Carmichael and Hamilton, *Black Power*, 69.

Manichean struggle between Black and White America whereby interaction denotes impurity and a negation of existence. Therefore, African Americans who integrate into middle-class America are interpreted as superficial images of European Americans.[20] Consequently, by advocating this theory, Carmichael equates impoverished Black communities as the antithesis to the White middle-class. Moreover, he never provides a detailed theory for Black social mobility. Carmichael merely portrays Blackness as retreating into an imaginary place to preserve, restore, and redefine itself through mythic Black sources that are undefiled by Whiteness.

Regarding Black integration, Carmichael argues, "Their kind of integration has meant that a few blacks 'make it,' leaving the black community, sapping it of leadership potential and know how."[21] Referring to them as *token Negroes*, Carmichael suggests that "they become meaningless show-pieces for a conscience-soothed white society."[22] He employs essentialist and racialized binary reasoning that articulates Black Power fighting *against* Whiteness, but also creating division *within* Blackness. For Black Power advocates, Blackness is subjected to a qualitative judgment according to the binary oppositional paradigms of poverty/middle-class, segregation/integration, and militant/conservative. This alludes to an Ideal-Blackness that is loosely constructed from the collective identities of impoverished Black people who are encouraged to be militant segregationists and are positioned *against* Whiteness. Likewise, Black identity that is loosely defined by middle-class America, and by concepts like integration, conservatism, and openness to Whiteness, is deemed a *fragmented* existence.

As a segregationist movement, Black Power advocates positioned themselves as the antithesis of King, the conservative African American Church, and the Civil Rights movement. They merely reversed the positions and principles that were established by King. Ironically, by doing so, some Black Power advocates imitated the goals and outcomes established by White supremacists. For example, during colonialism, racial segregation was enforced by Eurocentric notions of purity and African impurity. Some Black Power advocates replicated these beliefs by conjuring notions of Black purity by attempting to redefine Blackness apart

20. Carmichael also defined middle-class America as anti-humanist and a perpetuator of racism. Carmichael and Hamilton, *Black Power*, 46, 54, 55.

21. Carmichael and Hamilton, *Black Power*, 67.

22. Carmichael and Hamilton, *Black Power*, 67.

from Whiteness. I argue that Whiteness is also unable to redefine itself in European enclaves that are detached from the presence/influence of Blackness.

King employed integration as one of many principles to pressure White Americans into contexts whereby they worked/lived *alongside* Black Americans. This was a progressive goal that required both communities to work together. King stated,

> For many years the Negro tacitly accepted segregation. He was the victim of stagnant passivity and deadening complacency. The system of slavery and segregation caused many Negroes to feel that perhaps they were inferior. This is the ultimate tragedy of segregation. It not only harms one physically, but it injures one spiritually. It scars the soul and distorts the personality. It inflicts the segregator with a false sense of superiority while inflicting the segregated with a false sense of inferiority.[23]

For King, racial integration increased and strengthened the collective self-esteem of African Americans. It assisted African Americans in realizing and nurturing their humanity as they progressively viewed themselves as equal to European Americans. Yet, taking an oppositional stance, Carmichael argued,

> "Integration" as a goal today speaks to the problem of blackness not only in an unrealistic way but also in a despicable way. It is based on complete acceptance of the fact that in order to have a decent house or education, black people must move into a white neighbourhood or send their children to a white school. This reinforces, among both black and white, the idea that "white" is automatically superior and "black" is by definition inferior. For this reason, "integration" is a subterfuge for the maintenance of white supremacy.[24]

Carmichael presents an uncompromising decision between loyalty to Blackness as liberation and complicity to Whiteness as bondage. He is adamant that Whiteness is completely corrupt but powerful. This complements his assumption that Black integrationists represent the instability of Blackness. Any movement toward Whiteness deconstructs the identity of Blackness and makes it qualitatively different from the redefined Blackness that exists apart from Whiteness. Nonetheless, another

23. King, *Testament of Hope*, 85; Carson and Shepard, *Call to Conscience*, 62–63.

24. Carmichael and Hamilton, *Black Power*, 68.

controversial issue separating King and the Black Power movement was the practice of nonviolent activism.

THE PERMISSIBILITY OF VIOLENCE

Black Power advocates were not violent, but their rhetoric affirmed that violence through self-defense was permissible. There were slight disagreements regarding the relevance of nonviolent activism. Robert F. Williams remarks, "We must use non-violence as a means as long as this is feasible, but the day will come when conditions become so pronounced that nonviolence will be suicidal in itself. The day is truly coming when we will see more violence on the same American scene."[25] Williams is aware of White society's violence toward Black people. This influences his assumption that things will get worse and that nonviolent activism will become obsolete. Carmichael provides an alternative stance, stating, "Responsibility for the use of violence by black men, whether in self-defense or initiated by them, lies with the white community."[26] Carmichael relinquishes responsibility from Black society. In his mind, there is justification for Blacks to initiate violence at will in the name of liberation. Carmichael argued, "Those of us who advocate Black Power are quite clear in our own minds that a 'non-violent' approach to civil rights is an approach black people cannot afford and a luxury white people do not deserve."[27] We witness further Carmichael's opposition to King. He rejects nonviolent protest as a viable option without any legitimate replacement.

Washington insists that nonviolent protest was an affront to the fighting spirit of Black people and Black Power: "Nonviolence continues to be a direct repudiation of the Black Power dimension of blacks, which began on the slave ships and continued through the insurrections into the Civil War and Emancipation."[28] He argues that Black Power was present among the slaves during colonialism, and it provided them with a fighting spirit. Moreover, Washington claims violence has intrinsic value and that "violence is the means Black Power resorts to in the belief that all other means have been exhausted in the quest for freedom

25. R. Williams, "From Negroes with Guns," 158; see also Wendt, "Protection or Path," 320–32.

26. Carmichael, "Power and Racism," 63–64.

27. Carmichael and Hamilton, *Black Power*, 67.

28. J. R. Washington, *Subreption*, 61.

and equality with social justice."[29] His rhetoric is typical of some Black Power advocates. The imagery of an aggressive paramilitary organization against a racist White society created a sense of unity among its members. Ironically, individuals like Washington could not discern how their beliefs restricted them from finding pragmatic solutions to achieve Black liberation. Violence, according to Washington, is the final solution. King expressed noticeable disdain for militant rhetoric that feigned violence. He once critiqued Malcolm X on this topic:

> I know that I have often wished that he would talk less of violence, because violence is not going to solve our problem. And, in his litany of articulating the despair of the Negro without offering any positive, creative alternative, I feel that Malcolm has done himself and our people a great disservice. Fiery, demagogic oratory in the black ghettos, urging Negroes to arm themselves and prepare to engage in violence, as he has done, can reap nothing but grief.[30]

Williams, Carmichael, and Washington's views stem partially from misunderstanding, and this influenced their propensity to oppose most of what King taught and represented. Interestingly, King never disagreed with realistic principles of self-defense. Frustrated, King once stated, "The question was not whether one should use his gun when his home was attacked, but whether it was tactically wise to use a gun while participating in an organized demonstration."[31] For King, beyond a repulsion to violence, it was irrational to entertain the possibility of violence in a nonviolent protest or march throughout a community. Nor was it feasible to craft an aggressive rhetoric that feigned violence in the cause of liberation. King stated, "One of the greatest paradoxes of the Black

29. J. R. Washington, *Subreption*, 197; see also 198–202.

30. King, *Autobiography*, 265–66. I argue that Black Nationalism and Black Power shared similar principles. In many ways, Black Nationalism provided some basic theoretical structures which Black Power advocates mimicked. Nonetheless, King never withheld his thoughts about Black Nationalism: "In a real sense, the growth of black nationalism was symptomatic of the deeper unrest, discontent, and frustration of many Negroes because of the continued existence of racial discrimination. Black Nationalism was a way out of that dilemma. It was based on an unrealistic and sectional perspective that I condemned both publicly and privately. It substituted the tyranny of black supremacy for the tyranny of white supremacy." King, *Autobiography*, 269.

31. King, *Where Do We Go from Here?*, 33. King also stated that "the principles of self-defense, even involving weapons and bloodshed, has never been condemned, even by Gandhi, who sanctioned it for those unable to master pure nonviolence." King, *Testament of Hope*, 32; see also 12, 17–18, 26, 33.

Power movement is that it talks unceasingly about not imitating the values of white society, but in advocating violence it is imitating the worst, the most brutal and the most uncivilized value of American life."[32] King displayed a keen understanding of Black Power. He sympathized with its practitioners, and his critiques were always bestowed with compassion.

King also ascertained that despite Black Power's dysfunction, the problem was centered on White America's reluctance to support racial equality. He argued that every step of progress for racial equality was confronted by *White backlash*. This applied to the diminishing momentum of the Civil Rights movement. King stated,

> The white backlash of today is rooted in the same problem that has characterized America ever since the black man landed in chains on the shores of this nation. The white backlash is an expression of the same vacillations, the same search for rationalizations, the same lack of commitment that have always characterized white America on the question of race.[33]

This complemented his view that Black Power was a reactionary movement, created from frustration and despair at White America's indifference to racial equality: "Cries of Black Power and riots are not the causes of white resistance, they are consequences of it."[34] Yet, despite this, he still urged White Americans to participate in the movement to achieve racial equality.

King was aware of Black Power's inadequacies. He noted that it was emotionally and psychologically appealing to people who felt compelled to aggressively defend their racial identity from further degradation. Beyond this, Black Power never developed a progressive sociopolitical plan to implement. This led King to state definitively that "beneath all the satisfaction of a gratifying slogan, Black Power is a nihilistic philosophy born out of the conviction that the Negro can't win. It is, at bottom, the view that American society is so hopelessly corrupt and enmeshed in evil that there is no possibility of salvation within."[35] Black Power diminished as a movement within the early 1970s but continues to influence various people today. My concern is that it has deeply influenced the hermeneutics and methodologies of many African American academics and their scholarship.

32. King, *Where Do We Go from Here?*, 67.
33. King, *Where Do We Go from Here?*, 71; 116–17.
34. King, *Where Do We Go from Here?*, 21.
35. King, *Where Do We Go from Here?*, 49.

Racialized binary reasoning was a core aspect of *secular* Black Power. In various ways, Black Power advocates opposed White America through counterintuitive and counterproductive separatist ideologies. For some advocates, Whiteness was interpreted as a completely racist and corrupt existence that was *irredeemable*. This validated Black Power's separatist beliefs and attempts to redefine Blackness detached from Whiteness. Moreover, the process of redefining Blackness encouraged the discovery and implementation of untainted or pure Afrocentric/Black sources.

Black Power generated tension and eventually created division within Blackness by opposing King via the conservative evangelical African American Church and the Civil Rights movement. A paradigm of binary opposition developed between political divisions such as poverty/middle-class, segregation/integration, and radicalism/conservatism. Yet, the most destructive element was the qualitative judgment that described conservative Black people as a lesser essence of Blackness based upon their association with Whiteness. In doing so, Black Power advocates constructed an imaginative conflict between a mythic pure Blackness (liberal) and a fragmented, Whitewashed Blackness (conservative). I interpret this as alluding to the concept of an Ideal-Blackness. Nevertheless, I maintain that secular Black Power employed simultaneous expressions of essentialist and racialized binary reasoning *against* Whiteness and *within* Blackness.

An even darker turn is viewed with Black religiosity. The presence of racialized binary reasoning was endorsed by the proponents of *theological* Black Power. The religious advocates of Black power utilized the categories of secular Black Power and inherited its duality of racialized binary reasoning. I make this statement, in part, because the essence of Christianity vehemently opposes the basic tenets of Black Power endorsed by its advocates. Naturally, many people would disagree with me then, and there are those who would do so today. This brings us to the theological aspect of Black Power.

THE EMERGENCE OF THEOLOGICAL BLACK POWER

On July 31, 1966, the National Committee of Negro Churchmen drafted a Black Power statement that contributed to an alternative Christian identity, and influenced the future development of theological Black Power.[36]

36. The Black Power statement is a document by radical Black Christian clergy

Vincent Harding articulated one of the earliest attempts to Christianize Black Power.[37] His writings represented much of what secular Black Power argued, but contextualized it within underdeveloped Christian categories. Two of Harding's essays, "Black Power and the American Christ" and "The Religion of Black Power," display the normative themes of Black Power's prophetic message, the renewal of Blackness, critiques of American Christianity, the White Christ, and an interpretation of King's failures.[38] Harding identifies Black Power to Jesus and portrays the movement as a prophetic judgment from God. For Harding, the association is obvious, and any reluctance to accept this was representative of the individual's spiritual ineptitude:

> We have no choice but to hold Black Power in our black arms and examine it, convinced that Christ is Lord of this too. Anyone who is black and claims to be a part of the company of Christ's people would be derelict if he failed to make such an examination and to proclaim with fear and trembling and intimations of great joy what he has discovered.[39]

Harding makes a distinction between the real and false Christ. He states that the American Christ was "painted White and pink, blond and blue-eyed—and not only in white churches but in black churches as well."[40] Consequently, as Black Christians worshiped the White Christ, they were dehumanized, inflicted with a sense of shame and self-hatred: "This Christ shamed us for our blackness, for our flat noses, for our kinky hair, for our power, our strange power of expressing emotion in singing and shouting and dancing. He was sedate, so genteel, so white. And as

---

regarding sociopolitical power, freedom, love, justice, and truth. The document is directed toward four distinct groups: the leaders of America, White churchmen, Negro citizens, and the mass media. See Barbour, *Black Power Revolt*, 264–72; N. Wright, *Black Power and Urban Unrest*, 187–94; Cone and Wilmore, *Black Theology*, 2; Hopkins and Cummings, *Cut Loose Your Stammering Tongue*, xiii; Cone, *For My People*, 5–6; Ware, *Methodologies of Black Theology*, 2–5; J. Evans, *We Have Been Believers*, 1–10.

37. Joseph R. Washington Jr. and Albert B. Cleage Jr. had also written about Black Power and Christianity prior to James Cone. Washington, *Black Religion*; Washington, *Politics of God*; Cleage, *Black Messiah*. Cleage also published *Black Nationalism*.

38. Harding, "Black Power and the American Christ," 85–93. Originally published in *The Christian Century*, January 4, 1967. Harding, "Religion of Black Power," 715–45. Originally published in *The Religious Situation*.

39. Harding, "Black Power and the American Christ," 86.

40. Harding, "Black Power and the American Christ," 87.

soon as we were able, many of us tried to be like him."[41] From Harding's words, we witness another interpretation regarding the religious degeneration of Blackness. Harding insinuates that cultural and racial assimilation created the subsequent process of denying Blackness and affirming Whiteness as many Black Christians worshiped and desired to be like the White Christ. Harding creates binary opposition between Black Power advocates who worship the real Christ and the adversaries of Black Power that supposedly worship the White Christ. Yet, tragic irony is described by Harding as he states that the White Christ contributed to his own demise by assisting in the creation of Black Power.[42] Thus, Black Power is partially representative of the Blackness that Whiteness had created. King would be in agreement.

Harding articulates a secondary salvation experience for everyone who kneeled at the altar of the White Christ. For him, this justifies Black Power's existence as "a repudiation of the American culture-religion that helped create it and a quest for a religious reality more faithful to our own experience."[43] Thus, we witness the inverted process of denying Whiteness via the American culture-religion and affirming a new Black Christianity contextualized *solely* from the existence of Black people. There is another emphasis on recreating Blackness. Harding claims that a "gospel of Blackness" restores Black self-love and self-esteem within Black people who embrace the religious dimensions of Black Power. To justify this, he recounts a critique of King that was given at a Black Power forum. The spokesman stated, "Martin King was trying to get us to love white folks before we learned to love ourselves, and that ain't no good."[44] In this context, tension develops over priorities as Harding encourages a decision-making process determined by an either/or mentality. Black people can either love and affirm their Black existence or deny it by loving and

41. Harding, "Black Power and the American Christ," 87. Harding also suggests that God may be judging America for creating a Christ that represented "a white, middle-class burner of children and destroyer of the revolution of the oppressed." Harding, "Black Power and the American Christ," 93.

42. Harding expresses this by asking, "If the American Christ and his followers have indeed helped mold the Black Power movement, then might it not be that the God whom many of us insist on keeping alive is not only alive but just?" He further stated, "If these things are difficult to believe perhaps we need to look more closely both at the American Christ and the black movement he has helped to create." Harding, "Black Power and the American Christ," 87.

43. Harding, "Black Power and the American Christ," 87.

44. Harding, "Religion of Black Power," 716.

affirming Whiteness. Some Black Power advocates, who were Christian, rejected the possibility that an individual can subsequently love and affirm themselves along with a White person. Harding insinuates this by mentioning Stokely Carmichael's words regarding the process of building a Black community of love. Harding states that "at this juncture white persons are simply not considered as valid objects of black love. Such love (or, more accurately, its outward appearance) has been forced from blacks for too long."[45] He later maintained, "An interim goal is now to make white men 'invisible' while black men are brought into the light."[46] It is here that we see an ideological variant of Paul Tillich's concept of Being and Nonbeing, a theory Cone openly embraced.

Harding and other Black Power spokesmen employed racialized binary reasoning that established two opposing paradigms: visibility/existence and invisibility/nonexistence. For them, Black people had to cultivate self-love for each other to create a community of solidarity that represented Black Power. This occurred before any love was expressed toward White society. We also see semblance to the belief that liberation must occur first before reconciliation could develop between the conflicting races. It must occur in sequence, not subsequently. Segregation is implied as the Black community is encouraged to coalesce apart from and avoid acknowledging the existence of White society. A compromise does not exist whereby Black and White society can live alongside each other. Symbolically, as the Black community increases and strengthens its existence, the White community decreases and weakens to nonexistence.

Through Black Power, the Black community develops a specific and universal identity. Harmony is established between the communities of Black Americans and all non-White people throughout the world who are victims of White supremacy. Harding states,

> Actually, many sections of the world are already included in the concerns of Black Power, and one has the feeling that there is intimated in these concerns a universalism that is at least as broad as that known by most western religious traditions. Black Power calls for an identification between black people here and all the wretched nonwhites of the earth. (Some leaders, like Carmichael, now expand this to the poor and oppressed of every color.)[47]

45. Harding, "Religion of Black Power," 718. I interpret this as another passive critique of King's emphasis on universal love.

46. Harding, "Religion of Black Power," 718.

47. Harding, "Religion of Black Power," 722.

It is here that we witness the development of a universal Blackness. Yet, Harding never expounds upon Black Power's quasi-religious universalism. He only references Stokely Carmichael's inclusion of the poor and oppressed into the community of Black Power. Harding insists that Black Power and its universal community serve as God's judgments

> upon American religion, especially the faith of those persons who claim a master who came to set all broken victims free. For while such religious respectable stand silently or march weakly protesting, the devotees of Black Power identify themselves unambiguously with the oppressed and with the revolution made by the oppressed.[48]

I interpret this as criticism of the Black and White church along with the conservative Civil Rights movement. Harding continues to position theological Black Power *against* Whiteness, but he also creates tension *within* Blackness. He interprets conservative Black Christians as participating in futile marches and detached from the revolution of Black liberation.

Harding further argues that, through Black Power, God empowers the non-Whites and oppressed of the world to fight against American religion and the White Christ. This complements the belief that American religion, as well as the Black and White churches, need redemption through Black Power. Nathan Wright Jr. comments, "American religion needs to be regenerated. Black Power, as a concept emphasizing the need to bring a different focus to bear upon life itself and its possibilities, may open a pathway toward the renewal of American religious life."[49] Additionally, secular and religious categories merged through the Christianizing of Black Power. This is viewed in the newer conception of Blackness.

Wright emphasizes a transcendent form of power that is central to human development and the progressive nature of life. Thus, through his interpretation, power has a religious aspect that *glorifies* Blackness. Wright states,

> A possible clue to a resolution of our predicament lies in the glorification aspect of the Black Power emphasis. Blackness—which includes by definition all shades and complexions of non-whiteness—has been degraded in our culture. The glorification of blackness implicit in the term Black Power is a conscious or unconscious effort to stake a claim for the worth of those in our

48. Harding, "Religion of Black Power," 722.

49. N. Wright, *Black Power and Urban Unrest*, 143; see also 134, 141, 144, 145.

> nation who are termed non-white. Essentially it is a clarification. The root meaning of the term "glorify" is to clarify, to make clear and plain and straight.[50]

Wright is concerned about the regeneration and redemption of Blackness from being dehumanized by American religion and its White Christ. For Wright, Black Power humanizes Black people into an existence that God intended. Blackness becomes a global community of self-love and self-determination that is liberated from Whiteness. Harding contributes to Wright's interpretation by stating,

> If one follows this invaluable line of thought, it is obvious that Black Power has within it the possibility of setting black men in an entirely new light—the light of their Creator. They are called upon to see themselves as they were meant to be. This glorification has the potential of setting them at peace with themselves—and with the creative purposes of the universe; they no longer need to curse God and die. For their Blackness is now—like the rest of their createdness—a sign of His love and not His anger.[51]

Harding, like Wright, expresses a deep connection between Black Power and the real God. However, both men never outline exactly how God created Black Power. Rather, they insist Black Power is God's vessel to liberate and redeem Black people throughout the world. Thus, Wright insists that Black Power has a sacred aspect: "to the precise extent that Black Power affirms and extends God's truth and purposes, it is in the same degree possessed of sacred and eternal virtue. It is partially thus a sign of the presence of God's rule, which is what is meant by the term 'the Kingdom of God.'"[52] There is subtle wordplay between existence, light, and visibility. This complements the reoccurring themes of Blackness representing invisibility and nonexistence in the context of oppression. The wordplay is also associated with dehumanization and the loss of identity. Furthermore, through Black Power, glorification represents the revelation that Blackness is a beautiful creation of God. Harding also alludes to the destructive nature of Black self-hate by stating that some Black people maintained God had created them from anger. The reference to cursing God and dying is influenced by Job 2:9.[53] Harding and

50. N. Wright, *Black Power and Urban Unrest*, 139.

51. Harding, "Religion of Black Power," 728.

52. N. Wright, *Black Power and Urban Unrest*, 153.

53. Job 2:9, "Then his [Job's] wife said to him, 'Do you still hold firm your integrity? Curse God and die!'"

Wright provide us a glimpse into how Black Power was beginning to be contextualized into a Christian narrative.

Secular and theological Black Power shared the same agenda: Black liberation from White supremacy. However, theological Black Power, at least initially, was underdeveloped in comparison to its secular counterpart. We must remember that theological Black Power gained notoriety from non-academic Christian clergy and scholars who were not formally trained in academic theology. Thus, there was an opportunity for Black academic theologians to develop theological Black Power. This was fulfilled primarily by James H. Cone. Cone was an aggressive Black Power advocate who advanced theological Black Power beyond his predecessors. Cone is acknowledged as the most prominent Black theologian since 1969. Cone adopted and developed the categories/themes originally presented by his secularist and theological Black Power predecessors.

MIMESIS OF BLACK LIBERATION THEOLOGY

Cone is still considered by many people to be the most prominent contemporary Black theologian. Surprisingly, his theology has been the beneficiary of selective decontextualization. Predictably, his admirers have ignored the negative effects of Black Power upon his theology, resulting in the illusion that none exist. These same admirers selectively reference Cone's association to Black Power either abstractly or as a positive asset.[54] However, Cone's critics take a similar approach as they too ignore or minimize his identification with Black Power.[55] Cone's theology would

54. Murphy, "African American Christian Perspectives," 73–82; Kubic, "Between Malcolm and Martin," 448–67; Grant, "Black Christology," 366–75; Ruether, "Black Theology and Black Church," 347–51; Clay, "Black Theology," 307–26; L. Smith, "Black Theology and Religious Experience," 59–72; Erskine, "Black Theology," 176–85; Cumming, "Contrasts and Fragments," 395–416; P. Williams, "Ethical Aspects," 34–45; Fields, *Introducing Black Theology*, 14; Ware, *Methodologies of Black Theology*, 3, 4; Johnson, "Prophetic Persona," 266–85; Richie, "Theories of Cone and King Jr.," 86–106; McKinney, "Concept of 'Black Theology,'" 10–14; James, "Tillichian Analysis," 16–30; J. Evans, *We Have Been Believers*, 3–5, 110–11, 132; Burrow, "Who Teaches Black Theology?," 7–18.

55. Anderson, *Beyond Ontological Blackness*, 86, 134, 143; D. Andrews, *Practical Theology for Black Churches*; Bradley, *Liberating Black Theology*, 125, 162, 182; Carter, *Race*, 159, 161; C. Cone, *Identity Crisis*; Harden, "Toward a Practical Black Theology," 35–55; W. Jones, "Theodicy and Methodology," 541–57; P. Williams, "James Cone," 483–94; Witvliet, "In Search of Black Christology," 17–32; Sontag, "Coconut Theology," 5–12.

not exist without Black Power. His initial program, which was established prior to other Black Power advocates, was to provide an *advance* theological interpretation of the movement. As I interpret things, any neglect to critically reflect upon Cone's identification with Black Power, how it shaped his theology, and the possibility of it causing division with conservative African American Christians is extremely confusing. I connect this to my conviction that Cone's theology did not develop much throughout his career, because his Black Power hermeneutics and methodologies governed his work.

In the 1989 preface to his 1969 book, *Black Theology and Black Power*, Cone stated, "Considered within the sociopolitical context of the sixties, I still believe that my answer was correct: 'Christianity . . . is Black Power.'"[56] To my knowledge, Cone never rejected or distanced himself from Black Power. However, he had consistently published literature about the movement and its connection to Black theology.[57] As I understand it, sociopolitical movements increase and decrease, but all will eventually die. However, the *spirit* of a movement can transcend geography and time to influence anyone within knowledge of its existence.

WHAT IS BLACK POWER FOR CONE?

Black Power has always been an ambiguous sociopolitical concept, philosophy, and movement. Cone acknowledges its elusiveness. However, after three years (1969) of its prominence in America, Cone justifies this by stating, "the advocates of Black Power need time to define its many implications."[58] Yet, there is a deceptive and illusory aspect to ambiguous terms and the inability of practitioners to clearly define what/who they identify with. In this context, Black Power has consistently been defined as *self-consciousness* and *self-determination* that creates Black liberation from White supremacy. Thus, as I interpret it, Black Power is a vague concept sustained by vague concepts. This ambiguity allows for almost anything construed as self-consciousness and self-determination to be conflated as representative of Black Power. For example, Cone defines Black Power as "complete emancipation of black people from white

56. Cone, *Black Theology and Black Power*, ix.

57. Cone, *My Soul Looks Back*; and *Risks of Faith*.

58. Cone, *Black Theology and Black Power*, 5.

oppression by whatever means black people deem necessary."[59] Yet, it also embodies "an attitude, an inwards affirmation of the essential worth of blackness."[60] These statements also apply to Cone's concept of Black consciousness: "Black consciousness is Black Power, the power of the oppressed black man to liberate himself from white enslavement by making blackness the primary datum of his humanity. It is the power to be black in spite of whiteness, the courage to affirm being in the midst of nonbeing."[61] Cone also explains, "Black consciousness means rejecting the white oppressor's definition of being by re-creating the historical black being that is an antithesis of everything white."[62] Thus, as Cone describes them, Black power, self-consciousness, and self-determination are interchangeable concepts.

J. Deotis Roberts, Cone's peer, maintains that "Black Power symbolizes a number of images and ideas drawn from black history and the black experience: black consciousness, pride, self-respect, community control, reparations, empowerment, personhood, and peoplehood," and "a new mind-set, a new way of seeing life and relations between persons."[63] From these broad definitions, we witness the themes that were initially presented by secular Black Power advocates: the renewal and affirmation of Blackness, human dignity, segregation, and the desire for White society to acknowledge Black people's humanity. These categories were also present during the beginning stages of theological Black Power. There is a glimpse of Cone's racialized binary reasoning within the definition of Black Power: Blackness as being and Whiteness as non-being. This was also presented within the secularist argument against racial integration.

Black theologians used the ambiguity of Black Power to appropriate universal principles in an exclusive way. They created an illusion that Black Power was the only concept that embodied these universal principles or exemplified them beyond the conservative community of the Civil Rights movement. Yet, the conservative secular and religious traditions within African American history also advocated liberation, the affirmation of Black People's humanity, self-consciousness/determination, and stern critiques regarding White supremacy in America.

59. Cone, *Black Theology and Black Power*, 6.

60. Cone, *Black Theology and Black Power*, 8; see also 7, 12.

61. Cone, "Black Consciousness," 49–50.

62. Cone, "Black Consciousness," 51.

63. Roberts, *Black Political Theology*, 70.

Despite its ambiguity, Black Power was an important identity to Cone. He maintained that "Black Power is the most important development in American life in this century," and he embraced the task of theologizing it beyond his peers.[64] Black Power advocates were the minority in African American culture, and many did not identify with Christianity. Cone stated that "Black Power advocates made no claim to an identity derived from Christianity. Most were secular university students or adherents of African religions, and all tended to define Christianity as 'the white man's religion.'"[65] Thus, there was considerable tension and difficulty from theologizing Black Power and presenting a new Christian identity to the conservative African American Christians who rejected the secular movement and followed King. This is compounded by the fact that Cone initially boasted that "my style of doing theology was influenced more by Malcolm X than by Martin Luther King, Jr."[66]

Cone's brother, Cecil Cone, has crafted one of the most critical examinations of Cone's theology, but it is widely ignored. Cecil states, "The manner in which Cone utilizes Black Power in the development of his theology suggests an uncritical acceptance of the movement, which leads to problems in his work."[67] I maintain that Cone's loyalty to Black Power, and his identification to Malcolm X, in conjunction with his theological program, alienated Black theology from the conservative evangelical African American Church.

BLACK POWER AND BLACK THEOLOGY

It is common knowledge, at least to those aware of Cone, that Black Power provided the key themes and categories for his theology. My emphasis is on the structure of Cone's theology, whether it was borrowed or an original thought of his. We also must assess whether there was a considerable change in Cone's theology throughout his career. For example, Cone often employed two terms he treats as interchangeable: *Black self-consciousness* and *Black self-determination*. This sometimes causes confusion from the repetitiveness of defining each term with the same general

64. Cone, *Black Theology and Black Power*, 1.

65. Cone, *For My People*, 59.

66. Cone, *Black Theology and Black Power*, xix; see also Cone, *Black Theology and Black Power*, viii; and "God and Black Suffering," 709.

67. C. Cone, *Identity Crisis*, 95.

meaning. However, Cone attempts to make a clear distinction between Black power and Black theology by stating,

> Black power and Black theology work on two separate but similar fronts. Both believe that Blackness is the primary datum of human experience which must be reckoned with, for it is the *reason* for our oppression and the only *tool* for our liberation. Black Power investigates the meaning of Blackness from the political, economic, and social condition of Black people, explicating what freedom and self-determination mean for the wretched of the earth. Black theology places the Black Power concept in its proper theological context, analysing Black liberation in the light of the gospel of Jesus Christ. Black theology is the theological arm of Black power, and Black Power is the political arm of Black theology.[68]

Black Power and Black theology are interdependent and inseparable. Cone counterintuitively collapses the totality of African American existence into a universal expression of Blackness as the oppressed. He employs an inverted principle whereby Blackness as the sole reason for oppression becomes the singular motivation for liberation. Blackness also begins a process of reification or ontologizing. For Cone, race is not a simple social construction. Nor does he ever engage the concept of race as a construct of Eurocentrism. In this way, Black liberation is included within the network of Black Power, Black theology, self-consciousness, and self-determination.

Cone attempted to legitimize Black Power by associating it with everything he deemed representative of Black empowerment and liberation.[69] For example, this methodology frequently employed another broad term, *Black religion*. Generally, Black religion represents the complete and universal religious expression of African Americans throughout their historical existence. Thus, Cone attempts to construct an interpretation of Black Power that permeates the full spectrum of African American religious beliefs and practices. He suggests that

> Black Power and Black religion are inseparable. Both seek to free black people from white racism. It is impossible for Black Power to be effective without taking into consideration man's religious

68. Cone, "Black Power and Ethics," 209.

69. Cecil Cone observes, "Yet when one takes the time to scrutinize carefully Cone's efforts in his first book, there slowly emerges a deeper attempt at a theology of Black Power." Cone, *Identity Crisis*, 93; see also 118, 120, 159–60.

> nature. It is impossible for black religion to be truly related to the condition of black people and to the message of Jesus Christ without emphasizing the basic tenets of Black Power. Therefore, Black theology, as I see it, seeks to make Black religion a religion of Black Power.[70]

In this context, Black religion is included in the constellation of interchangeable terms that expand the ambiguity of certain aspects of Cone's theology. In part, this developed from basing a theology on the ambiguous concept of Black Power. Moreover, racialized binary reasoning is evident in Cone's statement that "Black religion, therefore becomes a revolutionary alternative to white religion."[71] Cone's binary reasoning permeated through every theme, category, and terminology of his theology.

Cone's binary reasoning developed in two general ways. First, he employed essentialist reasoning to totalize a group, community, concept, or race. Second, Cone's reasoning is filtered through the paradigms of positive/negative, either/or, and us/them. There is always a relationship of antithesis being employed within his reasoning. Victor Anderson provides one of the most influential critiques of Cone's binary reasoning through the category of *ontological Blackness*. Anderson defines ontological Blackness as "a covering term that connotes categorical, essentialist, and representational languages depicting black life and experience."[72] He further explains,

> Ontological blackness is a philosophy of racial consciousness. It is governed by dialectical matrices that existentially structure African Americans' self-conscious perceptions of black life. Under ontological blackness, the conscious lives of blacks are experienced as bound by unresolved binary dialectics of slavery

70. Cone, *Black Theology and Black Power*, 130.

71. Cone, *God of the Oppressed*, 120–21. Cone's interpretation of Black religion employs the affirmation of Blackness and the rejection of Whiteness: "There is another side in black religion that is rooted in blackness and its identify with Africa and its rejection of America and Christianity." Cone, "God and Black Suffering," 707. Cone also stated that he emphasized the term "Black Theology" as a constructive theological alternative to White theology. Cone, *For My People*, 20.

72. Anderson, *Beyond Ontological Blackness*, 11. I am introducing Anderson at this point because our methodologies differ. I interpret Cone's binary reasoning as deriving primarily from theologizing Black Power. I demonstrated how its advocates established themselves as the antithesis to White society and conservative-Blackness. Anderson does not theorize where or how Cone develops his reasoning. He only provides an extremely brief overview of binary reasoning within Black theology and does not speculate on how division is created *within* Blackness.

> and freedom, negro and citizen, insider and outsider, black and white, struggle and survival.[73]

Cone employs these categories throughout his interpretation of Christianity, the gospel, God the Father, and Jesus Christ. The binary serves as the means to legitimize Black Power and Black theology.

CHRISTIANITY, GOD, AND JESUS

Liberation is the central theme that connects all of Cone's terminologies. This applies to his interpretations of the gospel, God the Father, and Jesus Christ. Cone argues, "Christianity is not alien to Black Power; it is Black Power."[74] He interprets God the Father within the either/or paradigm as he states, "Either God is for blacks in their fight for liberation from white oppressors, or God is not. God cannot be both for us and for white oppressors at the same time." In principle, this statement is true; however, through essentialist reasoning, Cone interprets White America as representative of the oppressor, and there isn't a strong emphasis on God's desire for the oppressor, as Whiteness, to be redeemed.

Cone does not stop at this point but also associates this principle to God's love: "We will not accept a God who is on everybody's side—which means that God loves everybody in spite of who they are, and is working (through the acceptable channels of society, of course) to reconcile all persons to the Godhead."[75] To a certain extent, particularly in his early work, Cone's racialized binary reasoning created a conflicting interpretation of God that undermined aspects of basic Christian doctrine. He interpreted God through the either/or and us/them paradigms that determined his love according to human character and whether it represented righteousness or unrighteousness. Thus, there is a qualitative and quantitative assessment of God's love for humanity that is stipulated upon sociopolitical activity. Cone further states, "There is no use for a God who loves white oppressors *the same* as oppressed blacks."[76] For Cone, this was an element of divine love that needed to be expressed through Black Power.

73. Anderson, *Beyond Ontological Blackness*, 14.

74. Cone, *Black Theology and Black Power*, 38, 42–43, 48, 62. Cone also argued that "the politics of black power was the gospel of Jesus to twentieth-century America," because both were concerned with liberating the oppressed. Cone, *For My People*, 32.

75. Cone, *Black Theology of Liberation*, 74.

76. Cone, *Black Theology of Liberation*, 74. This linear reasoning is consistent with Cone as he reinterprets salvation as primarily a sociopolitical concept. Cone, *Black Theology of Liberation*, 136.

The difficulty with Cone's reasoning is that he is completely fixated upon the skewed logic and practices of *White supremacy*. He seldom reasons apart from this. It appears, at least in his early work, that he assumed merely reversing the principles of White supremacy would create progress toward liberation. He does not acknowledge that general methodologies of inversion are counterintuitive and counterproductive as they only create a cycle of oppression. This is exactly what King referred to when he stated that Black supremacy is just as problematic as White supremacy. The only change comes through the wielders of power and how they impose their human will upon others. Nevertheless, the origin of Cone's reasoning did not stem from a vacuum but from his predecessors within Black Power. Skewed Black logic and practices developed from a reactionary stance that mirrored the skewed White logic and practices by simply inverting principles. As the idiom states, "What's good for the goose is good for the gander."

Cone interprets Jesus within the same methodologies he employed for God the Father. Cone advocates that Jesus is Black to symbolize his identification with the literal and symbolic Black people of the world.[77] This interpretation was originally presented within the theological Black Power that preceded Cone.

Cone is aware of other interpretations of Jesus clothed in Black flesh.[78] The humanity of Jesus is also subject to Cone's binary reasoning. He makes a distinction between Jesus' *universal* humanity, which is an illusion created by White supremacy, and Jesus' Jewish humanity, which symbolizes oppressed Black flesh. Cone maintains, "Jesus is not a human being for all persons; he is a human being for oppressed persons, whose identity is made known in and through their liberation."[79] Cone is not interested in a colorless Jesus as he interprets that concept as advocating the oppression of Black people throughout the world. This complements his description of God being for or against Black liberation. A neutral or colorless God does not exist. Race, color, and their symbolisms have a dominant role in Cone's theology whereby he seldom theologizes apart from them. Yet, this shouldn't be a surprise if we categorize his theology as a sociopolitical theology of race.

77. Cone, *Black Theology of Liberation*, 126–30. Jesus is also interpreted as revealing and equipping people to experience the full potentiality of their Black humanity. Cone, *Black Theology and Black Power*, 149; and "Black Power and Ethics," 212.

78. Cone, *Black Theology and Black Power*, 68–69.

79. Cone, *Black Theology of Liberation*, 91, 90.

BLACKNESS AND WHITENESS

Cone's racialized binary reasoning depicts Black and White existence as the antithesis of one another. This also applies to their contextual expressions of politics, Christianity, and theology. For Cone, Blackness represented the literal existence of Africans, African descendants, and dark-skinned people. However, he also attributed Blackness symbolically as "all victims of oppression who realize that survival of their humanity is bound up with liberation from Whiteness."[80] The universal definition of Blackness was originally presented by secular Black Power advocates. This is a crucial aspect of Cone's theology. He consistently defines Blackness in relation to a *corrupt* interpretation of Whiteness and how Whiteness has treated Blackness. We have already seen this through some of Cone's previously explored principles. A further example is evident in his definition of the Black condition/experience. Cone describes it as "the tension between life and death, identity crisis, and white social and political power."[81] We also witness this in Cone's definition of Black theology: "Black theology is an earthly theology! It is not concerned with the 'last things' but with the 'white thing.'"[82]

Whiteness represented Europeans, European descendants, light-skinned people, and everyone who represented the oppressor. For Cone, any aggressive act of domination by Whiteness in the world was representative of the Antichrist.[83] He further states, "Whiteness characterizes the activity of deranged individuals intrigued by their own image of themselves, and thus unable to see that they are what is wrong with the world."[84] Anderson makes a strong observation regarding Cone's definitions of Blackness, and the relationship he establishes between Blackness and Whiteness. Anderson argued,

> The difficulty arises here: (a) blackness is a signification of ontology and corresponds to black experience. (b) Black experience is defined as the experience of suffering and rebellion against

80. Cone, *Black Theology of Liberation*, 8.

81. Cone, *Black Theology of Liberation*, 11; see also 12–18.

82. Cone, *Black Theology of Liberation*, 123.

83. Cone, *Black Theology of Liberation*, 8, 6.

84. Cone, *Black Theology of Liberation*, 8. Cone is also suspicious of sympathetic White liberals who seek to assist Blacks in their fight for equality. Cone rejects their attempt to mutually understand the perspective of Black and White society. Cone states, "But he is still white to the very core of his being. What he fails to realize is that there is no place for him in this war of survival." Cone, *Black Theology and Black Power*, 27.

> whiteness. Yet (c) both black suffering and rebellion are ontologically created and provoked by whiteness as a necessary condition of blackness. (d) Whiteness appears to be the ground of black experience, and hence of black theology and its new black being. Therefore, while black theology justifies itself as radically oppositional to whiteness, it nevertheless requires whiteness, white racism, and white theology for the self-disclosure of its new black being and its legitimacy. In this way, black theology effectively renders whiteness identifiable with what is of ultimate concern.[85]

In short, Anderson argues that Cone's interpretation of Blackness and Black theology is dependent upon Whiteness and White theology. Yet, the definitions of Whiteness and White theology are interpretations based on questionable binary opposition. This explains Cone's essentialist reasoning that relies upon the us/them and either/or paradigms.

For Anderson, Cone collapses the totality of Black existence into a quasi-universal reality of subjugation to Whiteness and an attempt of liberation from it. Therefore, Blackness, as Cone articulates it, cannot point to any transcendent meaning beyond Whiteness: "Without transcendence from the determinacy of Whiteness, black theology's promise of liberation remains existentially a function of black self-consciousness (to see oneself as black, free, and self-determined)."[86] As Anderson explains, Cone's definition of Blackness is one that Whiteness has created. This is a similar view presented by King, regarding the rise of Black Power among African Americans. As I interpret Cone, the tragic irony that Anderson describes is that Cone's Black theology not only fails to fulfill its ultimate objective, which is to assist in the liberation of Black people, but it is also symbolically in bondage to Whiteness. Cone's theological program owes its existence to Whiteness and would cease to exist if the corrupted Whiteness Cone interprets begins to change. Anderson points to the only success of Black theology: emotional and psychological empowerment whereby Black people view themselves as liberated.

Anderson's interpretation of Cone is similar to King's interpretation of Black Power. It was King who originally interpreted Black Power as a nihilistic philosophy that provided limited emotional and psychological benefits to Black people. Anderson and King are correct as Cone inherited his racialized binary reasoning from theologizing Black Power. Black

85. Anderson, *Beyond Ontological Blackness*, 91–92.

86. Anderson, *Beyond Ontological Blackness*, 92–93.

Power and Cone employed mirroring principles to White supremacy with the false assumption that by doing so they were creating progress toward justice and equality. However, we must entertain the possibility that aspects of their ideologies and theologies were in contradiction with itself and the basic tenets of Christianity. If so, these internal contradictions were unintentionally aiding the creation and sustaining of a cycle of oppression, as they sought to reverse the roles of the oppressed and oppressor. Anderson also points to an important aspect of Cone's theology: the principles of being and nonbeing.

The principles of being and nonbeing are extremely important to Cone's theology. Yet, as is the case with many of his theories, they were originally presented by his secular Black Power predecessors. This was seen in the issue of racial integration.[87] A central point for Cone is that Whiteness seeks to make itself the center of existence and consequently defines existence through the image of Whiteness. Therefore, Cone describes Whiteness as representative of a narcissistic, imperialistic, and consuming type of *being*. The process of defining reality involves Whiteness dehumanizing and oppressing non-Whiteness. Cone defines this as *nonbeing*, and Blackness represents this in binary opposition to Whiteness. Cone remarks, "This is the content of 'tension between life and death.' By white definitions, whiteness is 'being' and blackness is 'nonbeing,'" and he further maintained, "'To be or not to be' is thus a dilemma for the black community: to assert one's humanity and be killed, or to cling to life and sink into nonhumanity."[88]

Cone's statements provide examples supporting Anderson's critique. We witness how Cone defines the Black experience and the Black community within the either/or and us/them paradigms determined by Whiteness. His statements also show us why he constantly emphasized the necessity of affirming Blackness. However, it is always articulated through racialized binary reasoning that reverses the principles of oppression by defining Whiteness as nonbeing.

Blackness is not only identified with the Father, Son, and Holy Spirit of Christian scriptures, but it is also interpreted as synonymous with

87. Cone takes a similar position against integration and violence that was presented by his Black Power predecessors. Cone, *Black Theology and Black Power*, 17, 18, 77, 143; *Black Theology of Liberation*, 14, 104; *For My People*, 8, 14, 42; and "Christian Faith and Political Praxis," 132.

88. Cone, *Black Theology of Liberation*, 12; 13; 17; see also "Black Power and Ethics," 202, 208–10.

salvation. Cone maintains that it is Whiteness, not Blackness, that must experience a loss of identity to experience salvation: "But the misunderstanding here is the failure to see that blackness or salvation (the two are synonymous) is the work of God, not a human work."[89] For Cone, Whiteness as representative of the Antichrist is irredeemable and must cease existing. Whiteness must radically transform itself through an identification with God and the oppressed by becoming Blackness. Cone argues that "Whites will be free only when they become new persons—when their white being has passed away and they are created anew in black being."[90] This is a central principle not only in Cone's work, but it also dominates the discipline of academic Black theology in America.

For Cone, Whiteness has not only defined existence, but it has corrupted everything within it. Therefore, he maintains, "What we need is the destruction of whiteness, which is the source of human misery in the world."[91] Cone's interpretations of Whiteness as representative of sin and evil are often viewed as extreme statements. He also maintained that White theology, being an extension of Whiteness, is not a Christian theology. White theology is merely a religious instrument of the government to oppress non-White people. Cone referenced, "In order to be a Christian theology, White theology must cease being white theology and become black theology by denying whiteness as an acceptable form of human existence and affirming Blackness as God's intention for humanity."[92] For Cone, Whiteness exists beyond the reaches of God's love and redemptive work on the cross. Whiteness is an apostasy. It is both interesting and amazing to see a certain set of hermeneutics established by Black Power permeate within the discipline of academic Black theology. In some cases, they are embraced by scholars within the entire discipline of African American studies. I often wonder how many are aware of or oblivious to this possibility.

Cone's theology was at a considerable distance from conservative evangelical African American Christianity, and some would claim it was not a theology *strongly* rooted in the Black Church. His theology was indeed revolutionary because he succeeded in theologizing the secular sociopolitical philosophy of Black Power, solidifying his theology within

89. Cone, *Black Theology of Liberation*, 69.

90. Cone, *Black Theology of Liberation*, 103; and *Black Theology and Black Power*, 81–82.

91. Cone, *Black Theology of Liberation*, 114.

92. Cone, *Black Theology of Liberation*, 110.

the academy and around the world. Yet, Cone's Black liberation theology was positioned *against* Whiteness, but it subsequently created division *within* Blackness as he falsely assumed that Black Power and Black theology had usurped the theology of King, the conservative evangelical African American Church that existed during colonial slavery.

CONFLICT WITHIN BLACKNESS

Cone's essentialist and racialized binary reasoning had created a theology that caused division *within* Blackness. Cone's theology of Black Power was intended to be countercultural and a constructive theology to White American Christianity. Yet, Cone's theology also became an affront to some conservative evangelical African American Christianity. Ironically, scholars have relatively ignored not only Cone's indebtedness to Black Power but also his presumptions that Black Power and his theological program had usurped King's achievements during the Civil Rights movement.[93]

Cone has consistently spoken about King's influence on his life and theology. He has expressed a deep appreciation for King and the legacy he had established. However, by Cone's admission, Malcolm X and Black Power were more theologically significant to him.[94] Cone generally interprets King within the usual either/or and us/them paradigms that partially define his reasoning. This expresses itself through what Anderson described as an articulation of Blackness in subjugation to Whiteness. An example of this is evident in a theological assumption of Cone. He stated,

> Although Martin Luther King Jr. and other civil rights activists did much to rescue the gospel from the heresy of white churches by demonstrating its life-giving power in the black freedom movement, they did not liberate Christianity from its cultural bondage to white, Euro-American values. Unfortunately, even African-American churches had deviated from their own

93. Cone has written much about King. See Cone, *Martin and Malcolm and America*; "Martin Luther King, Jr.," 409–20; "America," 263–78; "Theology of Martin Luther King, Jr.," 21–39; "Martin Luther King, Jr., and the Third World," 455–67; and "Demystifying Martin and Malcolm," 27–37.

94. Cone is rather confusing on this issue. Early in his career, Cone had aggressively identified with Black Power and Malcolm X. However, there is a noticeable change during the later 1970s to early 1980s. Cone makes a greater effort to identify with King during the later stages of his career. I argue that this coincides with the failure of Black Power and Cone becoming aware of the church's rejection of his theology.

> liberating heritage through an uncritical imitation of the white denominations from which they separated.[95]

In this context, Cone makes strong assumptions in his assessment of King, other civil rights activists, and conservative African American churches. First, as I interpret King, there is no indication in his writing and speeches that he entertained the notion that Christianity needed rescuing from a corrupt White American church. However, King had habitually critiqued the White church for its complacency and complicity to White supremacy. King never employed essentialist and racialized binary reasoning that interpreted Christianity within an either/or and us/them paradigm. Nor did he advocate that a demographic of people could epitomize its principles beyond other groups. Second, Cone's critique of the African American Church is reminiscent of his predecessors. Black Power advocates habitually critiqued the African American Church for supposedly mimicking their European American counterparts. Except the more extreme members who didn't align with Christianity tended to promote the false belief that "Christianity is the White man's religion." In these contexts, it's easy to see the critique of the White Christ being worshiped within the African American Church. This theory was employed by Malcolm X and Cone's theological predecessors. Nevertheless, it is Cone who assumes that Whiteness has seized Christianity; therefore, Christianity needs to be reclaimed. This summarizes Cone's entire theological program, and once again, this hermeneutic has dominated the landscape of academic Black religiosity.

Occasionally, Cone is compelled to assess King's relevance to White America. In various ways, this is a way for Cone to employ the either/or and us/them paradigms that compare King to Black Power. For example, Cone has stated,

> One cannot help but think that most whites "loved" Martin Luther King, Jr., not because of his attempt to free his people, but because his approach was the least threatening to the white power structure. Thus, churchmen and theologians grasped at the opportunity to identify with him so that they could keep blacks powerless and simultaneously appease their own guilt about white oppression.[96]

95. Cone, *Black Theology and Black Power*, vii.

96. Cone, *Black Theology and Black Power*, 56. On another occasion, Cone stated, "King's words are what whites want to hear when there is a racial disturbance, always testing the limits of black patience with white supremacy." Cone, "God and Black

Cone insists that Black Nationalism through Malcolm X and the rise of Black Power after his death created a greater threat than King to White supremacy. Often, Cone pushes the issue to the extent of challenging and discrediting King's influence upon White America. For Cone, it was not King's theology nor his leadership abilities that influenced many White Americans to support the Civil Rights movement. Rather, it was White America's fear of Black Power and, secondarily, the presence of a more docile option of Black resistance advocated by King. At times, the nature of Cone's view partially insinuates that King was used or manipulated by White America to sustain the structures of White supremacy. Thus, the "progress" toward Black liberation and racial reconciliation presented by King through the Civil Rights movement was an illusion. Another example of this is viewed within Cone's interpretation of King and nonviolence:

> But when King brought his work north, many retreated and complained that he was confusing politics with religion. King only regained his popularity among northern churchmen after the emergence of the concept of Black power. They came to view King's nonviolence as the less of two evils.[97]

Gayraud Wilmore, Cone's peer and Black Power advocate, supports his claim that Black Power posed a greater threat to White supremacy than King. Referencing King's death, Wilmore stated,

> The King of love was dead and with his death an era of interracial church social action and theological innocence came to an end. Everyone knew that the memory of his commitment and faithfulness would never be permitted to die in the Black Church, but for those church leaders and theologians retreating from a city ready to burst into a strange, elegiac violence, a new challenge to America had to be mounted, one more consonant with the pragmatic sensibilities of the religious experience and theological maturity of a proud Black people come of age.[98]

Wilmore insinuates that King's theology and leadership did not represent a mature contextual expression of African American Christianity. Rather, King's approach was underdeveloped and innocent. Yet, it is interesting to witness Wilmore associating King's death with the demise of

Suffering," 212; see also *God of the Oppressed*, xv–xvi; and "Theology's Great Sin," 147.

97. Cone, *Black Theology and Black Power*, 79.

98. Cone and Wilmore, *Black Theology*, 21.

the Civil Rights movement's emphasis on the union of Black and White churches for sociopolitical purposes. This is not a surprise, considering many Black Power advocates disagreed with King on the issue of integration and opted for sociopolitical segregation. Cone echoes similar sentiments to Wilmore's words through his statement, "A black ecumenism that was defined by a radical commitment to the black poor sounded new to most twentieth-century black church persons. Martin King's civil rights movement created a similar ecumenical spirit, but it was destroyed with the rise of black power."[99] The first generation of Black theologians identified with and endorsed Black Power in a way that intentionally confronted and undermined the progress achieved by King. Despite their selective praise, Black theologians were clear that they disagreed with King on many issues and that he achieved some progress in comparison to Black Power. Cone's theological program initiated a conflict between conservative and liberal African American Christians, which widened the division between Black theology and the conservative evangelical African American Church.

There are a few scholars who have spoken about the division between Black theology and the African American Church. Anthony B. Bradley suggests, "Black liberation theology is not the dominant theological platform in most black churches across America."[100] For Bradley, the Black Church dismisses Black theology because "many theologians denied orthodox starting points such as the final authority of Scripture, biblical definitions of sin and redemption, the doctrine of God and redemption by means of substitutionary atonement, and the like."[101] Bradley suggests that Cone's theological program perpetually defined Black people as *victims* of White supremacy:

> The thesis is that James Cone's presupposition of black consciousness construed as victim supplies a fundamentally flawed theological anthropology for later developments in black liberation theology, leading to the demise of black liberation theology. In other words, reducing black identity primarily to that of

99. Cone, *For My People*, 85. Cone also stated, "Because of King's work we are now in the beginning stages of real confrontation between black and white Americans. He may not have endorsed the concept of Black Power, but its existence is a result of his work." Cone, *Black Theology and Black Power*, 109.

100. Bradley, *Liberating Black Theology*, 28.

101. Bradley, *Liberating Black Theology*, 24; 28.

> victim, albeit at times inadvertent, contributed to the decline of black liberation to obscurity.[102]

Some of Bradley's views are like those presented by Anderson. As I interpret Bradley, he also concentrates on various issues that I have identified within Black Power, one example being the ability to lose a racial identity through integration, and the emphasis on separatism to establish a new Black identity.[103] Dale P. Andrews states that a *chasm* exists between Black theology and the African American Church. For him, "the majority of black churches criticized the movement for its inherent reductionism and divisiveness. Black churches contested that black theology advanced black power in a neglect of the gospel message of universal love."[104] Andrews also states that the Black Church could not endorse sociopolitical violence in the name of liberation nor minimize the relevance of racial integration. Andrews does not fully examine the negative effects of theologizing Black Power and how it was possibly received by the African American Church. Nor does he introduce the theology of King as representative of conservative African American theology. Rather, for Andrews, the central problem that creates the division between the two institutions is centered on *American individualism*:

> An introspective analysis of the chasm reveals unexplored dynamics of faith by which black churches remain estranged from black theology. In short, black theology's sweeping disparagement of the "otherworldliness" of black churches indicates a misdiagnosis, which actually exposes a glaring "missed-diagnosis"—American individualism.[105]

Andrews maintains that American individualism had fragmented the secular and religious identities of African Americans. This skews the Black theologian's ability to articulate a theology relevant to the Black Church but also distorts how African Americans relate to the Black Church. Anderson complements the views of Bradley and Andrews in that he claims many Black churches argued that Black theology had rejected basic Christian doctrine which defined Black Christianity:

> Early critics, particularly those who pressed internal criticisms as black church theologians, asked how black theology could be

102. Bradley, *Liberating Black Theology*, 14–15.
103. Bradley, *Liberating Black Theology*, 21.
104. D. Andrews, *Practical Theology for Black Churches*, 4.
105. D. Andrews, *Practical Theology for Black Churches*, 7.

> a theology of the black churches if it fundamentally disentangles itself from the creeds and confessions, as well as the liturgical practices that structure the black churches. To some, black theology appeared to posit within itself a revolutionary consciousness that looked more like the mirror of white racism and less like an expression of the evangelical gospel that characterized most black churches.[106]

Anderson also mentions the contradictions within Cone's methodologies whereby he relies on White theologians and philosophers to articulate his radical Black theology. Anderson states that Cone could either acknowledge his debt to European Christianity, which helped shape the Black Church, or continue to disavow European Christianity, which would further alienate him from the Black Church. Anderson believes Cone chose the latter: "He attempted to overcome his academic alienation from the black churches by emphasizing the necessity of black sources for the construction of black theology."[107] Anderson insists that Cone inevitably created more problems by doing so.

Cone issued scathing critiques of the Black Church. He interpreted the institution within the categories of a pre–Civil War and post–Civil War contextual expression. For Cone, the pre–Civil War church had embodied the theme of liberation and earnestly fought against White supremacy. The pre–Civil War church had rejected White Christianity and made a clear distinction between the Black and White Christ. Cone insists,

> Freedom and equality made up the central theme of the black church; and protest and action were the early marks of its uniqueness, as the black man fought for freedom. White missionaries sought to extol the virtues of the next world, but blacks were more concerned about their freedom in this world.[108]

We witness in Cone's statement a major theme within his theology. He interprets White Christians as using *spiritual* principles to manipulate Black Christians into disavowing any interest in achieving sociopolitical liberation. Yet, Cone insists that the pre–Civil War Black Church had rejected this spiritual emphasis of Christianity, because it had no relevance to their sociopolitical bondage.

106. Anderson, *Beyond Ontological Blackness*, 90.

107. Anderson, *Beyond Ontological Blackness*, 90–91.

108. Cone, *Black Theology and Black Power*, 94; see also 95–103; and *Black Theology of Liberation*, 62, 134.

Nevertheless, Cone maintains that the post–Civil War church had extended to the Civil Rights movement. For him, the Black Church had lost its zeal for liberation, and this was partially influenced by an infatuation with *otherworldly* realities.[109] This led Cone to suggest,

> Just as the black church is a visible reminder of the apostasy of the white church, the current civil rights protest organizations are visible manifestations of the apostasy of the black church. Forgetting their reason for existing, the black churches became, as Washington appropriately describes, "amusement centers," "arenas for power politics," and an "organ for recognition, leadership, and worship." They became perversions of the gospel of Christ and places for accommodating the oppressed plight of black people.[110]

Cone insists that the Black Church became an apostasy by forfeiting its divine right to liberation at the expense of submitting to White supremacy. This renders the institution a mirror image of the White church as both fail to identify with the oppressed and fight for black liberation: "We may conclude that except in rare instances, the black churches in the post-Civil War period have been no more Christian than their White counterparts."[111] For Cone, the worship and glorification of God is derived from sociopolitical activity. Christian spirituality is informed and determined by our identities as either the oppressed or the oppressor. He consistently argued that it was White Christianity that initially developed an obsession with "otherworldliness" at the denial of its oppressive and dehumanization actions toward Black society. Cone maintained at one point that

> black theology believes that the emphasis on heaven in black churches was due primarily to white slave masters whose intention was to transfer slaves' loyalties from earthly reality to heavenly reality. In that way, masters could do what they willed about this world, knowing that their slaves were content with a better life in the next world.[112]

109. Cone, *Black Theology and Black Power*, 105.

110. Cone, *Black Theology and Black Power*, 106; see also 115.

111. Cone, *Black Theology and Black Power*, 108; Cone also posited this view in the form of a question: "If the white and black churches do not represent Christ's redemptive work in the world, where then is Christ's church to be found?" Cone, *Black Theology of Liberation*, 143.

112. Cone, *Black Theology of Liberation*, 149.

Therefore, Cone argues that the spiritual emphasis of conservative evangelical African American Christianity, which currently exists today, is a sign of the institution's indoctrination by White Christianity. This also contributes to the African American Church's inadequacy toward achieving Black liberation. This was a deviation from its divine purpose. Yet, Cone's interpretation of the church's purpose is primarily sociopolitical. This influences him to reference,

> Unfortunately black churches are also guilty of prostituting the name of God's church. Having originally come into being because they knew that political involvement in societal liberation of blacks was equivalent with the gospel, it is a sad fact that in subsequent decades they all but lost their reason for being.[113]

Cone rejects the African American Church's interpretation of Christianity as a spiritual religion, and having its spiritual principles inform the church' sociopolitical activism. This form of conservative Christianity was clearly seen through King's theology. Cone's statements are examples of Bradley's, Andrews', and Anderson's claims that the Black Church had distanced itself from and rejected Black theology because it detached itself from some of the basic Christian doctrine that defined evangelical African American Christianity. Nevertheless, Cone further argued that during this period,

> The black minister thus became a most devoted "Uncle Tom," the transmitter of white values, the admonisher of obedience to the caste system. He was the liaison man between the white power structure and the oppressed blacks, serving the dual function of assuring whites that all is well in the black community, dampening the spirit of freedom among his people. More than any other one person in the black community, the black minister perpetuated the white system of black dehumanization.[114]

Cone's comments represent the qualitative judgment of Blackness that was initially presented by his predecessors. He interprets the Black preacher as completely assimilated to White culture. This alludes to the problem of racial integration and the claim of the Black Church worshiping the White Christ. For Cone, the Black preacher was a race traitor and complicit to White supremacy as they pollinated White values into their Black congregations.

113. Cone, *Black Theology of Liberation*, 142.

114. Cone, *Black Theology of Liberation*, 105, 106.

Cone acknowledges the division between Black theology and the Black Church. However, he appears to avoid the conservative evangelical view of how and why the division occurred, as well as whether it currently exists. He remarks that during the early 1970s, the radical Black clergy and theologians had refrained from critiquing the Black Church. Instead, they chose to create religious organizations and obtain occupations as professors.[115] However, Cone reveals one of the more troubling reasons for the division:

> But more than I care to admit now and could not acknowledge at the time, one reason seems obvious: we had internalized too much of the theological values of the whites whom we were attacking. Therefore even when we attacked them for their racism, we could not separate ourselves from them, because we wanted to become like them, teaching at their schools and writing books to prove that we could think as well as they. In the meantime, we were separating black theology from the only source that could give it theological credibility—the black church and the black community.[116]

Cone's explanation partially accounts for the dominating theme of Whiteness within his theology. I interpret Whiteness as a hidden hermeneutic and methodology that determined Cone's employment of essentialist and racialized binary reasoning. His explanation also provides understanding of the fear of losing a person, group, or culture's Black identity through societal and religious assimilation to Whiteness.

115. Cone, *For My People*, 108–9.

116. Cone, *For My People*, 114.

3

The Afrocentric-Liberationist School of Black Religiosity

A BLACK BURDEN: THE QUESTIONING OF INHERENT AFRICAN RELIGIOSITY

CURTIS J. EVANS PRESENTS another example of racialized binary reasoning when he advances what he believes is the questionable colonial notion of an innate Black religiosity that was ironically constructed by White people. Evans argues that White antislavery leaders of the nineteenth century, whom he refers to as *romantic racialists*, embraced notions of Black inferiority although they sought to emancipate the slaves. Referencing Black religion, Evans maintains that these romantic racialists advocated that Black people were emotional and lacked progressive intelligence but were *innately religious*. Thus, for Evans, this assumption of innate African American spirituality was a construct among antislavery advocates who were unaware of their racist beliefs. Evans states, "The romantic racialist image of Blacks was often about what 'lost' values whites projected onto blacks to reclaim them as their own and rested on a theory of racial difference."[1] Evans's theories resemble Anderson's theory of *ontological Blackness*, the Blackness that Whiteness creates whereby some Black identities are constructed from the creativity of various White people.

1. C. Evans, *Burden of Black Religion*, 12.

Evans argues that the stereotype of being innately religious was eventually embraced by African Americans, but the notions of emotionalism and stupidity were rejected. Evans maintains,

> To be handed this image from mostly Northern White abolitionists did not seem to cause any conscious discomfort for black interpreters of African-American religion, perhaps because they came to accept it as their own creation. The interpretation of what it meant to be naturally religious was being transformed and refined even as blacks held onto the relatively benign romantic view of African-American religion.[2]

Hart M. Nelson, Raytha L. Yokley, and Anne Kusener Nelson reference similar sentiments to those of Evans. They argue, however, that the belief that African Americans were innately religious is a myth: "there prevails a persistent stereotype of the Negro as an exceedingly religious individual with a penchant for emotional forms of religious expression." Nevertheless, in disagreeing with Evans, these scholars suggest that the origin of this stereotype may have derived from African Americans, attempting to fight against racist notions of their inferiority.[3] According to Evans, many White abolitionists assisted in creating and promoting the image of a nonthreatening slave to complement the notion of the slave's innate religiosity. Evans explains,

> Romantic racialists argued that Africans were gentle creatures of feelings who were dragged from their natural habitat by avaricious and bellicose Europeans. This emphasis on slave meekness and religiosity was in part a counter to the worries and fears of slave owners that abolitionists were inciting slaves to rebellion and slave owners' views of African alleged natural barbarity and propensity for violence apart from white supervision or ownership.[4]

Evans's statement alludes to the presence of racialized religious paternalism that existed within European American Christianity. The identity of the supposed emotional, passive, and tender Black slave was seemingly endorsed by abolitionists to alleviate the concerns of proslavery advocates. For Evans, "The affectionate and naturally religious Negro

2. C. Evans, *Burden of Black Religion*, 102–3.

3. Nelson et al., *Black Church in America*, 38; see also Kruger, "Negro Religious Expression," 22–31.

4. C. Evans, *Burden of Black Religion*, 19; see also 41.

imagined and constructed by the romantic racialists became the emotionally extravagant Negro to white missionaries (and even to some black missionaries)."[5] Yet, despite these events, Evans insists that proslavery advocates continued to sift all information about slaves through the sieve of Eurocentrism. Ironically, as we shall see, various Black scholars, whom I refer to as Afrocentric-Liberationists, craft an interpretation that emphasizes the innate spiritual *superiority* of African American slaves as the antithesis to the supposed innate spiritual inferiority of their European American masters. This was partially witnessed within the discourse of some Black Power advocates and Black theologians.

It is interesting that Evans emphasizes that European missionaries sought to reconstruct a more positive image of African American slaves through conceptions of Black religion. He is never quite clear as to what contextual expressions influenced such missionaries. However, Evans continually references the accusations from proslavery advocates that the religious expressions of African Americans were immoral and primitive. The presumption is that the antislavery missionaries were attracted to elements of Black religiosity, exaggerated those elements, and framed them into an *oppositional* discourse that confronted the racist beliefs that European/European Americans held about African American slaves.

Evans suggests that during the late nineteenth century some Black social scientists sought to refute the supposed myth of the African American's innate spirituality. This research experienced a resurgence during the 1940s, 60s, and 70s.[6] Whether these intellectuals believed they accomplished their task, many African Americans have continued to advance the belief that they are indeed innately religious, and often this belief is interpreted in opposition to White irreligiosity. We must consider whether there is a secular sociopolitical counterpart to this innate religiosity. Perhaps it is an innate spirit of freedom and justice.

Evans's theories are rather provocative and would surely cause many African Americans discomfort, considering there are many who affirm an innate religious disposition. It is important to note, although he does not present it as such, that Evans is refuting the racialized binary reasoning employed by European Americans by creating the notion of an inherent African American spirituality. For him, the notion that Black people are inherently spiritual, and more religious than White people,

5. C. Evans, *Burden of Black Religion*, 65.

6. C. Evans, *Burden of Black Religion*, 9–10.

which many Afrocentric-Liberationists hold, is not an obvious fact. According to Evans, it is ironic that this theory was created by sympathetic White abolitionists (unaware of their Eurocentric dispositions) to refute various beliefs regarding African religious/spiritual inferiority and, more specifically, the claims that Africans were unable to grasp the nature of sophisticated religions such as Christianity. If Evans's theory has any merit, it is in the way he exposes another layer of irony, in that White abolitionists have created an influential religious principle that some Afrocentric-Liberationists consistently endorse.

Evans's interpretation provides a unique example of how racialized binary reasoning can create opposition *within* the Black community, rather than exclusively between Black and White societies. This is evident in that many African Americans do not claim religious superiority over European Americans. However, our ignorance can create division when we uncritically embrace belief systems that seemingly elevate our existence through the demotion of other people.

We must consider the natural practice of religion that is intertwined with culture. African slaves came from nations that had organic religious systems. Slavery did not strip them of the religious/spiritual element of their humanity. From a Christian theological perspective, humans are created as spiritual, religious, and worshiping beings. This is instinctual; even when the individual or group consciously decides to avoid organized religion, they eventually lapse into unacknowledged religious practice. Connected to this is the lack of self-awareness and self-degradation of European and European Americans who did not apply their basic understanding of humanity to the African slaves. Hence, we often observed the pendulum effect between two extreme poles: either the slaves are too unintelligent to grasp sophisticated religion, or they are gifted spiritually beyond other races.

For me, historical records do not demonstrate innate African religiosity. It merely articulates the reality of colonial Black humanity, which, largely within the American context, had experienced divine revelation intruding into their lives through the gospel of Christ Jesus. Many Black slaves experienced YHWH and engaged him as the God who was truly real. Through their genuine relationship with him, the distinctive contextual expressions of Christianity began to present themselves to White society in varied ways. As we reflect on these views, we must also discuss further the presence of essentialist and racialized binary reasoning found within the Afrocentric-Liberationist school.

AN OPPOSITIONAL BLACK CHRIST: RACIAL AND RELIGIOUS BINARY OPPOSITIONAL REASONING

Black womanist theologian Kelly Brown Douglas provides another example of racialized binary reasoning. Douglas's views are representative of contemporary Black liberation theology. In her early work, *The Black Christ*, she seeks to articulate the theological significance of the Black Christ in relation to the African slaves, and for African American culture from slavery to the present. Douglas employs essentialist and racialized binary reasoning as she reflects upon the relationship between African American Christianity as *slave Christianity*, and European American Christianity as *slaveholding Christianity*. She states, "During slavery the Black Christ emerged in contradistinction to the oppressive White Christ. The White Christ was at the centre of slaveholding Christianity, while the Black Christ was the centre of slave Christianity."[7] We originally witnessed this binary category employed by Black Power advocates and the Black theologian James Cone. The Black Christ, who is representative of Black Christianity, stands in opposition to the White Christ, who represents White Christianity.

For Douglas, the White Christ represented the supposed divine permissibility of slavery and the absence of any sociopolitical concern on the part of God for the enslaved. Douglas suggests, "This Christ gained stature in slaveholding Christianity as proslavery evangelists continued to support the idea that Jesus' liberating ministry was irrelevant to the Christian religion."[8] She advocates that the Black Christ represented Jesus' relationship to the slaves, their radicalization, and the enlightenment received regarding the contradiction between Christianity and slavery.[9] Douglas also insists that slave Christianity did not focus

> on the relationship between Jesus and God as did slaveholding Christianity. The significance of Jesus for the slaves had little to do with God becoming incarnate in him. Jesus' meaning had more to do with what Jesus did in their lives. Jesus was a living being with whom the slaves had an intimate relationship.[10]

7. Douglas, *Black Christ*, 10.
8. Douglas, *Black Christ*, 15; see also 17–19, 37.
9. Douglas, *Black Christ*, 20, 24, 27–30.
10. Douglas, *Black Christ*, 20–21.

This statement highlights Cone's influence on Douglas. Cone was the first Black theologian to minimize the importance of spiritual principles to create a heightened significance of sociopolitical activism. For Douglas, slave Christianity was guided by a hermeneutic of experience. Experience is reinterpreted through contextual expressions of sociopolitical liberation and equality. Jesus was the sociopolitical Savior who empowered the slaves for their emancipation. Douglas suggests that the slaves' experience relied very little on established doctrine within the church. Her interpretations of Black and White Christianity are articulated in broad strokes and according to the themes of contemporary Black liberation theology. In her work, one witnesses again how Black theologians distanced themselves from the basic Christian doctrine that is characteristic of the conservative evangelical African American Church.

Black theologian Noel Leo Erskine echoes similar sentiments. He advocates, "The truth is that Black people were not impressed by Christian doctrine but were concerned how the teachings of Jesus or the life of Jesus translates into strategies for liberation."[11] One of the more striking claims from Erskine arises from his theory that African American religiosity had originated in Africa, the Caribbean, and South America instead of America.[12]

Douglas and Erskine provide some indication as to how academic Black theology and African American religious studies, in general, tend to utilize essentialist and racialized binary reasoning in their interpretations of African American slave Christianity. Douglas creates a dialogue between proslavery Christianity and a radicalized slave Christianity depicted through the methodologies of contemporary Black liberation theology. Scant attention is given to the presence and activity of European/European American slavery-reform or antislavery Christianity. Nor is there a reference to other possible contextual expressions of African American slave Christianity beyond the Afrocentric-Liberationist motif, and how the Christian slaves defined the Black Christ, or if they advocated one at all. Therefore, Douglas constructs a theological historiography whereby Black and White Christianity stand in complete opposition with one another, as the Black experience confronts White traditional Christian doctrine.

11. Erskine, *Plantation Church*, 116–17.

12. Erskine, *Plantation Church*, 6, 28, 62.

Within this context, Evans's work provides a unique perspective of racialized binary reasoning within some forms of African American scholarship. He questions and rejects the lack of critical reflection employed by African Americans who embrace a stereotype or myth that supposedly uplifts the culture at the expense of demoting European American religiosity. For him, this becomes increasingly convoluted as the creators of the myth are those who are perceived to be religiously inferior, European Americans. Thus, there is the presence of parroting, and inverting the structures that demean African American religiosity, which subsequently demeans European American religiosity. This is an element of what I call *the cycle of dehumanization*.

Various Afrocentric scholars present enticing perspectives. It is helpful to explore their views regarding an Afrocentric emphasis on African cultural retention in America, the tendency to emphasize the inability of the slaves to create an authentic *American* culture, and the rejection of conservative evangelical Christianity by African/African American slaves. Certain scholars insist that most African slaves in America did not produce an African American culture or a conservative contextual expression of Christianity until roughly 130 years after their arrival to America.

AFRICAN PURITY OR AMERICAN ASSIMILATION: CONFLICT OF CULTURAL, NATIONAL, AND RACIAL IDENTITY

The historical approaches of Evans and Douglas are part of a much wider trend. Other examples of African American scholarship create various competing and conflicting interpretations of African American Christianity through concepts of cultural identity, racialized nationalism, and religious syncretism. Afrocentric racialized binary reasoning situated against Eurocentric discourse remains at the center of these interpretations. Some Afrocentric interpretations rely on the symbolic *power* and *purity* of what it refers to as an African heritage. Generally, African heritage is interpreted as the political, religious, and sociocultural realities that define Africa and the African. An example of this can be partially observed in Erskine's statement, "Enslaved people remembered Africa, and the memory of Africa became a controlling metaphor and organizing principle for Africans in the New World as they countered the hegemonic conditions imposed on them by their masters."[13] Afrocentric scholars emphasize that African slaves and their nomadic communities embodied authentic elements of African culture in various ways. Yet, they disagree on how each slave and community may have consciously relinquished or unintentionally withdrew from their indigenous heritage through sociocultural accommodation and assimilation.

African American scholars St. Clair Drake and Henry H. Mitchell are representative of this approach. There is difficulty in analyzing their work because they often present claims without establishing proper justification. An example of this is found in Drake's assertion that early African American slaves did not *sincerely* convert to Christianity between 1619 to 1750. Rather, he suggests that conversion was feigned as a sociopolitical ploy.[14] Indeed, there were slaves who used religion for sociopolitical advantages. However, Drake never provided any substantive evidence to support his claim that *most* slaves practiced this tactic. Mitchell, influenced by Drake and other scholars, makes similar claims. Drake and Mitchell represent examples of scholars that Curtis J. Evans challenged regarding the acceptance of presumptions that benefited Black people, as facts.

This form of African American historiography is problematic for the way it advances conceptions of African heritage that negate the authentic creation and development of distinct cultures from the African diaspora. An example of this is the origin and development of African American culture apart from the strong influences of African heritage. Afrocentric scholars seek to preserve African heritage through conceptions of racialized nationalism within the practice of religious syncretism. These scholars have developed an ambiguous criterion for determining the qualitative and quantitative degree of African heritage that was embodied by the African slaves of the diaspora. Some Afrocentric scholars advocate that the West Indies and South America had developed more authentic Afrocentric diasporic cultures than in America. For example, Drake mentions,

> The people in the Diaspora in North America never developed an *African-American* culture in the sense that the people of the Caribbean and South America did. Rather what might be called

13. Erskine, *Plantation Church*, 29. Erskine has also stated, "But Black people would fight back not only through revolts, running away, and insurrections but also by calling on their ancestors. Enslaved people remembered Africa, and Africa became a controlling metaphor of liberation." Erskine, *Plantation Church*, 69.

14. S. Drake, *Redemption of Africa*, 24–25.

> an *Afro*-American sub-culture evolved. Of the many factors that account for the difference—economic, demographic, and acculturation—perhaps the most important was the decision of the masters to encourage the Christianization of Africans as a means of social control to an extent that occurred nowhere else in the New World except in Barbados.[15]

It remains unclear as to what Drake's standard of African authenticity entails. He never discusses his criteria in relative detail. Yet, whatever criteria/standard Drake abides by is implied to be self-evident. His definition of culture and sub-culture is elusive. Drake's work never outlines why African Americans created sub-cultures and African Caribbean slaves created cultures. He relies upon the normative narrative that Eurocentric Christian evangelism was used as the means of diluting or expunging authentic African heritage from the slaves in America and Barbados.

Drake describes American *creole* culture as a fusion of African and European cultures, but with a strong disposition toward embodiments of African cultural survivals as philosophical, social, and theological points of reference.[16] Thus, an authentic African diasporic culture had to develop from, rely upon, and remain dependent upon indigenous African heritage. Yet, an African diasporic sub-culture is interpreted as lacking elements of African heritage, because Eurocentric Christianity mitigated or diminished the practices of authentic African heritage.

Drake also relies on a questionable assumption that Christianity was used to domesticate the slaves. However, Drake never outlines the initial presence or development of these attempts. It must be noted that Barbados had practiced proslavery Christianity since its initial colonization in 1625–27. The Puritans and Quakers of the colony saw no benefit in evangelizing their slaves. This was also evident in places such as Jamaica. In fact, the initial presence of evangelization developed among the slavery reformers and antislavery Christians from the mid 1670s to 1700s.[17] Christianization as a form of domestication may not have developed until roughly one hundred years after Barbados was colonized. There are

15. S. Drake, *Redemption of Africa*, 19.

16. S. Drake, *Redemption of Africa*, 15.

17. Chapters 6 and 7 of this book focus on the development of slavery reform and antislavery Christianity, as well as their distinct forms of evangelism toward the slaves. I theorize that these forms of Christianity assisted in the creation of conservative African American Christianity.

possibly over one hundred years of American cultural development that have gone unacknowledged in Drake's account.

Furthermore, Drake's views assume many questionable developments, or the lack thereof, regarding African American religiosity. For him, the Caribbean and South American colonies developed *authentic* African diasporic cultures, because they did not experience the intense Christianization by European colonists. Drake argues that the Caribbean and South American slaves practiced a high degree of religious syncretism between various African religions and European Christianity. The troubling part of Drake's interpretation is that the ambiguous nature of religious syncretism becomes the primary justification for his theory of African heritage retention. An example of Drake's attempt to minimize the legitimacy of conservative or non-syncretistic African American Christianity can be seen in his claim:

> There is no way of knowing how many slaves thought of themselves as sincere Christians on the eve of the Revolutionary War or participated in Christian worship or shared in the values or believed the mythology expressed in the spirituals. There is some evidence, however, that the great majority of the slaves prior to 1776 were not Christians.[18]

Drake never provides much detail or evidence to verify the supposed lacking development of African American culture and Christianity before 1776. Instead, he focuses on the effects of proslavery evangelism upon the slaves, and how it was used to strip away their African heritage. In principle, these are facts that cannot be disputed, but interpretations of them through essentialist and racialized binary reasoning do skew or exaggerate this development.

Drake largely ignores the initial presence and development of European slavery reform and antislavery Christianity during the late seventeenth century. Doing so negates the possibility that positive forms of European and European American evangelism were operative, as well as the sincere conversions of African slaves associated with them. Drake's claims regarding the *sincerity* of the slaves' conversion thus merit critical scrutiny. His perspective presumes that the very nature of evangelism, conversion, and discipleship was *exclusively* a political game of subjugation and liberation. This form of reasoning was also employed by Black Power advocates and Black theologians. Moreover, Drake exaggerates

18. S. Drake, *Redemption of Africa*, 24–25.

conceptions of power within the master and slave's relationship without any possibility of compassion, mercy, or love, negating the oppressive elements that typically defined their relationship. Thus, Christianity then becomes nothing more than a tool of oppression to achieve the sociopolitical self-interests of White society. Drake is not alone in this approach.

African American scholar Henry H. Mitchell has interesting views regarding the retention of African heritage and the conversion to Christianity by African American slaves. Mitchell suggests, "There is much hard evidence proving that Africans retained a great deal of their original heritage."[19] Elements of African heritage are taken to express themselves in the form of specific drums used, dancing styles performed, and an assortment of medicinal practices embraced by the slaves.[20] Yet, critically examined, it becomes clear that Mitchell's discourse is constructed from binary reasoning. This is evident in his reluctance to attribute any positive evangelistic effort on the part of European American Christians. They are presented as inherently anti-African. Referencing the inadequate efforts of evangelism from European Americans and American Anglicans during the early eighteenth century, Mitchell states,

> Regardless of the admonition of (non-resident) Anglican bishops, masters soon learned that slaves who could read a prayer book, as required, could read anything else they cared to read. This, along with a shortage of priests, meant that no significant number of the enslaved were converted to Christianity by white initiative during the so-called "silent years" from 1619–1750.[21]

If we recall, Drake referenced the *silent years* of 1619–1750 in his claim of inauthentic slave conversions by African Americans. For Drake, there is no record of European American Christians evangelizing the slaves; therefore, he concludes, the slaves had never been converted to Christianity. This line of reasoning leads Mitchell to advocate, in a similar fashion to Drake, that very few slaves *sincerely* converted to Christianity through the evangelistic efforts of European American society: "The fact

19. Mitchell, *Black Church Beginnings*, xvi.

20. Historian Lawrence W. Levine partially agrees with Mitchell. However, Levine has a less Afrocentric and essentialist view of Black and White cultural syncretism. For him, some fusions between Black and White cultures produced newer forms of Black cultural expression. Levine mentions these developments within folk beliefs, folk medicine, music, ritual of insult (sarcasm), and general tales. See Levine, *Black Culture*, 23–25, 36, 59–61, 66, 82, 351.

21. Mitchell, *Black Church Beginnings*, 26.

that Christianity took root at all among African Americans from 1619 to 1750 is not due in any appreciable measure to missions."[22] Furthermore, Mitchell suggests without supporting evidence that those slaves who did convert to Christianity were unlikely to be sincere Christians: "These converts were a tiny percentage of the total slave population, and the conversions were hardly credible or valid, by definition."[23] Mitchell makes broad assumptions regarding the quantity and sincerity of the slaves' conversion to Christianity. He assumes that the slaves did not have the ability or desire to accept Christianity on their own accord. Reminiscent of Drake, Mitchell has a criteria/standard of what an authentic conversation to Christianity is and how genuine Christian slaves should have lived. Yet, he never outlines this criteria/standard. In this context, we must question whether the evidence justifies the conclusion, or if a commitment to an ideology drastically skews how someone researches and interprets said evidence. Regardless of our opinion, it is clear Mitchell is adamant that most slaves retained their African heritage and rejected conversion to Christianity.

Early slave conversions were naturally scarce, because there was not a consistent effort to evangelize the slaves, and perhaps because the religion was indeed initially associated with the culture of the slave masters. Historical records and the lack of historical records point to this belief. However, the scarcity of conversions does not logically imply insincerity on the part of those who were converted. Furthermore, the attempt to qualitatively gauge the slaves' sincerity would be indeterminate based upon Mitchell's methodology. Mitchell does not reflect on the causal chain of engaging and converting to Christianity that many of the slaves experienced. Therefore, Mitchell's theories create a few problems that must be addressed.

First, some slaves became aware of and converted to Christianity in Africa. African Christianity developed in various ways within the Western side of the continent. Second, some slave conversions occurred in the Caribbean. The Caribbean was home to many slaves but was a temporary residence for most as they traveled to South America and the American colonies. Third, there was increasing evangelism toward the slaves during the middle and late seventeenth century through some efforts from the Church of England and the Quakers. Other groups like the Anglicans

22. Mitchell, *Black Church Beginnings*, 32.

23. Mitchell, *Black Church Beginnings*, 28; see also Erskine, *Plantation Church*, 183.

and Puritans had scarce attempts at evangelism as well. Last, extensive evidence is needed to justify Mitchell's claims. He continually suggests that over 130 years had passed whereby a growing population of people did not create authentic American cultures and sub-cultures, nor became increasingly affected by the dominant religion of the land, Christianity. Once again, it is difficult to critique most of Mitchell's views, because they are assumptions devoid of evidence.[24] Mitchell is obviously not the only scholar to cling to these views, which are connected to other important issues regarding African cultural retention by African American slaves.

RELIGIOUS IDENTITY: PRESERVATION OF THE AFRICAN GODS

Afrocentric scholars are relatively unified in proclaiming that the African slaves not only retained their cultural heritage but also practiced religious syncretism.[25] The ideological framework for articulating this belief bears similarity to the Afrocentric discourse regarding cultural confrontation, resistance, and retention against Eurocentric intrusions. Generally, Afrocentric scholars tend to advocate that

> Early African American religion was an effort by enslaved Africans to safeguard themselves against the disruption of their religious worldviews. Enslaved Africans gradually merged their composite African religiosity with western notions of Christianity through complex cultural processes of *enculturation*, adaptation, and assimilation.[26]

Nonetheless, there is disagreement among Afrocentric scholars regarding the slaves' practice of religious syncretism. Scholars who employ Afrocentric binary reasoning generally emphasize two principles of

24. The issues raised by Drake and Mitchell's scholarship will be resolved in chapters 6 and 7 of this book.

25. Frey and Wood, *Come Shouting to Zion*, 35, 40, 43; Hopkins and Cummings, *Cut Loose Your Stammering Tongue*; Erskine, *Plantation Church*, 120, 130, 134, 137, 153–54; Stuckey, *Slave Culture*; Blassingame, *Slave Community*, viii, 2, 64.

26. Floyd-Thomas et al., *Black Church Studies*, 5. Erskine makes a similar statement about the Black Church: "Although many of these churches took on the 'veneer of Christianity' they were at heart African churches." Erskine's comment represents the fragmented nature of racialized binary reasoning in the sense that Christianity is interpreted as European, and the real identity of the Black Christian church was inherently African. This implies that African and Christian are incompatible identities. Erskine, *Plantation Church*, 4–5.

African American religious syncretism.[27] First, Afrocentric scholars argue that the intellectual and spiritual sophistication of African religions are equal to European Christianity. Second, these same scholars suggest that the African slaves embodied and expressed this intellectual and spiritual sophistication by showing the compatibility of African religions with Christianity. African intellectual and spiritual sophistication could be observed from the slaves' abilities to *recreate* or *reimagine* new African identities within their current African syncretized religions.[28] Historian John W. Blassingame suggests, "Christian forms were so similar to African religious patterns that it was relatively easy for the early slaves to incorporate them with their traditional practices and beliefs."[29] Afrocentric scholars suggest that the preservation of African heritage is interrelated to, interdependent on, and inseparable from African traditional religions.

Christianity is defined as a monotheistic religion. West African religions are generally perceived as polytheistic. Theological and practical (rituals, etc.) inconsistencies would develop depending on how Christianity is syncretized with African religions. Monotheistic religions can be grafted into polytheistic religious structures, but not vice versa. Otherwise, the monotheistic religion would be reinterpreted as a polytheistic religion. For example, as Christians, some slaves understood that only Jesus was to be worshiped solely as Lord and Savior of their lives. No other deity was worshiped alongside him. Therefore, in an informal way, the slaves understood that polytheism was theologically inconsistent with Christianity, and any attempts by Christians to worship multiple gods were considered religious pluralism and syncretism.[30]

However, some Afrocentric scholars appear to avoid this dilemma or not view it as a dilemma at all. An example of this is expressed by Mitchell. He insists, "African traditional religion looked up to one omnipotent High God with power to enforce this ultimate justice. Africans

27. It must be noted that these principles assume that African religions must be preserved and proven to be equal or superior to Christianity (a European religion). Certain Afrocentric scholars reject the possibility that some slaves did not *racialize* Christianity by interpreting it as a European religion.

28. Frey and Wood, *Come Shouting to Zion*, 35.

29. Blassingame, *Slave Community*, 18.

30. Black slaves were evangelized into conservative contextual expressions of Christianity. These Black Christian slaves maintained an identity and practice of conservative African American Christianity. This will be partially explored in chapter 6 and expanded upon during my evaluation of the African American Christian slave Jupiter Hammon in the conclusion.

were not polytheistic as many suppose. Rather, their one distant High God ruled many deputy or intermediary deities, to whom various earthly functions were assigned."[31] Mitchell's view challenges the nature of how a deity, monotheism, and polytheistic religions are defined. Theological inconsistencies are overlooked because priority is reserved for expressing the compatibility and equality of African religions with Christianity. This is generally expressed by portraying the African *High God* as an omnipotent deity who was representative of or synonymous to YHWH of Judaism and Christianity.

Historian and theologian Gayraud S. Wilmore has a unique view that defends African traditional religions as the fusion of monotheistic and polytheistic beliefs. He expresses the attributes of the High God as compatible with the narratives within Christianity:

> Monotheism or "monarchical polytheism"; the concept of a High God and lesser divinities who open the way, serve, or are the messengers of God; the voluntary recession or forced separation of God from the creation, requiring appeasement through blood sacrifice, redemptive suffering, and other means of reconciliation and reunion; the necessity of rites of purification, glorification, thanksgiving, and supplication; the reality of many gradations of power—from personal charisma, to impersonal spiritual forces that can do no good or evil, to the omnipotence of a Supreme Being . . . all of these more or less characteristic aspects of African Traditional Religions from Senegambia, around the Gulf of Guinea, to the Congo and Angola (not to mention Equatorial and Southern Africa), find correspondences in the Judeo-Christian tradition.[32]

The very nature of a deity or divinity is elusive. Wilmore naturally equates the African High God with the YHWH of Judaism and Christianity. He also appears to suggest that the "lesser divinities" could be associated with angels. If so, Wilmore never clearly explains it in detail. Nevertheless, Erskine takes a similar position to Wilmore in stating,

> The will of the Supreme Deity was made clear through his assistants, the ancestors and lesser deities. This was one reason that made Christianity readily accessible to Africans; they were able

31. Mitchell, *Black Church Beginnings*, 17.

32. Wilmore, *Black Religion*, 20, 4.

> to see Jesus, the Holy Spirit, saints, and angels as emissaries of the High God who were assigned to carry out His will.[33]

I interpret Wilmore as representing the school of African religious pluralism and syncretism within contemporary Black theology.[34] Although Wilmore is a Christian, his desire to integrate West African religions with Christianity directly influences the possibility of polytheism. He establishes three sources for a constructive Black theology: the Black community, the writings/sermons/addresses of Black preachers and public citizens within Black history, and all traditional African religions. From Wilmore's perspective, Jesus Christ is not the primary theological norm. Rather, as I understand him, the primary norm is the collection of traditional West African religions. Wilmore maintains that African religious beliefs and practices can function as interpretive tools for articulating an *authentic* Black Christianity and an incorrupt understanding of Jesus Christ. Otherwise, the usage of Jesus Christ as the norm through European religious beliefs would only *Whitenize* any Black attempt at contextualizing Christianity. Wilmore is influenced by a cultural and political Afrocentric methodology, rather than a set of traditionally conservative Christian theological convictions.[35] He emphasizes the es-

33. Erskine, *Plantation Church*, 16.

34. See the following chapters by Wilmore in Cone and Wilmore, *Black Theology*: "General Introduction," 1–12; "Introduction to Part One," 15–22; "Introduction to Part Two," 67–79; "Black Churchman's Response," 93–99; "Introduction to Part Four," 241–56; "Black Theology and African Theology," 463–76; "New Context of Black Theology," 602–8. See also Wilmore, *Pragmatic Spirituality*.

35. Second generation Black theologian Dwight N. Hopkins has articulated two categories for the first generation of Black theologians. He categorizes them as "advocating a faith revealed in politics" (political theologians) and "advocating a faith based in black culture" (cultural theologians). Political theologians seek to oppose White racism within the American political system: "They expose White America's use of religion and theology to justify any maintenance of White rule over Black life." For Hopkins, theological articulation is their primary mode of confronting White supremacy. There are four theological categories identified with the political theologian. First, they aggressively proclaim the tenets of Black theology. Second, they emphasize the principles of liberation for Black (and all oppressed) people. Third, they have a strong Christology undergirding their message. Lastly, there is a message of reconciliation. James H. Cone and J. Deotis Roberts are representatives of the Black political theologians. Moreover, the cultural theologians place a greater emphasis on separation from White culture. They are conscious of cultural and social structures which sustain White supremacy. Cultural theologians seek to confront not only White structures but also the perceived misguided agendas of the Black political theologians: "From this perspective of the cultural trend, the black political theologians waste too much time and energy reacting to white racism while also accepting white definitions." Cultural theologians believe

sential value of African religions to assist African Americans in establishing a new liberated identity and contextualized Christianity.[36]

Wilmore and Mitchell agree with one another. Both advocate that the existence of a High God and lesser divinities does not imply a polytheistic belief system. Wilmore and Mitchell are influenced by the Nigerian theologian Osadolor Imasogie and others with similar beliefs. Imasogie disputed the claim that African religions should be defined as animism, fetishism, polytheism, and primitive monotheism. He argued that these categories were inappropriately placed upon African religions and were a product of Eurocentric theories of evolutionary development. Instead, Imasogie insisted that the phrase "'bureaucratic monotheism' adequately describes the belief in a Supreme Creator and the *de facto* prominence enjoyed by the divinities in the African religious expression."[37] Imasogie explains that the lesser divinities were created by the Supreme Being and were personifications of nature and symbols of God's providence.[38]

I argue that bureaucratic and monarchical monotheism are merely relabeled interpretations of *henotheism* and *kathenotheism*. Henotheism and kathenotheism share similar principles with polytheism, but differ regarding the form of worship that is practiced. Henotheism is broadly referred to as the belief in or worship of a single god while accepting the existence or possible existence of other deities. Kathenotheism is a refined form of henotheism and is defined as the worship of one god at a time, as

---

Black theology and African American culture must purge itself from all White or European-American definitions of reality. Cultural theologians insist Black theologians and African American culture must redefine themselves from their African heritage. Hopkins maintains that the cultural theologians maintain that Black people can create a new religion. For this to occur, new religious and theological structures from Black existence must be created. Thus, Wilmore argues that Christianity is corrupted by Whiteness, and African religious expression assists in avoiding those forms of corruption. In this way, Africanisms assist Black Christians in creating an authentic Black Christianity that is detached from the taint of Whiteness. Hopkins argues that the cultural theologians embody four methodological categories. First, they emphasize Black religious thought or language. Second, their sources derive from everything defined as culturally Black. Third, they have a strict allegiance to Africanisms. Lastly, the theme of liberation fluctuates throughout their message. Gayraud S. Wilmore and Charles H. Long are representatives of Black cultural theologians. See Hopkins, *Introducing Black Theology*, 52–53, 65–66.

36. Wilmore, *Black Religion*, 275, 276, 279, 281.

37. Imasogie, "African Traditional Religion," 289–90.

38. Imasogie, "African Traditional Religion." Erskine suggests that the Supreme Being was indirectly worshiped through the direct work of the lesser divinities. Furthermore, he argues that there were four classifications of spirits: the Supreme Being, lesser divinities, ancestral spirits, and bad spirits. Erskine, *Plantation Church*, 46, 50.

its practitioners acknowledge the existence of other deities. Afrocentric scholars are not necessarily united in defining the exact nature of a deity or divinities. This creates ambiguity and uncertainty in understanding the complexity of African American religious syncretism. Yet, there is another scholar who provides important insight into the process of African American religious syncretism that was practiced by the slaves.

DWIGHT N. HOPKINS: BLACK SLAVE LIBERATION THEOLOGY

Hopkins's theological interpretations are derived from the integrated hermeneutics and methodologies of Cone and Wilmore's Black liberation theologies. I argue that this results in Hopkins inheriting fragments of essentialist and racialized binary reasoning from his predecessors. In *Cut Loose Your Stammering Tongue*, Hopkins sought to

> Hold that the original premises of black theology, signified most clearly by James H. Cone (emphasizing Christian liberation) and Gayraud S. Wilmore (stressing non-Christian liberation), still remain true. The question is how to develop further that foundational framework—the unity and distinction between Christian and non-Christian, church and non-church, and theological and religious sources in African American faith and life.[39]

I interpret Hopkins's theology as an amalgamation of conflicting religious and secular concepts that adhere to an Afrocentric-Liberationist motif that relinquishes any strict identification to traditional Christian doctrine. This stands at least for his early work. Hopkins's interpretation of a Black slave theology is a synthesis of a few general Christian principles and ambiguous concepts from West African religions. I maintain that Hopkins's interpretation is problematic, because integrating the methodologies of Cone (Liberationist motif) and Wilmore (Afrocentric romanticism) produces a fragmented interpretation of contemporary Black liberation theology that is superficially juxtaposed with the African American slave narratives. Coincidently, Hopkins experiences the same problem as Wilmore, as both theologians argue that synthesized slave theologies existed but are unable to produce detailed models of these beliefs and practices. This is also applicable to Cone's theological project,

39. Hopkins and Cummings, *Cut Loose Your Stammering Tongue*, xiv–xv; Hopkins, *Shoes That Fit Our Feet*.

as he never produced the Black theology that was endorsed as being constructed *entirely* from *Black sources.*

My stance is not that religious syncretism was not practiced by African and African American slaves. Rather, I am questioning the beliefs of contemporary scholars who advocate religious syncretism was endorsed and practiced by orthodox/evangelical African and African American slaves.

There are a variety of concerns that I have about Hopkins's Black slave theology. First, Hopkins's interpretation assumes that Black slaves created theologies that never developed throughout the entire period of legalized slavery in America (1619–1865). He does not distinguish between time and geography. For example, the presumption is that a Virginian slave of the seventeenth century would have the same or similar theology as a slave of the eighteenth century from New Jersey. This creates the illusion that there is a solitary set of slave theologies that conforms to the theme of Afrocentric-liberation. Hopkins does not consider the natural influences from Christian denominations, diverse forms of Christian evangelism, or any sociocultural/religious developments throughout two centuries in America that would shape the slave's theological reflection. Instead, he articulates a slave theology that embodies the Afrocentric-Liberationist motif whereby all radical slaves opposed White America and its corrupt proslavery White Christianity that endorsed a White Christ.

Second, Hopkins employs the same essentialist and racialized binary reasoning that was observed by the Black Power advocates and Cone. Hopkins articulates European/European American and African/African American cultures as the antithesis to one another. He totalizes European/European American Christianity as proslavery Christianity and argues that these contextual expressions never established a positive influence upon the African American slaves. This also applies to any attempts to evangelize the slaves. Rather, for Hopkins, the slaves retained important elements of their African religious heritage and independently synthesized them within their Christian churches:

> And even as the African American phenomenon was eventually and partially created by the introduction of Christianity to black chattel, retentions of West African religions persisted. Africans and African Americans brought their own commitments to previous concepts and visceral lifestyles, a comprehensive spirituality, into the rituals and regularities of slavery churches. Slaves and masters could hear, repeat, and swear to the same

> biblical text, catechism, or sermon but think, feel, and interpret differently.[40]

This statement has elements of truth, but I argue it is exaggerated, because Hopkins never specifies with detail what these retentions, concepts, and visceral lifestyles entail.

Third, Hopkins argues that Black slaves practiced religious syncretism within the *Invisible Institution*, or the hidden Black slave church: "Enslaved Africans took remnants of their traditional religious structures and meshed them together with their interpretation of the bible. All this occurred in the 'Invisible Institution,' far away from the watchful eyes of white people."[41] On another occasion, he expressed that the "slaves met God in 'bush arbor' congregations of the 'Invisible Institution.' They had to meet secretly in order to worship a God who related divine compassion to the crucible of suffering of poor folk in pain."[42] These statements are true in the sense that the slaves indeed held secret church services without the permission or supervision of their slave masters. However, we must question how anyone can know in relative detail the manner of beliefs and practices that defined African American religious syncretism, if they were hidden from the public. Nevertheless, Erskine also supports Hopkins's view:

> Black people got around the laws forbidding their gathering by planning secret meetings. These secret meetings, the "invisible institution," not only provided space for enslaved persons to meet outside the gaze of White people but ensured a setting in which the virtue of respect, cooperation, compassion, hope, and faith would create a basis for them to carry on another day as they enjoined the help of ancestors through dancing, singing, and praying.[43]

He further stated, "Religion which assured them of the help of the ancestors and the God of Christianity and the gods of Africa was in the service of survival."[44] Erskine's interpretation is plagued with ambiguity also as he is unable to describe in detail the nature of African dancing,

40. Hopkins, *Down, Up, and Over*, 109.

41. Hopkins and Cummings, *Cut Loose Your Stammering Tongue*, 7; see also Raboteau, *Slave Religion*.

42. Hopkins and Cummings, *Cut Loose Your Stammering Tongue*, xviii; see also 1–45; Hopkins, *Down, Up, and Over*, 135–38, 140; and *Shoes That Fit Our Feet*, 15–20.

43. Erskine, *Plantation Church*, 121; see also 131, 135, 138.

44. Erskine, *Plantation Church*, 135.

singing, and praying that expressed itself within the hidden churches. Furthermore, we witness the reoccurring theme of survival that was originally emphasized by Cone in defining the central identity of Blackness, and Black theology.

Hopkins frames the Invisible Institution within an Afrocentric-Liberationist motif that emphasizes religious syncretism. He never entertains the possibility that conservative evangelical African American Christian slaves had secret church services. Hopkins also repeatedly explores the concept of the Invisible Institution with much ambiguity and romanticism. Despite his attempts, it is relatively impossible to describe with specificity the Invisible Institution because they were underground churches. Nevertheless, as other Afrocentric-Liberationists insisted before him, Hopkins maintains that there is obvious compatibility between Christianity and the plurality of West African religious beliefs:

> In a dynamic process, African precepts renegotiated the substantive terms of Christian plumb lines. Consequently, the voluntary acceptance of what the slave master thought was his Christianity by his human property occurred both because a fundamental structure in West African religions was somewhat compatible to a (reinterpreted) slave Christianity and because the malleability of African-American chattels' creativity wove together select portions of mainstream biblical teachings with remnants of the West African religious worldview.[45]

Once again, Hopkins remains vague regarding the details of this syncretizing process. His interpretation bears similarity to St. Clair Drake in that both scholars insist the slaves' Christianity was primarily political, as the core of their religious beliefs and practices were distinctly Afrocentric but clothed with the veneer of Christianity. Hopkins mentions a *fundamental structure* of West African religions but does not provide concrete examples of what this entails. This lack of specificity creates problems as Hopkins blurs the lines of distinction that define Christianity and uses that vagueness to project unverifiable correlations to West African religions. Anderson makes a similar observation:

> For all of Hopkins's talk about privileging African sources as an effective means for reassuring the legitimacy of black theology, these sources seem to fall out of or are simply consumed into Hebraic-Christian utterances. That is, so-called Africanisms are

45. Hopkins, *Down, Up, and Over*, 109.

> unidentifiable from the biblical utterances of Christian slaves. And instead of slave religion manifesting a hybridity, Hopkins's African slaves baptize the African gods into Hebrew faith.[46]

Anderson references the inability of Hopkins to specify how principles of traditional African religions were syncretized with Christianity. For Anderson, when Hopkins attempts to describe this process in detail, he is forced to reference Christian principles and their development, because there is no record of how African religious beliefs and practices were synthesized with Christianity. As I interpret Hopkins, he is confronted with the contradictions and inconsistencies of attempting to synthesize a pluralist religious structure (African traditional religions) into a monotheistic structure (Christianity) without detailed written accounts.

Nevertheless, Hopkins attempts to provide examples of this correlation, or synthesis, through basic concepts of God. For Hopkins, West African religions had a concept and system of worship that catered to one specific deity, the *High God*. He argues that West African worship of the High God was associated with YHWH of Hebraic scripture, and this eventually led to the worship of Jesus Christ through Christian scripture.[47] Hopkins also maintains,

> Captured and enslaved Africans, as they arrived on the shores of the thirteen British colonies and the United States of North America, did not know Jesus Christ, hence were not Christians; still they worshiped one God with similar attributes. For them there was only one ultimate divinity. This One was known by various local names but consistently embodied the same essential characteristics—creator, power, justice, beneficence, omniscience, and eternity. The Supreme Being constituted the beginning and the ending of all time, space, breathing, and non-breathing. God held power over life, death, rewards, and punishments. God was the final authority.[48]

Hopkins only required that the slaves believed in and worshiped one deity. Whoever this deity was, and whichever religion advocated it, did not matter. YHWH, Jesus Christ, and the Holy Spirit of Judaic and Christian scriptures were known and worshiped through different names within West African religions. The attributes of God are what connected

46. Anderson, *Beyond Ontological Blackness*, 97, 98.
47. Hopkins and Cummings, *Cut Loose Your Stammering Tongue*, 13–29.
48. Hopkins and Cummings, *Cut Loose Your Stammering Tongue*, 110.

these diverse religious systems. Critically reflecting upon Hopkins's interpretation incites a variety of questions: How did the slaves arrive at equating the High God of African religions to YHWH? In what ways did the processes of religious syncretism occur?

Hopkins has the burden of proving his claim that forms of religious syncretism had occurred repeatedly among the Black slaves. I support the view that religious syncretism was present among the slaves. However, I disagree with Hopkins and other scholars, whom I believe exaggerate this truth through attempts to minimize, undermine, and negate the presence of conservative evangelical African American Christianity.

In the end, I am convinced, Hopkins's interpretation of the slave's theology is a replication of contemporary Black liberation theology, constructed by the methodologies of Cone and Wilmore upon selective slave narratives. As Anderson has stated,

> Hopkins's hermeneutic of narrative return ends up justifying the black theology project by a vicious circulatory of reasoning that renders the legitimacy of slave religion coterminous with black theology and the legitimacy of black liberation theology coterminous with slave religion. When comparing the utterances properly ascribed to the slave narratives with those characteristic of the black theology project, there appears to be no significant differences that would suggest that the latter (black theology) is effectively indebted to the former sources (African traditional religion and slave theology). Both antecedent sources tend to be identified as liberation utterances. This is to say that there appears to be no difference between a source (antecedent) and its effect (consequent).[49]

We must come to our own conclusions about whether Hopkins is merely seeking to legitimate Black liberation theology by placing its supposed origins during legalized slavery in America. In this, we are forced to recall that his perspective was employed by Black Power advocates who interpreted Black Power as originating with radical African American slaves.

I argue that Hopkins creates a slave theology that is designed to be the antithesis of White proslavery Christianity. Moreover, his interpretation does not reflect any theological development from the slaves throughout the entirety of legalized slavery in America. Apparently, their theologies were unaffected by the cultural, social, and religious

49. Anderson, *Beyond Ontological Blackness*, 98, 99.

developments in America during this period. Hopkins interprets the eighteenth- and nineteenth-century African American slave narratives through the lens of twentieth-century Western liberal politics that are informed by the sociopolitical philosophy of Black Power. Hopkins provides another challenging interpretation of the slaves centered on their ability to recreate an identity apart from the dehumanizing treatment and perceptions of White America.

THE UNION OF GOD AND THE BLACK-SELF

Hopkins provides possibly the most complex Afrocentric-Liberationist theory of the *recreated human-Self* from the slave's innate religiosity and natural union with God. For Hopkins, the slaves recreated their identities from the fragments of three sources: the presence of African cultural and religious heritage, a sense of value within God, and an emancipatory relationship with God during their bondage. For Hopkins, these elements equipped the slaves to *re-imagine* and recreate their new lives in America: "In a word, aspects of African indigenous religions acted as key ingredient for the creation of and co-constitution of the black self in the United States. Black folk in America did not begin in slavery; they began in West Africa."[50] Hopkins seeks to preserve fragments of the slaves' cultural and religious heritage, and these fragments were symbolic bridges between African Americans and the continent of Africa.

The *co-constitution* of the new Black-self is interpreted as the relationship between an innate desire for freedom, fragments of African heritage, religious faith, and a union with God.[51] Hopkins argues, "Self co-constitution with God was a religious cultural act—a total way of life saturated with a quest for ultimate meaning. Self co-constitution with God was an epistemology of faith and a practical nurturing of an emancipatory way of being in the world on a daily basis."[52] Hopkins is adamant that the African slaves never embraced the belief of a sacred and secular paradigm or the separation of politics and religion. Moreover, Hopkins argues that the slaves rejected the notion that God was not concerned about their social existence. This is reinforced by his statements that conceptions of freedom were involved in the Africans' relationship with God,

50. Hopkins, *Down, Up, and Over*, 113.

51. Hopkins, *Down, Up, and Over*, 108.

52. Hopkins, *Down, Up, and Over*, 115–16.

and how Africans practiced "an emancipatory way of being in the world." This interpretation is typically advocated by Black liberation theologians. It was originally posited by Cone, but also expressed by Wilmore, Douglas, and Erskine.

Hopkins has two theories that describe the recreation of the slaves' culture, identity, and religion. Yet, it is difficult to comprehend their functionality and manner of sequence. Hopkins refers to the process of recreating one's identity as *the methods of the self.*[53] For him, the recreation of the human-Self was achieved by seizing sacred domains, the divine right to resist, and constructing a syncretized religion.[54] Furthermore, the process of recreating a new human-Self is secondary, and initiated when the slaves established a "substructure upon which they could then imagine, build, and refine methods of the self."[55] The *substructure* is created from commonsense folk wisdom, a reinterpretation of Christianity, and various aspects of African religion. Hopkins's theories of recreating a new human-Self and establishing a structure upon which to build their new identity are relatively synonymous. For example, both theories require a system of religious syncretism. This is problematic because the *methods* and *substructure* for the recreated human-Self are not easily distinguishable. Both theories are relatively the same and do not articulate a *first cause.* Hopkins never articulates how the slaves created their religious syncretism. Rather, he assumes a religious syncretism (substructure) was created beforehand, and it contributed to a second religious syncretism (methods of the self). The substructure and methods of recreating the human-Self are reliant upon an ambiguous religious syncretism. Nonetheless, Hopkins's theories suggest that all African descendants have a deep cultural and religious connection to Africa. Thus, it was relatively impossible for the slaves to create a new cultural and religious identity detached from their memories and innate African religiosity.

Once again, I do not dispute the presence of religious syncretism among the slaves. There is evidence that shows they practiced religious syncretism in various ways. However, I question why and how Afrocentric-Liberationist scholars exaggerate this fact in their attempts to make African cultural retention and religious syncretism the norm among *most* African American slaves. This is increasingly problematic if juxtaposed with evangelical colonial African Americans. Doing so creates

53. Hopkins, *Down, Up, and Over*, 108.

54. Hopkins, *Down, Up, and Over*, 115–47.

55. Hopkins, *Down, Up, and Over*, 108, 109, 113, 114.

multiple problems within African American scholarship. For example, there are no credible records that suggest that religious syncretism was a dominating practice among the slaves. Second, focusing primarily on religious syncretism minimizes and negates the origins and developments of conservative evangelical African American Christianity that was not influenced much, if any at all, by fragments of African heritage.

Afrocentric-Liberationist scholars within African American studies use a set of hermeneutics and methodologies reminiscent of the Black Power advocates and Black theologians. To my understanding, these Afrocentric-Liberationist scholars exaggerate and hyper-politicize the practice of religious syncretism among the African/African American slaves, whereby most slaves are interpreted as seeking to preserve their African heritage, as well as negate the process of racial assimilation through accepting European/European American Christianity. This interpretation is embellished and merely modified a position that was presented by the first generation of Black theologians who sought to undermine and negate scholarship concerning conservative evangelical African American Christianity/theology.

The Afrocentric-Liberationist scholars, establishing the most influential hermeneutics and methodologies within African American studies, have created what I believe to be some skewed interpretations of African American slave Christianity, that minimizes and ignores the presence of slaves that helped create the conservative evangelical tradition of African American Christianity/theology. Consequently, the dominant interpretation of African American slave Christianity/theology is parroted from, or represents a mirror image of, contemporary Black liberation theology influenced by James Cone and Gayraud Wilmore. This radical interpretation of militant sociopolitical slave Christianity establishes the concept of an Ideal-Blackness that some conservative slaves may not fit and therefore are relatively erased from the scholarship of the Afrocentric-Liberationist school of African American studies.

4

Racialized Politics Within African American Colonial Literature

Now these [Bereans] people were more noble-minded than those in Thessalonica, for they received the word with great eagerness, examining the Scripture daily to see whether these things were so.

ACTS 17:11

EXAMINING LITERATURE AND QUESTIONING INTERPRETATIONS

IN VARIED WAYS, CERTAIN scholars have employed a set of Afrocentric-Liberationist hermeneutics and methodologies derived from essentialist/racialized binary reasoning to construct what I refer to as an Ideal-Blackness. The issue isn't the Afrocentric or Liberationist elements, but how they are constructed, presented, and often imposed upon the reader. Connected to this is what seems to be elements of naivety and laziness, whereby some readers simply accept what the scholars present as truth without investigation, because it reinforces the reader's conception of an Ideal-Blackness.

I must admit, for me, it's irrational for African Americans, or those who prefer to be called simply "Black," to deny the birthplace, cultures, and existence of our African ancestors. Furthermore, freedom and liberation are central themes within African American culture and Christianity. Again, it would be irrational to deny this. My focus, and a more serious issue, is the driving force of essentialist/racialized binary reasoning, as it governs the construction and imposition of an Ideal-Blackness. My concern is that certain processes create a qualitative assessment of Blackness that displaces and ignores those African Americans who do not meet their standards. To a certain extent, the *potential* for this development stems from our natural disagreements and particularly any division between conservative and liberal expressions of African American existence. However, the manifestation of said processes occurs when our disagreements and division are hyper-politicized through racialized reasoning. Complications arise when some African American scholars are noticeably influencing certain European American literary scholars.

We can witness this in four areas, understanding there are more areas to be discussed that rest beyond the scope of this discussion. First, we must constantly examine the historical and sociopolitical issues regarding the education of African and African American slaves. There was extreme conflict in the secular world, reminiscent of what developed in response to attempts to Christianize the slaves, whereby European Americans deemed African and African American slaves as intellectually incapable of becoming educated. However, once again, from a historical perspective, eventually White slavery reformers and antislavery Christians influenced the initial stages of an educational movement that sought to empower African and African Americans.

Second, some contemporary scholars, understanding the historical issues regarding educating the slaves, have hyper-politicized things further through their essentialist/racialized binary reasoning, which enforces a concept of Ideal-Blackness by establishing a racialized binary paradigm between literacy and illiteracy. This structure is juxtaposed upon the African American slave narratives. The literate slaves/emancipated people who wrote their own narratives are held in high esteem over and against the illiterate slaves/emancipated people who relied upon European Americans to help write their narratives. Thus, we witness similar, if not the same, hermeneutics and methodologies employed by other liberal African American scholars. There is a persistent hyper-focus on conceptions of individualistic freedom from Whiteness that causes further fragmentation within contemporary Blackness, one that didn't have a widespread presence during colonialism.

Third, we can witness this firsthand through certain scholarship that elevates specific narratives above the other. One elevated narrative is by an ex-slave, Olaudah Equiano (?–1797). Equiano was a literate ex-slave who wrote and published a narrative about his life. Some scholars hold Equiano in high esteem because his account displays a form of literary sophistication and political astuteness that was rivalled by a select group of his peers. However, recent scholarship has revealed some dramatic contradictions and inconsistencies that, at least for me, undermine the legitimacy of Equiano's narrative.

Last, as a contrast to Equiano, some scholars have neglected and demeaned the writing of some conservative African American Christians, who are viewed as somewhat the antithesis of the Ideal-Blackness. I am fascinated by an African American slave named Jupiter Hammon (1711–1806). Hammon produced a collection of poems and prose articles that most early twentieth-century scholars have been indifferent toward. My belief is that this stems from the fact that Hammon, at least in their eyes, does not reproduce certain conceptions of a literary freedom or emancipation from Whiteness.

BRIEF HISTORICAL DISCUSSION: THE RACIALIZED POLITICS OF COLONIAL EDUCATION

It is widely held by scholars that colonialism marked a period in which education was a privilege seldom provided to African slaves.[1] Even the basics of learning the English alphabet, constructing a coherent sentence, and the importance of arithmetic were deemed beyond the intellect of the slaves. The overwhelming assumption among Europeans throughout colonialism was that Africans were innately inferior, and notions of inferiority inevitably involved their intellectual capabilities. This was partially witnessed through the etymology of race and Eurocentric racial classification. Naturally, these theories of African inferiority spread throughout the British colonies. Thus, European Americans adapted these beliefs and maintained that African American slaves lacked an adequate intellect to function independently from their masters.

1. Woodson, *Education of the Negro*, 67. A full examination of education among the slaves lies beyond the scope of this chapter. However, Woodson has written possibly the most comprehensive book on the subject. He discusses a wide range of conflicts, tensions, and agreements among Americans that led to public and private Negro schools. See also Webber, *Deep Like the Rivers*; Cornelius, *When I Can Read*.

Generally, most European Americans argued that even if education was offered, the slaves lacked the minimum intellectual faculties required to become literate. Carter G. Woodson (1875–1950) insists, "Those who had theretofore justified slavery on the ground that it gave the bondmen a chance to be enlightened, fell back on the theory of African racial inferiority. This they said was so well exhibited by the Negroes' lack of wisdom and of goodness that continued heathenism of the race was justifiable."[2] Woodson states one of the many contradictory theories that justified the enslavement of Africans. For some people, theories regarding the advancement of African civilization through European guidance were paramount to justifying the transatlantic slave trade. However, this was eventually revealed as sociopolitical and religious propaganda, since anything that established equality between the two races would ultimately undermine the institution of slavery. Therefore, we see a concentrated effort to minimize, if not eliminate completely, any attempts to educate the slaves. Nevertheless, notions of African inferiority became widespread, and it was an important belief within conceptions of racial classification.

Some European American masters insisted that the slaves had the ability to become literate but cautioned that education would eventually enlighten them on the principles of freedom and equality. From this we witness the presence of awareness and unacknowledged accountability as these European American masters knew that true equality was obtainable, but it would not satisfy their self-interest. Woodson speaks on this, maintaining,

> Yet, believing that slaves could not be enlightened without developing in them a longing for liberty, not a few masters maintained that the more brutish the bondmen the more pliant they become for purposes of exploitation. It was this class of slaveholders that finally won the majority of southerners to their way of thinking and determined that Negroes should not be educated.[3]

Sustaining the master's control over the slave was the primary purpose for keeping them illiterate. Absent was any desire to humanize the slaves, nor assist them in receiving salvation through the gospel of Christ. Present is White self-dehumanization through the withholding of freedom and education for the Black-Other. Enforcing illiteracy upon a

2. Woodson, *Education of the Negro*, 67.
3. Woodson, *Education of the Negro*, 1–2.

person or group is beyond immoral. It strikes at the core of our humanity as it wars against what is natural for us.

European slavery reformers and antislavery Christians encouraged society to critically reflect upon educating the slaves during the late seventeenth century. Their collective efforts created controversy and conflict to the extent that it not only encouraged a minority of masters to educate their slaves but also fuelled the passion within the slaves to become educated. Groups such as the Quakers partially led this fragile educational movement into the eighteenth century. Woodson states, "The first settlers of the American colonies to offer Negroes the same educational and religious privileges they provided for persons of their own race, were the Quakers."[4] This testifies to the influence of reformers and antislavery Christians such as George Fox (1624–91), William Edmondson (1627–1712), the Germantowners (1688), George Keith (1638–1716), and others. Likewise, the Anglican minister Morgan Godwyn (1640–ca. 1690) was a strong advocate for educating the African slaves and Indians during his missionary journeys.[5] The first organization to attempt a global effort in evangelizing and educating the non-European world was the Society for the Propagation of the Gospel in Foreign Parts, which was established in 1701 by the Church of England.[6]

My central concern, at this point, is this: We cannot avoid or minimize the historical reality that many African American slaves were reliant upon their masters, or members of White society, to obtain an education and to learn the basic tenets of Christianity. Historian Peter Kolchin (1943–2025) remarks,

> Fearing that literacy would promote excessive independence among slaves, most (although not all) slave owners opposed teaching their people to read or allowing them to attend Sunday school, thereby subverting the central Protestant tenet that each individual must be able to read the Bible. Instead, many masters read the Bible to their slaves, prayed with them, encouraged them to attend church, and arranged special services to them.[7]

Kolchin succinctly describes the divergent and opposing positions that masters held regarding educating their slaves. Generally, the slaves

4. Woodson, *Education of the Negro*, 4.

5. Woodson, *Education of the Negro*, 24.

6. Woodson, *Education of the Negro*, 18; Glasson, *Mastering Christianity*; Bennett, *Shaping of Black America*, 116.

7. Kolchin, *American Slavery*, 116.

that resided within the southern states, and primarily on plantations, were unlikely to be literate or be openly allowed to attend church services. Northern slaves had slightly more accessibility to education and were inclined to be taught the basics of Christian doctrine, sometimes within integrated churches. Yet, regardless of the slave's geographical location, various states had imposed laws that prohibited educating the slaves. However, enforcing these laws was subject to the individual or local community's discretion:

> Most states passed laws designed to keep slaves illiterate, but these laws were surprisingly vague, inconsistent, and ineffective, and were poorly enforced. Only four states—Virginia, North Carolina, South Carolina, and Georgia—had laws on the books throughout the last thirty years of slavery totally prohibiting teaching slaves to read and write; other states had such laws for briefer periods or banned the teaching of *assembled* slaves but not individuals.[8]

The eighteenth century marked a period in which African American slaves and emancipated people went to great lengths to educate themselves. This was complemented by European and European Americans creating numerous schools throughout this period. The influential historian Ira Berlin (1941–2018) places a strong emphasis on the desire for education from emancipated African Americans:

> Nothing spoke more loudly of the free people's aspirations than the schoolhouses that appeared "like mushrooms after a storm" among newly liberated slaves. Slaves and sometimes free blacks had been denied—by custom and often by law—the right to a formal education, and they believed access to the word to be an essential element of freedom as well as a practical means of self-advancement. Literacy would enable them to crack the secret code white men had used to enslave them. Newly freed slaves flocked to schools established by northern missionaries, who testified to the enthusiasm for education among former slaves. When denied schooling, freed people petitioned federal agents and missionaries for its establishment so they might "become a People capable of self support." And when schools were not forthcoming—and sometimes even when they were—freed people pooled their scant resources to hire teachers, build schoolhouses, and establish libraries. Aspirations long pent up in slavery burst into the open.[9]

8. Kolchin, *American Slavery*, 129.
9. Berlin, *Generations of Captivity*, 254–55.

Berlin describes the general passion for literacy that symbolically emancipated African Americans. Education, for them, was a central element of psychological and sociopolitical emancipation. This passion for education was further incited by the presence and sporadic development of Black schools throughout the land. These schools represented the relationship between European American philanthropy, a minority of citizens seeking to teach African Americans, and African Americans' acquisition of literacy. Berlin's reference to educated African Americans cracking the code of the White man is rather ambiguous. He is possibly insinuating the broad understanding of how the transatlantic slave trade developed and everything this entailed. Furthermore, another important point to mention is Berlin advocates Christian missionaries were active in educating African American slaves and emancipated people. However, even the short existence of most Black schools, a consequence of oppression from proslavery European Americans, did not restrain the passion many African Americans had cultivated for education.[10] Janet Duitsman Cornelius (1938–) insists that for some African Americans, literacy represented more than generic freedom, but symbolized a self-sufficient life and the accumulative ability to create their own identities:

> For enslaved African-Americans, literacy was more than a path to individual freedom—it was a communal act, a political demonstration of resistance to oppression and of self-determination for the Black community. Through literacy the slave could obtain skills valuable in the white world, thereby defeating those whites who withheld the skills, and could use those skills for special privileges or to gain freedom.[11]

There were many ways African Americans became educated. Some achieved education through institutions, but this was extremely rare. Cornelius provides an interpretation that emphasizes the politics of education whereby manipulation and forced coercion were central elements within the teacher and student relationship: "Slaves maneuvered whites into teaching them, so whites were often casual, even unwitting, instructors, not realizing the impact of the power they were giving slaves. Other whites taught purposefully, for practical reasons; they could use literate

10. Bennett, *Before the Mayflower*, 81, 161, 194; Franklin and Moss, *From Slavery to Freedom*, 125, 126–27; Bennett, *Shaping of Black America*, 127–28, 185, 199–201.

11. Cornelius, *When I Can Read*, 3.

slaves for their own needs."[12] Cornelius also provides further insight into the politics of education by maintaining:

> For slaves, literacy was a two-edged sword: owners offered literacy to increase their control, but resourceful slaves seized the opportunity to expand their own powers. Slaves who learned to read and write gained privacy, leisure time, and mobility. A few wrote their own passes and escaped from slavery. Literate slaves also taught others and served as conduits for information within a slave communication network. Some were able to capitalize on their skills in literacy as a starting point for leadership careers after slavery ended.[13]

Surprisingly, contrary to many Afrocentric-Liberationist views, an influential number of African Americans were willfully taught by European Americans devoid of ulterior motives that deviated from their desire to edify them. A popular way was through European American children teaching African American children and adults. Thomas L. Weber (1947–) explains, "Of those slaves who did learn to read and write, many were taught by whites, especially by the sons and daughters of their masters."[14] Moreover, possibly influenced by the European slavery reformers and antislavery Christians, within America the Bible became a primary source for achieving literacy.[15]

Many African American slaves, their masters, and sympathetic European Americans had understood the importance of education. This importance was not only toward conceptions of freedom and empowerment, but also for the development of racial reconciliation and the undermining of colonial slavery. Most literary scholars are keenly aware of the political dynamics that defined the issue of educating the slaves. Yet, I will demonstrate that some scholars, through essentialist/racialized binary reasoning, have exaggerated the political contours of education and contributed to the fragmented scholarship regarding the slaves' narratives. I'm not attempting to present a romanticized form of White altruism and its contribution to Black literacy. Rather, I seek to incite more scrutiny on the dynamics of slave literacy and the realistic consequences of its absence, within the passion to present one's testimony to the world.

12. Cornelius, *When I Can Read*, 4.

13. Cornelius, "'We Slipped and Learned to Read,'" 171.

14. Webber, *Deep Like the Rivers*, 131.

15. Cornelius, *When I Can Read*, 68, 76, 88, 100, 107.

TEXTUAL CONFLICT: EXPRESSIONS OF WHITE DOMINANCE AND BLACK LIBERATION

Some scholars suggest that the collection of African American slave literature consists of over six thousand documents of autobiographies, biographies, and the overall written accounts of the African American slaves' experiences during colonialism. These narratives are generally divided into three categories. First, there are the narratives created during the abolitionist era before the American Civil War (1861–65) between 1760 to the 1820s. The second group of narratives were the testimonies of ex-slaves regarding their experiences between 1831 and 1865. The most extensive collection of narratives was compiled by the Federal Writers Project Administration during 1936–38.[16]

The African American slave narratives are accepted as a particular genre, composed in the context of extreme politics. However, some controversy was created from the fact that some European Americans were writing on behalf of some slaves. Dickson D. Bruce (1946–2014) alludes to this by stating, "Though sometimes exaggerated by historians and critics, there was a tendency among white abolitionists to control the African American voice, to define and delimit the content and character of the narratives."[17] Bruce is correct about the general conflict between the African American slave orator and the European American narrator. My issue is the extent of the exaggerations, as I believe certain scholars embellish most of these conflicts. My concern derives from the view that some scholars, such as William L. Andrews (1946–), Beth A. McCoy, and John Sekora, have partially, though unintentionally, decontextualized the narratives by minimizing the methods of how the slaves were educated during colonialism.

For me, reframing the narratives into their educational contexts minimizes the inclination to focus exclusively on the conflict between the orator and writer, because a broader understanding of *positive* European American assistance is achieved. We discover a significant number of European Americans who politicized education for the African American slave's emancipation and the abolishment of institutional slavery. Restating a previous point, I'm not attempting to present a romanticized view of Whiteness. Rather, I'm attempting to elicit re-examination of Black

16. Rawick, *American Slave*, xv–xvi; D. Bruce, "Politics and Political Philosophy," 28–29; Foster, *Witnessing Slavery*, xi, 17; Olney, "'I Was Born,'" 46–73.

17. D. Bruce, "Politics and Political," 36.

slave illiteracy and the realistic ways the Black slaves used to reach the consciousness of colonial White America.

Some historians and literary scholars have interpreted the slave narratives as a site of turmoil regarding the education of African American slaves, their ability to construct an autobiography, and the participation of European Americans in this process. I maintain that essentialist/racialized binary reasoning is expressed within the stories of the slave narratives. However, these accounts are often exaggerated by the interpretations of some scholars that seek to articulate conceptions of an Ideal-Blackness, which is sometimes complemented by conceptions of unredeemed Whiteness.

For some scholars, literacy is representative of emancipation from Whiteness and slavery, as well as a form of empowerment that equips the slaves with the ability to craft their own identity *apart* from European Americans. Lindon Barrett (1961–2008), referencing a general understanding of literacy in the context of the slave narratives, observes, "Literacy is conceived in terms of empowerment and the transformation of identity it grants those long excluded from it in a society in which letters were indispensable."[18] We witness here the connection between literacy, power, and self-identification. Subsequently, as a binary opposite, illiteracy is interpreted as a form of perpetual bondage, dependency upon Whiteness, and the absence of self-identity. Barrett alludes to this by explaining, "Thus, African Americans who are forced to live illiterate lives, who are forcibly identified with the limited sphere of the body, are in as manifest a fashion as possible seemingly restricted to being the objects of thought and never its subjects."[19] Barrett also mentions,

> To restrict African Americans to lives without literacy is seemingly to immure them in bodily existences having little or nothing to do with the life of the mind and its representation. Conversely, to enter into literacy is to gain important skills for extending oneself beyond the condition and geography of the body.[20]

18. Barrett, "African-American Slave Narratives," 418. Barrett also crafts a personal definition of literacy that is associated to the African American body: "Literacy determines for whom the physical, the geographic, and the bodily will remain an overwhelming concern and source of identity and for whom it will remain an index of power and valuable apparent remove." Barrett, "African-American Slave Narratives," 421.

19. Barrett, "African-American Slave Narratives," 419.

20. Barrett, "African-American Slave Narratives," 419.

Barrett emphasizes principles of power between the master and the slave as illiteracy was forced upon the slave, not chosen. Moreover, we witness an interpretation of a binary paradigm between illiteracy and literacy. For Barrett, literacy is a requirement for achieving higher levels of human development. Literacy has provided the slaves with the ability not only to emancipate themselves, but also to transcend the limitations of the *enslaved* human body. However, Barrett never explains the processes of how illiterate slaves establish self-identification.

We cannot afford to decontextualize the slave narratives, nor minimize and ignore the accumulative variables that defined their contexts, as well as the slave narratives themselves. Colonialism was a period of extreme persecution and represented the dehumanization of the non-European world. This occurred to the extent that people genuinely argued about whether Africans were truly human. Regarding America, it was natural for conflict to develop from the mere notion of educating the slaves. Education was a privilege and a sign of equality that European Americans had generally refused to share with their African American slaves. Similar views surrounded the question of whether it was realistic to evangelize the slaves. Nevertheless, historians have convincingly shown, and the slave narratives testify, that a significant number of slaves and emancipated people were educated toward the middle and end of the nineteenth century.

In this regard, there are a variety of things we must consider. First, in this context, the definitions of education and literacy are extremely ambiguous. We cannot assume educational equality extended among the slaves. Nor can we conclude that the slaves received an adequate level of education per the standard of the era. It is only safe to infer that most educated slaves achieved a minor level of literacy. Second, achieving the basics of literacy does not determine an adequate ability to construct a new Black identity and, by extension, a *refined* autobiography. A cursory reading of the self-written slave narratives reveals a variety of literary sophistication per the writer's educational level, personal experiences, intended purposes for writing, and everything these aspects entail. Stephen T. Butterfield broadly alludes to this: "But the best writers in the history of black autobiography are able to share the same political involvement of the mediocre ones without being noticeably crippled by monotonous style or a one-dimensional outlook."[21] Third, educational competence

21. Butterfield, "Use of Language," 73.

and the ability to create an autobiography do not presuppose a sufficient aptitude for understanding and the ability to communicate with European Americans.

For reasons which are the consequences of slavery, some African American slaves were reliant upon European Americans to construct their narratives in a way that effectively communicated their views and influenced their readers to reject, as well as undermine, the institution of slavery. Frances Smith Foster (1944–) insists,

> The black, who in the antebellum society attempted to define himself and to assess the factors which had marked him as he was, found that the process of communicating this knowledge to a group which had doubts about his human status and which was guilty of his enslavement was fraught with special problems. He had to overcome the incredulity of persons whose surprise that a black could write overshadowed any attempt to understand or to consider what he was writing about. He had to convince his reader to accept the validity of his knowledge and conclusion, which in many instances profoundly contradicted their own. Furthermore, if he was to obtain their sympathy and aid, he had to do this in a manner which did not threaten or embarrass his reader.[22]

Foster delivers one of the more balanced and realistic interpretations of the slaves' burden. They had the unacknowledged responsibility of simultaneously affirming their humanity and proving their capability to exist in sociopolitical equality with those European Americans who enslaved them.

Yet, Foster is not alone in this grounded assessment of American slavery. Sterling Lecater Bland Jr. (1961–) echoes similar sentiments. Bland Jr. reaffirms the view that the context of slavery demanded the presence and activity of European American authority in relation to African American existence. However, there was a distinct difference between relationships created from oppression and dehumanization by proslavery European Americans to relationships of progressive equality and humanization influenced by the slavery reformers/antislavery/abolitionist European Americans. Bland Jr. comments,

> Because of the source of the narrative, slave narratives required white corroboration in order to achieve any kind of resonance

22. Foster, *Witnessing Slavery*, 9; 45, 55–56; Stepto, "I Rose and Found My Voice," 3–31.

> with readers. This layer of validation was particular to black autobiography writers for a white audience, since white narratives of Native American captivities or explorations of inhospitable places around the world seldom used these same kinds of framing devices to add a patina of legitimacy.[23]

Thus, to a certain extent, European American authority was necessary, because a racist society required it as a prerequisite to engaging the slave narratives. Generally, the presence and activity of sympathetic European Americans were not a consequence of some compulsive drive to dominate and continue to enslave African Americans. Bland Jr. accurately mentions the callousness of a Eurocentric society that refused to acknowledge any semblance of independence and equality expressed by African Americans.

There are scholars that either focus solely on the destructive practices of proslavery European Americans or conflate the natural conflict between the African American slave orator and the European American writer. For these scholars, certain aspects of the slave narratives represented White dominance over Black existence. It's fascinating to observe that some of the ideological beliefs of Black Power advocates, the first generation of contemporary Black theologians, and the Afrocentric-Liberationist scholars are located within the work of some literary scholars such as William L. Andrews and Vincent Carretta (1945–). For example, aspects of Andrews's and Carretta's scholarship employ essentialist/racialized binary reasoning that depicts Whiteness as a corrupt existence that seeks to dominate Blackness. This is complemented by depicting Blackness in a perpetual state of survival, fighting for emancipation from Whiteness, and ceaselessly attempting to define its multifaceted identities.

My difficulty with these interpretations lies in their absence, at least partially, of what I view as historical realism. These scholars accurately describe the racism that permeated throughout American society; yet, some scholars typically neglect a healthy articulation of the slave's burden, whereby the presence and activity of European Americans were required, because the nation was defined by Eurocentric sociopolitical and religious beliefs that demanded it during that era. Such scholars characterize most of these perceived and literal power struggles as *editorial conflicts*.

Andrews strongly emphasizes the power and editorial control that many European American writers wielded over their African American

23. Bland, *African-American Slave Narratives*, 18; see also Nichols, *Many Thousands Gone*, xi.

orator counterparts. He is well informed on this topic of slave narratives, but creates what I believe is an unnecessary shroud of suspicion upon the European American writers who assisted in the production of these texts. For me, Andrews's views make it relatively impossible to conceive of a healthy partnership between the orator and writer, whereby a balance of editorial collaboration was achieved. Andrews states,

> From a literary standpoint, however, it is not the moral integrity of these editors that is at issue but the linguistic, structural, and tonal integrity of the narratives they produced. Even if an editor faithfully reproduced the facts of a black narrator's life, it was still the editor who decided what to make of these facts, how they should be emphasized, in what order they ought to be presented, and what was extraneous, or germane. It was the editor who controlled the manuscript and thus decided how a "statement of facts" became a "fiction of factual representation," a readable, convincing, and moving autobiography. Editors of early Afro-American autobiography assumed the right to do everything to a dictation from "improving" its grammar, style, and diction to selecting, arranging, and assigning significance to its factual substance.[24]

We must question whether Andrews's statement minimizes and rejects the variables that required the presence of European American authority. With this, we must critically reflect on the ways a White supremacist society would receive any Black person educating, rebuking, and attempting to correct them. Otherwise, we are likely to lapse into a romanticized conception of illiterate Blackness which existence is detached from Whiteness, yet somehow is equipped to effectively communicate with said Whiteness through structured writing. The moral intent of the White writer is important. Some aspects of editorial control are rational and required. The character of the White editor provides insight toward their relationship with the Black orator and whether there were possible nefarious motives to discredit the narrative. I struggle to understand if it is beneficial to minimize the moral intent of the writer yet place a hyper-emphasis on the moral outcome from their actions.

It is indeed a moral issue because Andrews critiques the editorial choices of the European American writer from a set of presumptions. First, Andrews implies that the African American orators did not express

24. W. Andrews, *To Tell a Free Story*, 20; see also Stepto, "I Rose and Found My Voice," 7; Casmier-Paz, "Slave Narratives," 91–116.

opinions of their own, nor provide any major decisions that ultimately shaped their narratives. Second, he appears to reason from a theoretical narrative written apart from European American assistance, and this alternative narrative reveals the inconsistencies of the former narrative. Andrews assumes that on most or all occasions, the Black orator would partially or completely disagree with the decisions presented by the White writer. Andrews further argues,

> Transcribed narratives in which an editor delimits his role as explicitly as Eliot did undoubtedly may be regarded as more authentic and reflective of the narrator's thought in action than those edited works that flesh out a statement of facts in ways unaccounted for. Still it would be naïve to accord dictated oral narratives the same discursive status as autobiographies composed and written by the subjects of the stories themselves. There is much that we do not know about the circumstances in which these oral narratives were dictated, for instance. Obviously the work was done in the context of a power relationship that gave the supposed passive amanuensis ultimate control over the fate of the manuscript and considerable influence over the immediate future of the narrator.[25]

Samuel A. Eliot had written the narrative of a slave named Josiah Henson (1789–1883). Eliot explained that he at no point embellished or fabricated any part of Henson's narrative. Everything recorded was solely from Henson's testimony. Andrews insists that this is evidence of Eliot's credibility. Ideally, this was the sole purpose of having the presence and activity of European American authority within the African American slave narrative. I'm not suggesting we shouldn't be suspicious of certain slave narratives edited by European Americans. Rather, I'm questioning whether some contemporary scholars are projecting certain issues onto the slave narratives that the narratives themselves don't express. I'm also questioning if said projections stem from the contemporary scholar's views on racialized politics, not the racialized politics of the colonial White editor and slave orator. Bland Jr. provides some insight into this issue:

> The introductory material is customarily written by White abolitionist supporters or white editors and authors who served as literary benefactors to the slave writer. The function of these prefaces [is] to emphasize the fundamental truth of the narrative to follow, the connection between the preface writer and

25. W. Andrews, *To Tell a Free Story*, 21.

> the narrative writer, and the fact that the narrative understates rather than overstates the effects of the slave system.[26]

I find Andrews's position somewhat confusing and contradictory. Andrews persistently approaches European American written narratives with extreme suspicion and regards them with less reliability than the narratives written by African Americans. Yet, he accepts the statement of Eliot, a European American, regarding his integrity and the genuineness of Henson's narrative. For Andrews, conceptions of power define the relationship between African American orator and European American narrator. This is applicable to some narratives, but there is not enough evidence to assume that every or most relationships functioned as such. Moreover, playing devil's advocate, we cannot assume, as Andrews does, that the literate slaves were unlikely to embellish portions of their narrative any more than those who wrote on behalf of illiterate slaves. This is an important point that will be examined through the self-published narrative of Olaudah Equiano. The unavoidable reality is that there are always issues of power within every relationship. The presence of disagreements to overt arguments is not synonymous with oppression. If so, possibly, contemporary authors could claim to be oppressed by their publisher.

Andrews is not alone in advocating this perspective. John Sekora provides similar sentiments: "Whatever the circumstance, the slave narrative is born into a world of literary confinement—designated by otherness, plainness, facticity, and dictated forms."[27] For Sekora, an unacknowledged element of the slave narratives involves the master controlling the contours of the slave's language and how this bears upon the narratives.[28] Thus, there is a duality of White dominance upon Black existence in African American autobiographies, and those written by European Americans. Sekora insists,

> The beginnings and endings of slaves' lives are thus institutionally bound. Put another way, the slave is witness in a double sense: eyewitness to a system that must be exposed, and witness called before abolitionist judges and jurors to reply to specific questions—no more, no less. Once again, white sponsors compel a

26. Bland, *African-American Slave Narratives*, 16. Like Bland, John W. Blassingame has a more positive view of European American editorial assistance. See Blassingame, *Slave Testimony*, xviii, xix, xxii, xxiii, xxvii.

27. Sekora, "Black Message/White Envelope," 488.

28. Sekora, "Black Message/White Envelope," 485.

> black author to approve, to authorize white institutional power. The black message will be sealed within a white envelope.[29]

Sekora accurately describes the slaves as witnesses to, as well as the recipients of, the oppression and dehumanization during colonialism. However, Sekora conflates this view into conceptions of bondage as the slaves' testimonies are supposedly determined by European Americans. The narratives are interpreted as a site of African American literary subservience to *White institutional power*. Beth A. McCoy adheres to a similar interpretation of Andrews and Sekora. McCoy, referencing the fugitive slave narratives, maintains,

> The paratext crafted by white prefacers and editors, however, reduces fugitive author to fugitive reporter, a construction that accommodates Thomas Jefferson's distasteful declaration that "never yet could I find a black had uttered a thought above the level of plain narration." In this way, serving neither the text nor its author, the paratext serves something else: an indirect white supremacy, different from the brutality against which white abolitionists fought but one that interferes with the fugitive writer's authorial primacy nonetheless.[30]

Generally, the main context is framed within broader contexts. An understanding of the broader contexts helps further clarify the message(s) of the main context. Thus, the pretext, which McCoy argues is determined by the White editor, frames the narrative within boundaries without the consent of the Black orator and writer. The White editor's authority is interpreted as transcending both the Black orator and writer. For McCoy, the voice and message of African Americans are shaped by, as well as become, a mere parroting of European American discourse. This view is complemented by the reference to Thomas Jefferson's demeaning statement regarding the inferiority of African American literature. However, McCoy takes her interpretation further by claiming that European American editorial control is a cloaked form of White supremacy. We are forced to ask ourselves whether these principles can be adequately applied to issues of gender and social status.

Contemporary Black theologian J. Kameron Carter provides an interesting perspective regarding the relationship between Black orator, White narrator, and the emergence of an authentic Black identity. His

29. Sekora, "Black Message/White Envelope," 502.

30. McCoy, "Race and the (Para)Textual Condition," 157.

approach is distinct from the scholars above, in that Carter's interpretation is theologically centered. He explores the subtle Christology within *A Narrative of the Uncommon Sufferings, and Surprizing Deliverance of Briton Hammon* (1760).[31] Briton Hammon was an African American slave credited for publishing the first African American slave narrative. Carter maintains that he is attracted to Hammon's narrative because,

> Hammon's literary gesture insinuates a decidedly theological response to the racial indexing of existence. In employing Christological categories and ideas within which to materialize the black self, the Hammon *Narrative* reclaims Christianity as salutary for Hammon's own, and thus for human, flourishing. His textual reclamation invests Christology with liberative possibilities that were yet to be realized at the time of his writing.[32]

Much of Carter's project examines the theological problem of Whiteness and how it has dislodged, as well as replaced, Israel as God's chosen people. In this context, Carter maintains that Hammon's narrative displays a subtle Christology that provides a counternarrative to Whiteness as the theological center within Christianity. Moreover, Hammon's Christology articulates a constructive theology that subsequently dislodges Whiteness, reclaims the universality of Christianity, and creates a new Black-Self which is independent of Whiteness.

Carter is aware that a major problem presents itself within Hammon's narrative: it was the beneficiary of one or more White editors. Citing Carter's critical view of White editorial authority, he surprisingly states,

> The editors of Hammon's story sought to employ Christian theological ideas to reaffirm, reinforce, and further establish "the color line," to employ an anachronism, is no small matter. In its literary pantomime, it parrots much of the logic of white slaveholding Christianity. In many respects, the story reinforces the codes of Enlightenment racial thought and the central place accorded to Christianity in founding and maintaining its discourse and social vision. The way *Narrative*, or perhaps more accurately, its amanuensis—editor, employs Christology as a frame within which to materialize the black author, albeit stripped of authority, affirms as much. It suggests, on one level, a Christology wedded to white racial supremacy and non-white subservience.[33]

31. Hammon, *Narrative*. Coincidently, 1760 is the year Jupiter Hammon published his first poem, "An Evening Thought. Salvation by Christ with Penitential Cries."

32. Carter, *Race*, 268.

33. Carter, *Race*, 269.

As I interpret Carter, he agrees with other liberal scholars that European American editorial authority created a conflict within the African American text, whereby White supremacist beliefs not only aided in the creation and presentation of a Black-identity, but also subtly forced this Black-identity into the service of White supremacy. For him, this is a central issue within Hammon's narrative. However, some readers may ask why Carter would choose Hammon's narrative as a testimony to a constructive universal Christology and the emergence of a new Black-Self.

In short, Carter, influenced somewhat by Andrews's scholarship, insists that Hammon is indeed a co-author with the unnamed White editor(s). Thus, his voice, albeit in confrontation with the voice of the White editor(s), can be discerned if or when we locate the ideological inconsistencies within the narrative.[34] From this perspective, Carter initiates a rereading of Hammon that is conscious of the internal racialized conflict within the text, but concentrates on Hammon's voice to discern his Black Christology.

Carter's interpretation of Hammon's narrative is problematic for various reasons. First, Carter presents similar contextual expressions of essentialist/racialized binary reasoning that was employed by the Black Power advocates, Black liberation theologians, and Afrocentric-Liberationist scholars. I am *not* placing him within these groups. I am merely emphasizing that Carter interprets Whiteness as a corrupt existence and requires Blackness to renew itself apart from Whiteness. Second, it is questionable whether Hammon's narrative truly supports Carter's claim, because it is not typically recognized as a spiritual or theological document. In saying this, I am not suggesting we blindly ignore references to Christianity or YHWH. Indeed, Carter may be merely theologizing the supposed conflict between Hammon and the White writers of his narrative, as a conflict between Black and White theology.

THE PRESENCE OF A COLONIAL IDEAL-BLACKNESS

In any case, there are over two thousand slave narratives. The narratives are an important part of a greater collection that incorporates a variety of letters, poems, prose articles, and everything alike. This extends the collection to roughly six thousand documents in entirety. Yet, some scholars have committed a disservice to the knowledge within, the integrity of, and

34. Carter, *Race*, 275.

the overall value of this extensive collection by giving a disproportionate amount of attention to a minority of narratives.[35] There are roughly ten to fifteen slave narratives of the six thousand documents that receive an inordinate amount of scholarly attention. Furthermore, there are possibly four to five narratives within this group that are elevated as representative of Black literary sophistication.

Scholars have every right to focus on the narratives they are interested in and passionate about. This isn't the issue. I'm merely calling for the re-examination of the established standards constructed by some scholars. My central concern is that some narratives are ignored or their value minimized, because they don't fit the scholar's construction of an Ideal-Blackness. Their conceptions seem to always coincide with their personal sociopolitical and theological convictions. This fragmented scholarly approach to exploring the narratives is determined by a binary paradigm between literacy and illiteracy constructed through essentialist/racialized binary reasoning. Furthermore, some historians and literary scholars have passively contextualized the Afrocentric-Liberationist principles of interpreting Whiteness as corrupt, Blackness as existing in a perpetual state of survival, the endorsement of ideologies that justify Blackness separating from Whiteness, and a newly created Blackness that is constructed without the influence of Whiteness. Thus, the literary contextualism of an Ideal-Blackness is represented by an elite set of narratives. However, these narratives do not accurately represent the complexity of African American existence during colonialism nor the depths of their literary achievements. The construction and employment of a literary Ideal-Blackness have produced some contradictions and inconsistencies regarding which narratives are interpreted as sophisticated as well as distinct from others. A powerful example of this is witnessed within scholarship regarding the popular narrative of Olaudah Equiano (1745–97). Equiano was a literate ex-slave who had written and published his narrative. He is praised as an exemplar of the Ideal-Blackness within African American colonial literature.

35. Example of such popular narratives are Equiano, *Interesting Narrative of the Life of Olaudah Equiano, or Gustavus Vassa* (1745); Bibb, *Narrative of the Life and Adventures of Henry Bibb* (1815); Douglass, *Narrative of the Life of Frederick Douglass* (1845); and Jacobs, *Incidents in the Life of a Slave Girl* (1861).

EQUIANO: THE AFRICAN OR AFRICAN AMERICAN?

Olaudah Equiano, also known as Gustavus Vassa, is considered by many historians and literary scholars as a pioneering Black author during colonial America.[36] He is held in such high esteem that, despite other African and African Americans publishing their narratives before him, the sheer influence, as well as sophistication, of Equiano's narrative has scholars relegating his predecessors behind him in terms of literary importance.[37] Anthony Carrigan (1980–2016) summarizes the perspective of many scholars that Equiano's narrative "has come to be widely regarded both as one of the most influential slave narratives of the eighteenth century and as one of the earliest examples of black diasporic life-writing."[38] Vincent Carretta proudly makes the claim, "No one has a greater claim to being called a self-made man than the writer now best known as Olaudah Equiano."[39] Arthur P. Davis (1904–96) and Joyce Ann Joyce (1949–) state, "Most American scholars interested in black literature claim Gustavus Vassa as the first important writer of African American autobiography."[40] Indeed, Equiano's narrative influenced many people during the eighteenth century, and being a literate slave who wrote his narrative without anyone's assistance, he was able to craft multiple identities for himself in a world that believed this right was designated solely for European/European Americans.

However, Equiano's level of importance within Black literature may be a result of scholarly exaggeration, as well as political agendas, and less about the *credibility* of his *personal* testimony. Some scholars have employed a double standard that elevates Equiano's narrative above other African American narratives without effectively justifying the minimizing or complete overlooking of other narratives that may display equal to greater levels of literary sophistication, according to alternative criteria

36. Equiano's narrative is extensive as it encompasses two volumes. My aim is not to explore his narrative in entirety. Rather, it is to briefly examine an overt contradiction/inconsistency of his narrative that challenges its credibility and reveals how some scholars ignore this issue, as well as attempt to reinterpret it as a positive attribute. This double standard is not applied to other narratives.

37. Some examples of black literature published before Equiano's autobiography are Hammon, *Narrative of the Most Uncommon Sufferings* (1760); Gronniosaw, *Narrative of the Most Remarkable Particulars* (1772); and Wheatley, *Poems on Various Subjects, Religious and Moral* (1773).

38. Carrigan, "Negotiating Personal Identity," 42.

39. Carretta, *Equiano, the African*, xi.

40. Davis et al., *New Cavalcade*, 34.

from non-Afrocentric scholars. Many scholars have portrayed Equiano as the epitome of Black self-consciousness and self-determination that defined his complex identities apart from the influence of Europeans/European Americans. Opinions are divided on this, as there are persistent and growing levels of interrogation, dismay, and denial regarding the accuracy of Equiano's narrative. Some scholars continue to uphold him as a representative of the literary Ideal-Blackness, despite newer scholarship that questions and overtly contradicts parts of Equiano's narrative. One of the more contentious areas of Equiano's narrative lies in the accuracy and detailed account of his birthplace.

Equiano delivers one of the most compelling descriptions of his homeland imaginable. The reader is captivated by Equiano's vivid portrayal of his people and the specific aspects of their culture. Equiano states that he was born in a kingdom called Eboe, located in the valley of Essaka in 1745, which is known today as Nigeria.[41] Regarding his family, Equiano had a mother, sister, brothers, and a father who was an influential elder/chieftain of the community. Equiano loved each member of his family and provided specific moments that testified to the love they shared for one another.[42]

Equiano also provides an impressive portrait of his people. For example, he characterized them as highly skilful in the arts and stated that "we are almost a nation of dancers, musicians, and poets. Thus, every great event, such as a triumphant return from battle or other cause of public rejoicing is celebrated in public dances, which are accompanied with songs and music suited to the occasion."[43] Yet, Equiano testifies that they had other natural talents. For example, they were gifted warriors to the extent that the women of the nation had actively participated in battle: "All are taught the use of these weapons; even our women are warriors, and march boldly out to fight along with the men. Our whole district is a kind of militia: on a certain signal given, such as the firing of a gun at night, they all rise in arms and rush upon their enemy."[44] Impressive as this may be, Equiano explains that his people were not limited to excelling in dance, music, poetry, and war. His people were also proficient artisans and agriculturalists. Common among them were the practice of spinning and weaving cotton, making dye for their garments, creating

41. Equiano, *Interesting Narrative*, 4–5.

42. Equiano, *Interesting Narrative*, 5, 25, 28–29, 36–37.

43. Equiano, *Interesting Narrative*, 10, 11.

44. Equiano, *Interesting Narrative*, 25, 24.

earthen vessels and tobacco pipes, and making an assortment of luxury perfumes.[45] Equiano maintains,

> Agriculture is our chief employment, and every one, even the children and women, are engaged in it. Thus we are all habituated to labour from our earliest years. Every one contributes something to the common stock; and as we are unacquainted with idleness, we have no beggars. The benefits of such a mode of living are obvious. The West India planters prefer the slaves of Benin or Eboe to those of any part of Guniea, for their hardiness, intelligence, integrity, and zeal. Those benefits are felt by us in the general healthiness of the people, and in their vigour and activity; I might have added too in their comeliness.[46]

Equiano goes to great length to portray what some readers may regard as a utopian interpretation of his people. For him, they were not only hardworking but also physically attractive in comparison to other African nations. Albeit disturbing, Equiano justifies this view by stating that West Indian slavers preferred the people of his region to work on their plantations. Nevertheless, Equiano makes continuous references to the practice of slavery by Africans. His culture, and every African nation discussed within the narrative, are described as active participants within the institution. Yet, Equiano maintains that his people, and by extension most African nations in general, practiced slavery as a means of punishing immoral people:

> They [people called the Oye-Eboe] always carry slaves through our land; but the strictness account is exacted of their manner of procuring them before they are suffered to pass. Sometimes indeed we sold slaves to them, but they were only prisoners of war, or such among us as had been convicted of kidnapping, or adultery, and some other crimes, which we esteemed heinous.[47]

Equiano does not typically define the *African* institution of slavery as immoral, except in relation to wars derived from the desire to acquire European goods: "Perhaps they were incited to this by those traders who brought the European goods I mentioned amongst us. Such a mode of obtaining slaves in Africa is common; and I believe more are procured

45. Equiano, *Interesting Narrative*, 12, 14, 17.

46. Equiano, *Interesting Narrative*, 20–21.

47. Equiano, *Interesting Narrative*, 19; see also 7, 13, 15, 26, 46, 71, 72.

this way, and by kidnaping, than any other."[48] Although they were often interconnected, Equiano had two opposing moral standards for African and European institutions of slavery. This is fascinating considering slavery and morality are guiding themes within Equiano's narrative. Of course, we must realize Equiano is speaking from his cultural and socio-political context, with the awareness of those contexts from surrounding African nations. Yet, it's difficult to assume every or most African nations abided by the same standards as Equiano's people. Regardless of our interpretation of things, Equiano clearly viewed a strong distinction between African and European forms of slavery.

An example of this is witnessed in Equiano's initial enslavement. Equiano was sold to various African masters as he traveled to the western coast of Africa. Yet, he never condemns these African masters, nor their African nations that participated in slavery. Rather, Equiano romanticizes his relationships with these African masters and their families. Equiano stated, "At length, after many days traveling, during which I had often changed masters, I got into the hands of a chieftain, in a very pleasant country. This man had two wives and some children, and they all used me extremely well, and did all they could to comfort me; particularly the first wife, who was something like my mother."[49] Regarding Equiano's views, Yael Ben-Zvi comments, "Thus, slavery in Africa seems almost egalitarian, as the only distinction between slaves and slaveholders is that the former are prohibited from eating 'with those who were freeborn.'"[50] As I interpret things, Equiano appears to intentionally create tension between accepting and rejecting the general institution of slavery, by viewing a qualitative difference between African and European slavery despite their interrelated existence.

Regarding religion, Equiano keenly associates his people with the Old Testament Israelites and the colonial Jews. This was accomplished through the socio-religious aspects of cleanliness, rituals, and theocratic governance. Equiano also describes a rather vague account of his people's religious beliefs as relatively monotheistic:

> As to religion, the natives believe that there is one Creator of all things, and that he lives in the sun, and is girted round with a belt that he may never eat or drink; but, according to some, he

48. Equiano, *Interesting Narrative*, 23–24.
49. Equiano, *Interesting Narrative*, 51; see also 63–65.
50. Ben-Zvi, "Equiano's Nativity," 404–5.

> smokes a pipe, which is our own favourite luxury. They believe he governs events, especially our deaths or captivity; but, as for the doctrine of eternity, I do not remember to have ever heard of it.[51]

Thus, we see the underpinnings of an omnipotent African deity that may or may not have had an interest in colonial slavery. Nevertheless, there were some people who held distinctly traditional African religious beliefs. Equiano testified that people advocated the transmigration of the soul, and that some ancestral spirits remained on the earth to protect their loved ones. Furthermore, Equiano stated, "We practiced circumcision like the Jews, and made offerings and feasts on that occasion in the same manner as they did."[52] Yet, according to Equiano, the similarities between African and Jewish cultures extended also to the custom of social cleanliness: "I have before remarked that the natives of this part of Africa are extremely cleanly. This necessary habit of decency was with us a part of religion, and therefore we had many purifications and washings; indeed almost as many, and used on the same occasions, if my recollection does not fail me, as the Jews."[53] Black theologian Willie James Jennings comments,

> Equiano draws an analogy between Jewish ways of life and those of his own people. They share purification rites, circumcision, offerings and feasts, the significance of naming, and the "law of retaliation," as he called it. His drawing attention to these cultural analogies sets the reader up for his more serious conclusion: "that the one people had sprung from the other." His people came from the Jews, directly from the seed of Abraham. By drawing the black body next to the Jewish body, Equiano suggests a reorientation for his white readers—toward kinship.[54]

Jennings is correct. Equiano crafts an ambiguous racialized sociopolitical theology that posits two vague connections between the Israelites of the Old Testament and some West African nations. First, there is a vague assumption that his people, and possibly other nations within their region, had distinctly originated from the Israelites. Second, one could interpret Equiano as advocating that the Israelites received much of

51. Equiano, *Interesting Narrative*, 27–28.

52. Equiano, *Interesting Narrative*, 30.

53. Equiano, *Interesting Narrative*, 31–32.

54. Jennings, *Christian Imagination*, 189–90.

their sacred religious practices from certain African nations such as his. Each interpretation assumes a natural cross-cultural pollination when the Israelites lived in Egypt. Equiano indeed frames the memories of his childhood, family, and nation into racialized politics. He also provides details regarding the similarities between African and European cultures through principles of morality and socioeconomics. Yet, recent scholarship has challenged and undermined some of Equiano's claims.

Vincent Carretta is a notable scholar of Equiano's narrative. Referencing himself, Carretta has stated, "Recent biographical discoveries have cast doubt on Equiano's story of his birth and early years. The available evidence suggests that the author of *The Interesting Narrative* may have invented rather than reclaimed an African identity."[55] Carretta discovered baptismal records from 1759 and naval records from 1773, which revealed Equiano was not born in Africa in 1745. Rather, Equiano was an African American who was born in South Carolina in 1747.[56] Regarding Equiano's baptismal records, Carretta states, "The parish register of St. Margaret's church, Westminster, records the baptism on 9 February 1759 of 'Gustavus Vass a Black born in Carolina 12 years old', indicating a birth date of 1746 or 1747."[57] Moreover, Anthony Carrigan mentions that his birth is recorded "also in the muster book of a ship on which Equiano worked as a freeman."[58] This raises a series of questions. What compelled Equiano to create false accounts of his childhood, family, and African nation? Was there a clear benefit for Equiano to construct African and British identities at the expense of denying his American heritage? The troubling part is not only that Equiano fabricated a significant part of his narrative and ultimately created suspicion regarding the credibility of his entire autobiography, but that some scholars have erroneously sought to justify Equiano's embellishments.

Carretta is forced to grapple with the fictitious nature of Equiano's African heritage. Yet, he displays a subtle dismissal of its severity. Carretta attempts to provide some possible explanations for Equiano's fabrications: "The discrepancy between the ages and dates Vassa records in his *Narrative* and the external documentary evidence may be due simply to a confused memory of childhood events recounted some 40 years later. Or

55. Carretta, *Equiano, the African*, xiv; Carretta, "Olaudah Equiano or Gustavus Vassa?," 96.

56. Carretta, *Equiano, the African*, 2.

57. Carretta, "Olaudah Equiano or Gustavus Vassa?," 102.

58. Carrigan, "Negotiating Personal Identity," 42.

the discrepancy may have been rhetorically motivated."[59] I maintain that an unreliable memory was highly unlikely. There were obvious cultural distinctions between African and American cultures during colonialism. Furthermore, even if a child was not conscious of them, they would have understood the differences as they grew older. Equiano was roughly forty-two to forty-four years old when his narrative was published, and he spent over thirty years as a seaman traveling throughout Europe, the West Indies, and the American colonies. This makes it relatively impossible for him to have forgotten or misunderstood the location of his birthplace. Furthermore, Equiano displayed a nuanced interpretation of his fabricated African identity which encompassed two of the six chapters within the first volume of his narrative.

Carrigan provides another interesting attempt to justify Equiano's false accounts. Yet, this pursuit is achieved not through an interpretation of a faulty memory, but from a concept of *retranscribed imagination*. Carrigan argues, "Further, if he never personally experienced the horrors of a slave ship then this is an example of a profoundly intense cultural memory being retranscribed imaginatively, forming part of a narrative construction which renders these 'members' forcefully and tangibly 'real.'"[60] For Carrigan, defining what is *real*, a *memory*, and the nature of *personal* experience is partially determined by the emotional, as well as psychological, stimulus we undergo from reflecting upon an imaginary event(s). Thus, we can *personally* experience almost anything our imagination conceives, and the false memories that develop from this can be redefined as *real*, because we established a profound connection to them. We see this in our contemporary era whereby certain scholars *reimagine* certain events and people, to introduce imaginative elements, in the construction of new interpretations.

Ben-Zvi provides a rather confusing philosophical approach to Equiano's African tale. Ben-Zvi acknowledges that the African account was false and insists that it is "a complex adaptation and revision of contemporaneous Anglophone depictions of Africa."[61] He justifies Equiano's embellished African heritage on the premise of symbolic identification:

> I argue that Equiano mounts a diasporic indigenous critique of Eurocentric denials and subversions of the universal entitlement

59. Carretta, "Olaudah Equiano or Gustavus Vassa?," 103.

60. Carrigan, "Negotiating Personal Identity," 43.

61. Ben-Zvi, "Equiano's Nativity," 408.

> decreed by eighteenth-century conceptions of reason and Christian theology. He affirms a commitment to human rights by aligning himself not only with his African or Eboe "countrymen" but also with a broader spectrum of "those who are called barbarians," including the "Samaide" and "Hottentot," which Eurocentric geopolitics posited as exotic peoples occupying the northern and southern margins of a geopolitically divided humanity.[62]

I interpret Ben-Zvi as contextualizing a similar concept of racial-identification through Blackness that was exhibited by the Black Power movement of the 1960s in America, and the conceptualizing of symbolic Blackness that James Cone, the influential contemporary Black liberation theologian, has actively endorsed. Moreover, Ben-Zvi's interpretation is unconvincing since he does not acknowledge the irony of Equiano's use of European sources to construct his *imaginary* African heritage, which partially expressed how some Africans nations were civilized/Westernized, as he subsequently critiqued the same European nations that influenced his life.

Furthermore, constructing arguments for Black solidarity from Equiano's racial and nationalistic beliefs is difficult and would be confusing since he actively showed a deep affection for Europeans. An example of this is seen between him and one of his many masters. On one occasion, Equiano stated, "When he was going he wished me to stay on board the Preston, to learn the French horn; but the ship being ordered for Turkey I could not think of leaving my master, to whom I was very warmly attached; and I told him if he left me behind it would break my heart."[63] Statements like this are dispersed throughout Equiano's narrative to the extent that some scholars have argued that he was fully assimilated to British culture, since he routinely reinforced an African and British identity.[64] This too has caused scholars problems as they grapple with Equiano's American birth and false African heritage.

Yes, Equiano's narrative is impressively written, and everyone should engage it. My point isn't to discredit Equiano's character and place within African American literature. My previous discussion regarding the education of the American slaves should be held in conjunction with Equiano's narrative to demonstrate how the concept of an Ideal-Blackness,

62. Ben-Zvi, "Equiano's Nativity," 402.

63. Equiano, *Interesting Narrative*, 118.

64. Paul, "'I Whitened My Face," 848–64.

along with the hermeneutics and methodologies that created it, have influenced scholarship within African American literature. Despite some contemporary scholars discovering the contradictions and inconsistencies within the narrative, Equiano is still held in higher esteem than those who were truthful in their narratives and/or needed White editors to help them share their testimony. Equiano and his narrative have been touted as representative of Black self-consciousness and self-determination. He is applauded as a literate slave who earned his freedom and published his autobiography independent of White authority/approval. Scholars tend to ignore the fact that he lists close to three hundred subscribers of his narrative, most of whom were White.

Nevertheless, we should accept the facts of Equiano's life and narrative. They provide us with a glimpse of who he truly was, not who he portrayed himself to be, nor how we want him to be for us. Some of us must grapple with the reality that, despite the fact Equiano misrepresented an important part of his narrative, and a shroud of suspicion is now placed upon his entire autobiography, scholars continue to overlook, even seek to justify, this to hold him as a representative on the Ideal-Blackness. This raises the question as to what is being forfeited, or who is being ignored within African American history, because of the hyper-politicized scholarship that greatly influences the direction of contemporary African American studies.

5

The Politics Within Politics

The Ambiguity of Racialized Politics and Relations

So for one who knows the right thing to do and does not do it, for him it is sin.

James 4:17

"Woe to you, scribes and Pharisees, hypocrites, because you travel around on sea and land to make one proselyte; and when he becomes one, you make him twice as much a son of hell as yourselves."

Matthew 23:15

HISTORICAL TRUTH OR DECEPTION

History is a peculiar reality. It requires human existence in action, the progression of time, and contemporary interest from people to understand the past. History, as factual reality, may not be completely known with extreme detail, but often we can know enough, because someone took the time and care to record it. In certain ways, history functions as a double-edged sword. It can inform us, strengthening our resolve for betterment, and assist in nurturing our humanity. History can also manipulate us, by aiding in how we are shaped into who the historian and interpreter desires. Both trajectories develop through our faith in history and submission to it in a way that allows the *knowledge* to transform us. Knowledge, faith, and belief are connected. Thus, history can aid in either oppressing or emancipating us. Yet, things become even more complex when we are forced to reflect on the intent and agenda of the historian, relating to the intent and agenda of the interpreter of the historian's work. This brings me to another issue: the relationship between the interpretation of history and the intentional and unintentional deception of the interpreter.

Self-deception is metaphorically a place on the map of human existence. We can intentionally seek to travel to that location. However, as we continue this journey, we begin to lose healthy levels of self-awareness and will eventually lose the ability to determine if we've finally arrived.

Self-deception, and the consequential deception of the human-Other, appear to be central presences in some contemporary racialized sociopolitical historiographies. I speak as an outsider, someone who doesn't abide by such popularized historiographies, and never identifying with them to the extent that I believe those things that never happened, as actually existed. Yet, those things defined as nonexistence to some, are viewed in the minds of others, as irreplaceable moments in our concrete reality. In this context, I'm emphasizing how one generation can intentionally seek to be misleading through their historiographies in the aims of satisfying their self-interest, but at the expense of the following generations' intelligence, morality, and self-awareness.

Generally, there are often two poles situated at both ends of a spectrum, and both ends represent conservative and liberal extremism. In this context, I'm including two seemingly opposing historiographies regarding the transatlantic slave trade and colonial American slavery. One interpretation could be interpreted as derived from contemporary White Christian nationalism. In varied degrees, from this perspective, slavery is viewed as a humane institution, whereby the slaves generally enjoyed their life of servitude. They had food, clothing, and shelter. Beyond this, they received exposure to advanced European cultures and Christianity. This view tends to interpret racism and White supremacy as later constructs upon American soil, most African slaves rarely experienced abuse, and it was the Northern Whites that encouraged slave rebellion to their Southern masters.

The other historiography appears Afrocentric in nature, not based entirely from a realist perspective, but more through racial and sociocultural romanticism. These forms of historiographies are amalgamations from fantasies. They are products of the interpreter reimagining people and events into someone and something that is slightly different from who and what they are. From this view, generally speaking, these Afrocentric romanticized historiographies are grounded upon forms of militant Black liberation and consciousness, whereby Blackness is independent from the deteriorating influence of Whiteness. These historiographies don't lie as some White Christian nationalist historiographies do, but instead, inconspicuously ignore or minimize important people and events to portray specific conceptions of Ideal-Blackness.

Sometimes our understanding of historical facts will only create a veil of ambiguity. The ambiguity stems from partial knowledge of a particular person and event. Differences of interpretations are often birthed within this space of ambiguity. Yet, we still have the responsibility to seek and obtain the truth, regardless of how difficult it is for us to accept things. In many ways I view this within certain areas of racial relationships throughout colonialism.

A NECESSARY REMINDER

One of the more sensitive issues surrounding the transatlantic slave trade is examining the initial contact and developing relationship between some West African nations and the Portuguese during the fifteenth century. There are scholars who avoid this issue in its entirety. Other scholars appear uncertain, and their work seems vague as to how these events may have come about. There is a third group advocating that Europe's political and religious corruption was the primary influence in their attempts at creating relationships with Africa. However, there are even fewer scholars who seek to examine just how active and complaisant some African nations were in creating a political alliance with the Portuguese and eventually Europe in general. For some people, these issues aren't important, and others may simply bracket this information as common knowledge.

I, on one hand, deem this information as highly important and am firmly convinced it isn't common knowledge for certain people worldwide. There are forms of revisionist histories that surface through the research of Black and White scholars, which in their own way deviate from specific historical events to express the agenda of the scholar. Corrupt revisionist histories are intended to deceive the masses to make them more compliant to the dominant, skewed racialized political agendas of those wielding power. Hence, there is always the necessity of maintaining historical interpretations grounded upon truth and reality, no matter how difficult learning them may be. We, as African Americans, have the *responsibility* to know our history, regardless of who or what we agree or disagree with. This is applicable to all African Americans who also confess Christ as their Lord and Savior.

Any conception of an Ideal-Blackness, if taken seriously, must grapple with the reality of the transatlantic slave trade, regarding the complicity of some West African nations. Otherwise, conceptions of Ideal-Blackness are constructed more from Afrocentric romanticism and not historical realism. My concern is that some influential Black historiographies are grounded more on fantasy than reality. The partial result is that we continuously commit the same sins of our ancestors, but with greater knowledge, responsibility, and judgment.

INITIAL CONFLICT TO DECEPTIVE ALLIANCE

The relationship between some African nations and the Portuguese regarding the transatlantic slave trade may be forever recognized as the convoluted, dehumanizing, and manipulative reality of what I refer to as the *politics within politics*. It is here that the relationship between groups is established to fulfill one another's political self-interest. In the context of this discussion, the politics within politics is also the reality whereby naiveness, narcissism, and deception immerse themselves into the political agendas of Africa's *local* imperialism and Europe's *global* imperialism. I want to emphasize the words *local* and *global* as representative of each group's worldview and sociopolitical aspirations. How did the relationship between some West African nations and Europeans develop? Were those African nations innocent participants in their own enslavement? Did they perceive their relationship with Europe as contributing to their political self-interests?

There is a consensus among some historians that the transatlantic slave trade began generally around 1441–44 by the Portuguese.[1] However, it must be stated that the institution of slavery was already embedded within African societies well before the Portuguese arrived. As historian Stephanie Smallwood states, "The Portuguese had not introduced slave

1. James H. Sweet suggests that the slave trade within the Portuguese colonial world existed in four stages. The first stage began from 1441 to 1518. The second and third stages were 1518 to the 1580s, and 1580s to the 1690s. The last stage lasted from the 1690s to the 1770s. Sweet, *Recreating Africa*, 15–18. See also Blackburn, *Making of New World Slavery*, 95–123.

trading in African regions where no such commerce had existed prior to their arrival."[2] Yet, despite this information, few scholars have undertaken the task of examining the function of slavery within African societies and how it contributed to the continent's enslavement to Europe. Researching African slavery in totality is beyond the scope of this chapter. Yet, a brief discussion is necessary to understand some of Africa's political relations with Europe. These political relations ultimately influenced the creation of diverse Black cultures from the African Diaspora through the transatlantic slave trade. Furthermore, this discussion and others should be held within the world of African American Christians, especially those who are articulating Black theologies and theologically centered historiographies.

Historian John Thornton (1949–) has suggested that the Portuguese had established the intent of fulfilling their political self-interest through military violence, acquiring foreign land, and the enslavement of conquered people well before their initial interaction with west coast Africans. For example, the Portuguese were involved in the enslavement of the people from the Canary Islands. "The raiding and commerce of the Canaries provided the base and the motives for European activities farther down the Atlantic coast of Africa."[3] This aggressive form of imperialism was already embedded within Portuguese culture and politics. To complement this claim, historian Donald Wright explains that by the end of the thirteenth century a system of plantations was developing by Europe on the island of Cyprus. The institution of slavery had increased in the expanse of over two centuries. Eventually the institution would spread from Crete, Sicily, coastal Spain, and Portugal: "By 1450, on the eve of European expansion into the south Atlantic, slave-based sugar plantations existed in the western Mediterranean and even on nearby Atlantic islands."[4] It can be suggested that this same form of imperialistic politics would eventually cloak itself in peaceful intent during Europe's developing relationships with some West African nations.

Aggressive politics and violent military activity were a normal part of Portuguese travel along the west coast of Africa. However, things would change as they reached the Senegal region. Unlike the people of

2. Smallwood, *Saltwater Slavery*, 31. See also Thornton, *Africa and Africans*, 73–75, 86–91, 94, 103–12.

3. Thornton, *Africa and Africans*, 29.

4. D. Wright, *African Americans in the Colonial Era*, 9.

the Canary Islands, Africans within the Senegal region had a naval military. Thornton makes the point,

> Although African vessels were not designed for high-seas navigation, they were capable of repelling attacks on the coast. They were specialized craft, designed specifically for the navigational problems of the West African coast and the associated river systems. From the Angolan coast up to Senegal, African military and commercial craft tended to be built similarly.[5]

The African naval military was not equal to those of Europe; however, it still posed a serious problem as it did not allow Europeans to easily reach the shores of West Africa. Even when Europeans reached land, they still had to contend with African foot soldiers. Thus, in an interesting way,

> the Africans were unable, in most circumstances, to take a European ship by storm, and the Europeans had little success in their seaborne attacks on the mainland. As a result, the Europeans had to abandon the time-honored trading and raiding and substitute a relationship based more or less completely on peaceful regulated trade.[6]

If what Thornton suggests has any legitimacy, one may reject the belief that Africans were defenseless and submissive toward the initial attempts of European imperialism. The difficulty is then seeking to understand what benefits some West African nations believed they could receive, and what they actually received through trade and political alliances with Europe. Yet, another difficult issue to reflect upon is how conceptions of racial solidarity were forming within the European mind, which were absent within the African mind.

Thornton states that Europe had never presented any material or resources to Africa that the continent did not already possess. He lists these materials and resources in specific categories of cloth, metal (iron, copper, etc.), types of currency (cowry shells), jewelry, alcohol, and things as such.[7] If these materials were already present to some degree, what would be the benefit received by Africans for establishing a relationship with Europeans at all?

5. Thornton, *Africa and Africans*, 37.
6. Thornton, *Africa and Africans*, 38.
7. Thornton, *Africa and Africans*, 45.

> It was, in short, not to meet African needs that the trade developed or even to make up for shortfalls in production or failures in quality of the African manufactures. Rather, Africa's trade with Europe was largely moved by prestige, fancy, changing taste, and a desire for variety—and such whimsical motivations were backed up by a relatively well developed productive economy and substantial purchasing power. The Atlantic trade of Africa was not simply motivated by the filling of basic needs, and the propensity of import on the part of Africans was not simply a measure of their need or inefficiency, but instead, it was a measure of the extent of their domestic market.[8]

From this perspective, Africa was a relative equal to Europe. Initially, Africa did not have to either initiate or sustain continued trade with Europe out of *necessity*. Rather, the combination of intrigue, admiration, and the desire to use the foreign-Other and their products as means to achieving a higher status, prominence, and authority within their own societies appears to have been the primary benefits of a sociopolitical relationship. Furthermore, it must be understood that Africa was not the primitive or barbaric continent of backward nations that Europe would eventually record them to be. Africa had developed societies that were complex and contextualized according to African, not European, existence.

Corruption can overtake every individual, group, and nation. This is the reality of imperialistic self-interest consuming them in entirety. Imperialism was present within African politics as it was in European politics. However, it can be interpreted that the nature of African local imperialism differed greatly from that of European global imperialism. African local imperialism had no political admiration to conquer the European world. Yet, European global imperialism had every intention of eventually conquering the African world. What united both forms of imperialism were the institutions of slavery from which each group of nations had openly participated and benefited. We must also remember that both groups had religious differences. Portugal claimed itself as a Christian nation of sorts, abiding by Christian principles according to their faith in and love of Christ. Thus, it can be argued that the dominant view of colonial Portuguese Christianity was imperialistic and, by extension, an obvious proslavery contextualism. Returning to a previous point, Thornton mentions:

8. Thornton, *Africa and Africans*, 45.

> The reason that slavery was widespread in Africa was not, as some have asserted, because Africa was an economically underdeveloped region in which forced labor had not yet been replaced by free labor. Instead, slavery was rooted in deep-seated legal and institutional structures of African societies, and it functioned quite differently from the way it functioned in European societies.[9]

It may be helpful to understand that the transatlantic slave trade was possibly an institutionalized product of three different contextualized forms of slavery. It may be suggested that the transatlantic slave trade was derived in part from African slavery, European slavery, and the hybrid Afro-European institution that was created from both continents, forming an alliance to satisfy their own political self-interests.

The participation of some African nations in the enslavement of their African neighbors cannot be ignored. Their activity should not be romanticized through contemporary ideologies of Black liberation and solidarity that minimize this historical truth. African nations had a different conception of ethnicity and group solidarity than those from Europe. The concept of race and racial solidarity did not exist in their consciousness. Here lies the double-edged sword. In some sense, the African worldview transcended the divisive barriers of ethnic/racial ideology and practice. However, it can also be interpreted that the African worldview accomplished this through greed, ignorance, and naiveness.

Race as a sociocultural construct was gradually developing as a reality within the European worldview. The fact remains that Europe was indeed divided within itself based on ethnicity, race, and nationalism. Yet, those internal divisions were set aside and became a means of uniting with one another over and against those whom they deemed as the *inferior-Other*, the Blacks. The idea of a race or groups of races was not conceivable within the African worldviews. At this point, Africans understood Europeans as the foreign-Other. However, they did not conceive the continent of Africa as a collection of Africans or merely the Black race within humanity. Nor did they view humanity as a collection of diverse races. A racial alliance was not a concept within African politics. Thus, in an odd way, the truces and political alliances some Africans held with Europeans were stronger than those established among their neighboring African nations. Some African nations created an alliance with Europe as a means of fulfilling their local-imperialistic goals. Slavery in some

9. Thornton, *Africa and Africans*, 75.

African nations (such as the Denkyira, Akwama, and Asante) developed further into a complex system of acquiring wealth. Wealth was obtained through the acquiring of land from those conquered African people, free labor from their enslavement, and the selling of those conquered Africans to their European allies.[10]

It can be interpreted that parts of Africa became politically fractured and eventually conquered because of its gradual internal instability. This instability did not originate from a foreign threat. As certain African nations such as the Akwamu, Tafo, Assin, Akyem, Agona, Fantine, Akwapim, Ladoku, and others waged war with one another, the populations of some nations decreased dramatically, if not were completely removed by extermination or enslavement.[11] Through European aid, many African nations received advanced weapons of warfare against their enemies. In hindsight, it can be interpreted as a wise political move by Europeans to aid certain African nations against one another to increase the continent's sociocultural and political instability. Within the world of Christianity, it isn't wise, but demonic, as it represents an anti-gospel and a pseudo-Christ endorsing European imperialism.

There are scant accounts from Europeans as to the nature of African warfare. A man by the name of Samuel Brun, who lived along the Gold Coast from 1614 to 1620, testifies that "the Blacks say it is better to strangle women and children than men." He goes on to state their reasoning: "because then they will not reproduce quickly; and the children, if they come of age, would want to seek revenge."[12] It is interesting to note that Brun mentions Africans as "the Blacks." This testifies, at least in part, to the presence of racial ideology during the early seventeenth century. Furthermore, the beheading of captives was a common ritual in African warfare. During the 1640s, Michael Hemmersam had witnessed wars in the town of Elmina, located in the modern-day country of Ghana. He stated that all conquered people of war were eventually killed, and that "even if they shoot someone dead, they nonetheless cut off their head."[13]

African local-imperialism aided in the continent's developing internal instability and eventual subjugation under European political rule. For some African nations, the obsession with fulfilling their self-interest

10. Smallwood, *Saltwater Slavery*, 21–28.

11. Smallwood, *Saltwater Slavery*, 28; D. Wright, *African Americans in the Colonial Era*, 18–19.

12. Smallwood, *Saltwater Slavery*, 21.

13. Smallwood, *Saltwater Slavery*, 21.

had created forms of self-deception that blinded them to their own demise. Ironically, through the conquering, enslavement, and killing of their African neighbors, certain elite African nations created a reality whereby they would be subjected to the same events. Regardless of these suggestions, the nature of African politics did not justify nor usurp the dehumanizing institution of slavery that Europe had constructed. It does not dismiss the level of unacknowledged self-degradation Europeans committed in the name of Christ, to impose inhumane practices upon their enslaved Africans, as they distorted aspects of European civilization beyond their collective self-awareness.

In part, European slavery differed from African slavery in that it utilized a new sociocultural construct of human categorizing, philosophy/theology of human development, and a conception of relational superiority/inferiority referred to as *race*.[14] Some scholars may be correct in stating that racism was not the primary influence in Europe's involvement in the slave trade. However, the elements of racism, referred to by some as proto-racism, were present well before Europe had contact with the coastal West Africans.[15] The elements of racism can be interpreted as deriving from notions of ethnocentrism and any other sociocultural theory of superiority/inferiority in relationships among humans. It can be suggested that racism, the notion of racial superiority/inferiority through biological and even divine ordination, had developed subsequently with Europe's refining of the transatlantic slave trade. Additionally, these elements may have contributed to the creation of what some scholars refer to today as Eurocentrism, the belief in Europe's superiority over the rest of the non-European world. Notions of superiority over another person or group are merely psychological. These thoughts and beliefs are a product of psychological distortions and are the elements of which other psychological distortions are created. Thus, ethnocentrism, Eurocentrism,

14. Thomas McCarthy discusses race, racism, and notions of human superiority in relation to human development. See McCarthy, *Race, Empire*.

15. For a scholarly discussion on the concept of proto-racism and its development, see Isaac, *Invention of Racism*. Isaac states, "In this book I shall argue that early forms of racism, to be called proto-racism, were common in the Graeco-Roman world. My second point in this connection is that those early forms served as prototype for modern racism which developed in the eighteenth century." Isaac, *Invention of Racism*, 1.

This book disagrees with Isaac regarding the claim that racism developed during the eighteenth century. Rather, it is during the eighteenth century that European world scholars from the academia sought to concretize the concept with their various teachings. Emmanuel Chukwudi Eze provides a brief introductory examination of this. See Eze, *Race and the Enlightenment*.

and racism can be interpreted as systematized psychological distortions of one's supposed superiority over and against another person or group. Regardless of labels, it is certain that an idolatrous understanding of themselves relating to the distinct collective-Others produced one of the highest levels of demonic dehumanization within human history. Benjamin Isaac suggests,

> Racism is never based on solid facts, objectively analysed; it changes over time and between peoples, depending on a multitude of factors. It mixes up inherited features with cultural phenomena and confuses reality and fantasy, language and religion, real and non-existent differences. In its interpretation it always distorts the facts for its own purposes, for its aim is always to prove that the other group is inferior and the racist superior, and that these qualities are permanent and cannot be changed. Hence it claims that the attributed characteristics are not subject to control by those so characterized. They come from the inside, that is, from essential traits of the body, or from the outside, from climate and geography. Moreover, they are collective and override any individual differences that may be the result of education, personal circumstances or a human will.[16]

African humanity was redefined through the transatlantic slave trade. African humanity was not only referred to but treated as *cargo* and *property*. The labels of cargo and property did not signify the actual nature of African existence. Rather, it represented the sociopsychological state of the European slave trader, slave trade sympathizer, and various aspects of European societies. To think of and treat another person or group's humanity as a pseudo-lifeless object stems from a psychological distortion of one's supposed superiority over another. This distortion signifies not only the lack of belief regarding human equality between the enslaver and enslaved, but also the perceived absence of intelligence, consciousness, human will, and determinism that is believed to partially define human existence. Smallwood asserts,

> Turning captives into commodities was a thoroughly scientific enterprise. It turned on perfecting the practices required to commodify people and determining where those practices reached their outer limits (that is, the point at which they extinguished the lives they were meant to sustain in commodified form). Traders reduced people to sum of their biological parts,

16. Isaac, *Invention of Racism*, 22.

> thereby scaling life down to an arithmetical equation and finding the lowest common denominator.[17]

The enslavement of another human being is never coincidental. Nor is the gradual development of the practice into a complex institution. They require the basic beliefs of human superiority over another which the enslaver claims to embody. They also require the human will and political means to enforce the reality of enslavement upon another person or group. As Smallwood suggests, they are elements of a *scientific enterprise*. The slave was reduced to an economic tool valued only in relation to the capital they could produce. Therefore, the land, labor, and products derived from the slave toiling the land were valued above and beyond the humanity of the slave.

From 1580 to 1640, an estimated 700,000 Africans boarded slave ships headed to the New World.[18] These slaves would be pioneers in establishing new cultures, ethnicities, and nations from the African Diaspora.[19] African Americans, like many other ethnicities, are the descendants of such slaves. They were conquered and stolen from a continent that was at one point, at least partially, consumed with its own localized-imperialistic self-interests. Exactly how did some Africans arrive in North America? How was the state of those American colonies regarding ethnic and racial equality between Africans and Europeans? Did notions of slavery and racial superiority reside within the British colonies prior to the arrival of African slaves?

CULTURAL ORIGINS: AFRICANS IN AMERICA

In May of 1607, the first successful British settlement in America was established in Jamestown, Virginia. The settlement's religious identity was believed to be that of Anglicanism. The land and people of the colony would soon embody the paradox and hypocrisy of proslavery Christianity. Twelve years later in August of 1619, the first group of Africans had arrived on American soil as stolen slaves. Twenty Africans were

17. Smallwood, *Saltwater Slavery*, 43.

18. Smallwood, *Saltwater Slavery*, 16.

19. Sweet lists roughly forty-four African nations and ethnicities which were recorded in a Brazilian document discussing slavery within the colonies under Portuguese rule. These nations and ethnicities stem from four regions within Africa. They are Upper Guinea (Guine), Lower Guinea (Mina), Central Africa (Angola), and East Africa (Mocambique). Sweet, *Recreating Africa*, 21, 26.

kidnapped from their homeland by Spaniards who were involved in the transatlantic slave trade. On their journey to the West Indies the ship was attacked by a Dutch man-of-war, commanded by Captain Jope and pilot Marmaduke.[20] From the words of Sir John Rolf, a leader of the settlement, the slaves were traded for food and drink for the crew of the Dutch warship: "About the latter end of August, a Dutch man of Warr of the burden of a 160 tunnes arrived at Point-Comfort. . . . He brought not any thing but 20. And odd Negroes, the Governo and Cape Marchant bought for victualle."[21] Eventually, all twenty African slaves were to be divided among the settlers.[22] Early accounts of the slaves on the settlement are difficult to discern. Out of the twenty, history records the names of three African slaves: Antoney, Isabella, and Pedro. Antoney and Isabella eventually fell in love and conceived a baby boy by the name of William. William is recognized by some as possibly the first African American.[23]

THE GRADUALIST: INNOCENT ACCEPTANCE OF AMERICAN SLAVERY

Scholars differ regarding how the *institution* of slavery had developed within the Jamestown settlement and British colonies in general. Some scholars adhere to a gradual enslavement theory, whereby they claim that the concept of slavery and the term itself were not present during Jamestown's initial development. For them, Africans had enjoyed a relatively peaceful existence as indentured servants and as free citizens within society. Slavery was then gradually enforced upon the African servants as the colonies developed. Lerone Bennett Jr. (1928–2018) remarks,

> In Virginia, then, as in other colonies, the first Black settlers fell into a well-established socioeconomic groove that carried with it no implications of racial inferiority. That came later. But in the interim, a period of forty years or more the first Black settlers

20. Bennett, *Before the Mayflower*, 28; Harding, *There Is a River*, 26; Hopkins, *Down, Up, and Over*, 16–17; Morgan, *American Slavery*, 105; Quarles, *Negro in the Making*, 33–35; Sarson, *British America*, 43, 57, 73; G. Williams, *History of the Negro Race*, 159–62.

21. D. Wright, *African Americans in the Colonial Era*, 23; see also Bennett, *Before the Mayflower*, 28; Hopkins, *Down, Up, and Over*, 17.

22. In a footnote, Morgan states that "it is perhaps no coincidence that in 1625 Yeardley (governor in 1619) and Abraham Peirsey (cape merchant in 1619) held 15 of the 23 Negroes then in the colony." Morgan, *American Slavery*, 105n56.

23. Bennett, *Shaping of Black America*, 12–13.

> accumulated land, voted, testified in court and mingled with Whites on a basis of equality. They owned other Black servants, and certain Blacks imported and paid for White servants when they apparently held in servitude.[24]

Historian Vincent Harding (1931–2014) also testifies to a gradual enslavement theory. "For several decades, indeed, blacks in Virginia and elsewhere had a status within the labouring classes that varied from indentured apprentice and servant to free man and free woman; the nature of the quest for justice, the definition of the struggle for freedom was also fluid."[25] Furthermore, historian Benjamin Quarles (1904–96) makes the bold assertion, "At the start of the English settlement in America, no one had in mind to establish the institution of Negro slavery. Yet in less than a century the foundation of a peculiar institution had been laid."[26] Oddly enough, Quarles never provides an adequate theory as to how this peculiar institution developed. He can only assert that an institution of oppression and dehumanization had mysteriously developed within a context of mutuality and equality.

It is interesting to note that Sarson, although advocating a gradualist perspective, suggests that slavery as a concept was present within the colony of Jamestown. However, he recounts the arrival of those African slaves as a matter of happenstance. This is in the sense that Sarson claims the Dutch man-of-war could not sell those African slaves anywhere else but in Jamestown, Virginia. Sarson never provides any historical documents to verify this claim. Yet, he states,

> Even so, New World slavery was over a century old by this time and was by no means unfamiliar or alien, and Governor George Yeardley readily accepted the slaves in exchange for food. With a ready supply of cheap servants from England, though, slavery remained a minor institution in Virginia for some 40 years.[27]

Historian Michael Guasco (1968–) takes things a bit further. For him, the nature of slavery within the British colonies before 1660 is relatively absent, if not difficult to discern at all.

> Unfortunately, characterizing anything as "slavery" or anyone in particular as a "slave" during the first half century of

24. Bennett, *Before the Mayflower*, 34.
25. Harding, *There Is a River*, 25.
26. Quarles, *Negro in the Making*, 44.
27. Sarson, *British America*, 73.

> English colonialism tends to produce more confusion than clarity because, from a strictly technical point of view, slavery was not legal in the English-speaking world before the mid-seventeenth century.[28]

How are we to interpret Guasco's statement of "from a strictly technical point of view"? He continues to add, "Before the 1660s, Africans may have seeped into the colonies and may have been held in perpetual bondage, but slavery was neither systematic nor routine."[29] Guasco recognizes that there was an increase in the population of Africans from 1619 to 1660. He is also aware that they had been possibly forced into perpetual bondage. However, he does not view these events as contributing to the concretizing of institutional slavery. These events do not signify any intentionality from the European settlers. Africans had increasingly arrived in Jamestown coincidently. Guasco hinges his definition of slavery on *legality*. For slavery to have existed in a technical sense, it must have been sanctioned by the authority of the government. Thus, since there were no slave laws until roughly 1660, the sociocultural practice of slavery from 1619 to 1659 should not be fully recognized.

Lastly, one of the more striking interpretations of African American origins comes from T. H. Breen (1942–) and Stephen Innes (1946–2005). They, too, take a legal approach to discussing the initial development of slavery within the British colonies. For them, the colonists were unfamiliar with the global institution of slavery but embodied forms of xenophobia.[30] In their work, they sought to reveal the institution of slavery

> was more circuitous than many have imagined. The process of black debasement and degradation was not linear and foreordained. As the following examination of free blacks in seventeenth-century Northampton County, Virginia, suggests, Englishmen and Africans could interact with one another on terms of relative equality for two generations. The possibility

28. Guasco, *Slaves and Englishmen*, 4.

29. Guasco, *Slaves and Englishmen*, 4.

30. John H. Russell has a similar view. However, his particular interpretation seemingly implies a higher level of innocence, ignorance, and naiveness in regard to the colonists. "Since it is the fact that the white population in the colony in 1619 had not been familiar in England with a system of slavery or with a model slave code, and since they had developed in Virginia a system of servitude and were fortifying it by law, it is plausible that the Africans became servants in a condition similar to the status of white servants, who, after a term of service varying from two to eight years, were entitled to freedom." Russell, *Free Negro*, 23.

> of a genuinely multiracial society became a reality during the years before Bacon's Rebellion in 1676. Not until the end of the seventeenth century was there an inexorable hardening of racial lines. We argue that it was not until the slave codes of 1705 that the tragic fate of Virginia's black population was finally sealed.[31]

However, one of the more confusing pieces of evidence they present is on Antoney, one of the three Africans we know by name to have supposedly arrived in 1619. Breen and Innes briefly mention the arrival of twenty Africans in 1619, but never mention their names.[32] Rather, they suggest that there was another slave named "Antonio a Negro" who arrived in 1621 on a vessel called the *James*.[33] Antonio eventually had his name changed to Anthony Johnson. Anthony worked on the Bennett plantation for over twenty years of his life.

AMBIGUOUS RELATIONS: FRAGMENTED WHITENESS AND EMANCIPATED BLACKNESS

The patriarch of the Bennett family was Edward Bennett (1577–1651). He was a London merchant who moved to Virginia in 1621. Edward is recorded as establishing the first large plantation in American history. It is estimated that during his lifetime he and his family brought over roughly eight hundred immigrants to the English colony. He is also known to have owned a fleet of vessels. As John Bennett Bodie (1880–1965) notes, Edward was the first to receive a land patent from the London Company of Virginia.[34] The significance of this fact will be discussed further in the chapter. Yet, the records do not explain this.

It must be considered that Edward's kin Rev. William Bennett was one of the original settlers who resided in a place called "Warroscoyack," in 1609. Therefore, it could be interpreted that Edward came from a wealthy and politically influential family from London who established their roots within the new Virginian colony. It must also be mentioned that Edward "was elected a free member of the London Company of Virginia and on May 2, 1621, was elected auditor. He was on various

31. Breen and Innes, *"Myne Owne Ground,"* 5.
32. Breen and Innes, *"Myne Owne Ground,"* 18–21.
33. Breen and Innes, *"Myne Owne Ground,"* 8.
34. Bodie, "Edward Bennett," 117.

commissions of the London Company."[35] Edward would periodically travel from London to Virginia. He would leave the operation of his plantation to his brother Robert, and upon Robert's death, he brought his nephew Richard to Virginia to oversee operations in 1628. Richard would eventually become governor of Virginia from 1652 to 1655. How could Edward receive a land patent (headright patent) before his arrival in the colonies?

During Anthony Johnson's service to the Bennett family, he met and married another African slave by the name of Mary.[36] They were the parents of four children. Breen and Innes suggest that the records discuss only three of the children: two daughters and one son. This second Anthony of 1621 has great significance for Breen and Innes. Anthony would eventually gain his freedom, amass great land, and live prosperously within the Virginian colony. For Breen and Innes, Anthony and the Johnson family are representative of the fact that not *all* Blacks lived in dehumanizing standards of inequality to White citizens. However, their language and presentation of certain facts are problematic and present a picturesque utopian society.

First, Breen and Innes never settle the tension presented by the awareness of two African slaves named Anthony. One arrived on the Dutch man-of-war in 1619, and the other in 1621 on a ship called the *James*. If both slaves named Anthony are distinct, there should be historical documents that express this. However, it is at this point where things become rather ambiguous. Historian Alden T. Vaughn (1929–2024) has remarked, "Neither John Rolfe, it will be remembered, nor any other contemporary claimed that the Dutch ship brought the *first* Negroes to Virginia."[37] Vaughn emphasizes the first Africans to have arrived. This becomes problematic if one perceives Vaughn as playing on words to present a particular suggestion. Vaughn decides to examine the 1624 General Court Records from Virginia and a 1625 census regarding the Negroes living within the colony. In those records, Vaughn indeed verifies that there was a Negro by the name of Anthony and he had married a Negro woman named Isabella. Both had a child named William Theire who was baptized. However, a problem surfaces once Vaughn continues by stating that this particular Anthony "undoubtedly was the Anthony Johnson who subsequently became free and later owned black servants

35. Bodie, "Edward Bennett," 119.

36. Bodie, "Edward Bennett," 10.

37. Vaughn, "Blacks in Virginia," 474.

himself."[38] Breen and Innes are aware of Vaughn's contradictory suggestion. Breen and Innes suggest that the Anthony who married Mary became the famous free Black of Virginia, not the Anthony who married Isabella. Is there a possibility that some documents were interpreted incorrectly? Or could someone have falsified various documents regarding Anthony's initial arrival, marriage, and supposed accumulation of wealth within Virginia?

Historian Ira Berlin has seemingly avoided the tension of possibly two distinct Negroes named Anthony. Berlin does mention the arrival of twenty African slaves in 1619, but he too, like Breen and Innes, does not mention the names of any slaves. Rather, Berlin states, "The story of Anthony Johnson, sold to the English at Jamestown in 1621 as 'Antonio a Negro,' reveals something of a history of Atlantic creoles in the Chesapeake region."[39] Berlin does not associate Anthony with the arrival of the Dutch man-of-war in 1619. Instead, Johnson is described as arriving two years later in Jamestown, Virginia. Anthony, as Berlin interprets him, is married to another African slave named Mary.[40] This implies that Isabella and William do not exist. Kathleen M. Brown provides a more detailed discussion of Mary. For Brown, Mary had arrived in Virginia during 1622 on a ship called the *Margarett and John*. Mary is believed to have given birth to several free-born children.[41] Did Anthony Johnson arrive in 1619 or 1621? Did he marry a Negro woman named Isabella whom he initially arrived in Jamestown with? Or did Anthony marry a Negro woman named Mary whom he met years later during his service on the Bennett plantation?

Breen and Innes may have interpreted the social mobility and accumulated wealth of Anthony and the Johnson family through the lens of American self-help ideology. Again, for them, the Johnsons represented how *free* Blacks lived in relative equality with Whites from roughly 1619 to 1705: "Johnson's movements between 1625 and 1650 remain a mystery. Court records from a later period provide tantalizing clues about his life during these years, but they are silent on how 'Antonio a Negro' became Anthony Johnson."[42] Ambiguity and mystery surround the second Anthony of 1621. Breen and Innes state their uncertainty as to why Anthony

38. Vaughn, "Blacks in Virginia," 475.

39. Berlin, *Many Thousands Gone*, 29.

40. Berlin, *Many Thousands Gone*, 30.

41. Brown, *Good Wives*, 107–9.

42. Breen and Innes, *"Myne Owne Ground,"* 10.

and his family relocated with their former master, Edward Bennett, to Northampton, Virginia. However, they do state, "it is curious that the Johnsons appeared in the Eastern Shore records at precisely the time that Bennett became a major political force in the area."[43] This is an interesting point which will be explored further. However, before this takes place the nature of a particular immigration law and the usage of that law in shaping Virginia's planters' class must be discussed. This suggests there may be a faint correlation between this immigration law, the increased political influence of Edward Bennett, and the prosperity of the Johnson family.

Throughout the seventeenth century, England was concerned with developing Virginia and establishing the colony as an important investment in the British Empire. England sought to devise ways that would entice more immigrants to the colony. In so doing they created a law which was referred to as a *headright*. Thomas J. Wertenbaker (1879–1950) explains,

> In the early days of the settlement a law passed designed to stimulate immigration, by which the Government pledged itself to grant fifty acres of land to any person who would pay the passage from Europe to Virginia of a new settler. Thus if one brought over ten indentured servants he would be entitled to 500 acres of land, if he brought 100, he could demand 5,000 acres. But the headright, as it was called, was not restricted to servants; he was entitled to the fifty acres. Should he bring also his family, he could demand an additional fifty acres for his wife and fifty for each child or other member of the household.[44]

The headright law was a great means of acquiring socioeconomic stability and the potential to obtain considerable wealth within the colony. Essentially, the British government would give land to established settlers for the sole purpose of cultivating that land and providing a percentage of the profit obtained back to the government. However, there were multiple layers of investment to be made. The established settlers had to cover the travel costs and lodgings for every immigrant they managed to relocate to America. In theory, the indentured servant would become an

43. Breen and Innes, *"Myne Owne Ground,"* 11.

44. Wertenbaker, *Planters of Colonial Virginia*, 34–35. Craven, *Southern Colonies*, 121, 127. See also Weiseger, "Virginia Land Office"; Library of Virginia, "About the Virginia Land Office Patents."

established settler once their debt was paid. Then, they, too, could obtain the right to use the headright law.

It may be suggested that there are a few forced assumptions surrounding the role of indentured servants within the British colony. First, some scholars may imply that the living conditions of indentured servants were extremely poor, if not closely related to that of the slave. However, this could be an odd stretch of the facts. Many White indentured servants were enticed into relocating to the colonies to experience a better life. For most, the travel to America was purely optional and was considered an opportunity that could reap considerable benefits. Although the guidelines for their service were strict, one cannot forget that the cost of travel and lodgings to America was extremely expensive. Many immigrants could not afford to relocate on their own initiative. Wertenbaker asserts,

> The necessity for placing him under a stringent contract or indenture is evident. Had this not been done the immigrant, upon finding himself in Virginia, might have refused to carry out his part of the bargain. But the indentured was in no sense a mark of servitude or slavery. It simply made it obligatory for the newcomer, under pain of severe penalties, to work out his passage money, and until that was accomplished to surrender a part of the personal liberty so dear to every Englishman.[45]

To assume one's agreed-upon service to another is slavery may be a stretch of the imagination. Furthermore, certain indentured servants were indeed criminals. All colonies were intended to be self-sufficient and able to contribute their resources to the expansion of their homeland. Thus, we must at least consider that "the bulk of the servants were neither criminals nor political prisoners, but poor persons seeking to better their condition in the land of promise across the Atlantic."[46] Yet, it must also be stated that there were individuals who indeed paid their own cost of relocating to America.[47]

The Virginia Company (also known as the London Company, or the Charter of the Virginia Company of London) was given authority in 1617 to partially regulate the activity of the headright system. Under certain circumstances, the company disbanded in 1624. It may be suggested that corruption was present during the Virginia Company's operation, and

45. Wertenbaker, *Planters of Colonial Virginia*, 32.

46. Wertenbaker, *Planters of Colonial Virginia*, 34.

47. Craven, *Southern Colonies*, 128.

upon its demise, corruption had extended itself throughout the colony beyond rationale.

Regarding the headright system, the defining of land, land rights, and the level of accountability each citizen had to the British government seemed to be in constant dispute. For some Virginians, land ownership was an endowment. Other citizens had seemingly perceived it as a commercial concern. According to Parent Jr., investors in the Virginian plantations wanted to become more active in the English commercial world. However, many elite London merchants and even smaller ones as well had actively avoided trade with America. These same British merchants had opted to continue trade with Asia, India, and the rest of Europe. This, in turn, left a void of commerce to be filled within America. Eventually, there were British citizens who began to invest in the Virginian colony, and they reaped economic benefits from the tobacco trade. Some of these investors decided to return to England as merchants. Others chose to remain in Virginia to operate their plantations. Collectively both groups formed a network of merchant planters.[48]

Parent Jr. suggests that the men who formed this network of merchant planters had gained control of the tobacco trade in Virginia. In part, this is how the headright law became such a powerful tool within the political system of the colony. Greed and the obsessive attempt at fulfilling one's self-interest soon created an irrational form of corruption within the socioeconomic and political systems of Virginia. Not only did a planter's class establish itself, but a hierarchy within that class arose as well. It can be interpreted that there were multiple layers of political corruption which existed during the development of the Virginian colony. If this is so, could the Bennett family have played an influential part in this?

During the early part of the 1630s the governor of Virginia, John Harvey, had stopped issuing headright patents for imported servants.[49] Governor Harvey was not upset that individuals were using the headright law as a means of establishing socioeconomic mobility. Rather, he believed many individuals had accumulated an inordinate amount of land without any intention of cultivating it. In 1634, Charles I had appointed William Laud (1573–1645) to investigate Governor Harvey's dispute with certain political elites of the colony (the Council of State). This resulted in Governor Harvey's expulsion from Virginia in 1635.[50] John West would

48. Parent, *Foul Means*, 25–26.

49. Parent, *Foul Means*, 26.

50. Robert Brenner discusses the political alliances, tensions, and battles which led

become the new governor of Virginia. West began to proceed with issuing the headright patents in a way that the Council State had approved. Governor West issued 377 headright patents for 18,850 acres to "councillors and merchant-planters."[51] In what could be interpreted as a sign of political corruption, Governor West had received 2,000 acres from the Council "in the right of his son being the first born Christian at Chischiak."[52] Was there justification for Governor West to have received 2,000 acres of land, simply because his son was the firstborn Christian of a city?

Additionally, the councillors had initiated an audit in 1627 to investigate the land grants which were issued under the authority of the Virginia Company (1617–24). The councillors were intent on obtaining authority over these land grants and eventually dividing the land among themselves and their associates. Thus, it can be interpreted that a monopoly had gradually been formed by some elite politicians and elite planters through the usage of the headright law. Parent Jr. summarizes this theory:

> After mid-century, the elite secured their economic interests through the headright system. They amassed acres, at first hundreds of thousands and then tens of thousands, for both speculative and productive purposes. The watershed of Bacon's Rebellion shaped the course of this landgrab. The rebellion exposed ridges of discontent among the English poor, reversing the flow of immigration to Virginia. The poor were responding to the constrained economic opportunity in Virginia, especially their access to land. The decline in immigration drained both the number of headrights issued and the potential market of new land buyers.[53]

How are we to interpret these series of events? Might it be suggested that life within the Virginian colony was a far cry from a utopian existence that transcended race, class, and gender distinction?

Throughout the seventeenth century, there were continual sociopolitical conflicts that created and sustained class distinctions and, ultimately, class conflict. Not only was a poor class established within the colony, but a poor planter's class was as well. It may be suggested that amid class oppression was the developing reality of race, racism, and

---

to Governor Harvey's expulsion. Brenner, *Merchants and Revolution*, 140–48; P. Bruce, *Institutional History of Virginia*, 269, 318.

51. Parent, *Foul Means*, 27.

52. Parent, *Foul Means*, 27.

53. Parent, *Foul Means*, 27–28.

slavery. In part, these elements may have been tools used by the elite of the colony to satisfy their self-interests.

Political corruption became so widespread that it was not until roughly 1695 that England became fully aware of it. Edward Randolph, the colonial administrator, had undergone a three-year investigation (1692–95) and reported that there was indeed fraud in the tobacco trades in Virginia, Maryland, and Pennsylvania: "He attributed the greater planters' avarice, pluralism in office holding, and duplicity in landholdings in the royal colony of Virginia as the chief problem with tobacco revenues."[54] In 1696, the Administrators of the House of Orange through the Board of Trade had assigned John Locke to investigate matters further.[55] In explaining Locke's investigation of Virginia's land grants, Parent Jr. stated,

> He described the perversion of a land system that parceled out fifty-acre tracts for either headrights or kickbacks. Since cultivation was [in] neither case given consideration in awarding great tracts of acreage, the peopling of Virginia was retarded. The resultant poverty of population left Virginia without a proper defense, without economic diversification, and without an adequate labor force to produce tobacco revenues. The amassing of titles complicated fixing the land system; he nevertheless proposed elimination of the headright system, enforcement of the land-use laws, and regular collection of the quitrents, with delinquent landholdings returning to the crown.[56]

From roughly 1640 to 1650, Anthony and his family acquired an extensive amount of land and developed an impressive livestock. It is rather vague as to how he managed to accomplish this. In 1651, Anthony claimed the "headright" of five men. These men were Thomas Bembrose, Peter Bughby, Anthony Cripps, John Gesorroro, and Richard Johnson.[57]

54. Parent, *Foul Means*, 41.

55. Parent, *Foul Means*, 41. See also Laslett, "John Locke," 371–73, 382, 398.

56. Parent, *Foul Means*, 41–42.

57. There may be some confusion in regard to the identity of Richard Johnson. Breen and Innes imply that he is the son of Anthony Johnson. "Whether Anthony Johnson actually imported these five persons into the colony is impossible to ascertain. None of them, with the exception of Richard Johnson, his son, appeared in later Northampton tax lists." Breen and Innes, *"Myne Owne Ground,"* 11. However, James H. Brewer has a different interpretation of Richard Johnson. "The next member of the African community to acquire land under the head-rights was a carpenter by trade, Richard Johnson. Richard was perhaps among the 5 servants imported in 1651 by Anthony Johnson. Three years later he was assigned 100 acres adjoining the property of John and Anthony

How did Anthony and Mary earn their freedom? Once free, why did they travel with their former masters, the Bennett family, to the eastern shores of Northampton? Could the Johnson family's social mobility be attributed to the political influence of the Bennett family? Is there a possibility that the Johnson family had benefited from the widespread corruption of the headright system?

We do not have any direct answers to these questions. However, it's realistic to suggest that these events are not coincidental. There is a strong possibility that the Johnson family and many other emancipated Blacks still maintained faint political relations with their former masters. These former slaves may have received a variety of socioeconomic benefits that they would not have otherwise enjoyed as slaves or as free members of society who had to survive on their own. Parent Jr. provides further theories regarding the corruption of the headright system regarding enslaved Blacks within the colony: "Headrights on enslaved Blacks were accepted in violation of the 'great charter,' which stipulated that servants could serve for only seven years and then be entitled to the fruits of their labor. Enslaved workers never completed their term of service, however, for their condition became perpetual."[58] We can discern two things from Parent's perspective. First, there were Black slaves within the colony, some of whom were smuggled.[59] Second, White planters had illegally received land by claiming those slaves under the headright law. By implication, the headright law was designed to bring immigrants to the colonies, not slaves. It is here that we see a distinction between Africans and Europeans regarding how immigrant, indentured servants, and slaves were defined.

The gradual enslavement theory is difficult to accept for a variety of reasons. First, the theory tends to ignore the concepts of human superiority over another. Ethnocentrism, Eurocentrism, and imperialistic nationalism were extremely influential in people's communication and relationships with one another. These elements were developing as Europe maintained its sociopolitical relationship with Africa. From this relationship came the creation of race theory and racism as an accepted belief system and

---

Johnson." Brewer, "Negro Property Owners," 576–77. Breen and Innes state that the headrights were only "claimed" in 1651, whereas Brewer states that the five individuals were imported in 1651 and the headrights were subsequently claimed. Ira Berlin goes further by suggesting that not only is Richard the son of Anthony Johnson, but that Anthony's fourth child is a son by the name of "John." Berlin, *Many Thousands Gone*, 30.

58. Parent, *Foul Means*, 43.

59. Parent, *Foul Means*, 43.

practice. However, Sarson would likely disagree. Regarding African and European relationships in Jamestown, "Racism and oppression existed in these early years, but they had no force of law and little force of custom."[60] Second, there tends to be an overemphasis by some scholars who focus on the role of an indentured servant. The overemphasis sometimes develops into a shallow label. This is in the sense that the usage of the term tends to designate notions of equality and mutuality within the social position. Scholars imply that any concept of human superiority over, and discrimination toward, another did not affect the role or status of an indentured servant. Therefore, all Africans and Europeans were treated the same within society, regardless of the presence of ethnocentrism, Eurocentrism, and racism in the world. Are these beliefs ample evidence that slavery did not exist from 1619 to 1660 in the British colonies?

Collectively, it can be interpreted that the views of the gradualist may imply the projection of a utopian America infused with a self-help ideology whereby race and class discrimination had been transcended.

SLAVERY: A SOCIOPSYCHOLOGICAL REALITY WITHIN COLONIAL SOCIETY

Other scholars believe that the concept of slavery and the usage of Africans as slaves was well understood during the initial development of the colonies. For them, the gradual enslavement approach may be a set of false assumptions derived from mistaken interpretations of historical documents. Historian Robert McColley explains,

> The textbooks tells us that the first Negroes to arrive in Virginia—or in any English colony of North America—came on a Dutch ship numbered twenty, and were not slaves at all but only servants for a fixed period of time. This information is partly accurate, partly conjectured, and wholly misleading. It leaves the impression that an unexpected foreign ship quite accidently traded black laborers to Virginians who had not expected them, and through their innocence and inexperience of slavery, were disposed to treat them just like their indentured white servants.[61]

60. Sarson, *British America*, 43.

61. McColley, *Slavery and Jeffersonian Virginia*, x.

The gradualist perspective may have some false presumptions based on the institutionalizing of slavery. The construction of an institution can be a complex process in which people participate naturally. Generally, an institution could be defined as a collection of beliefs and practices assembled to establish and govern cultural and social order. Thus, an institution can be interpreted as an element within culture and society as well as a transcended reality that is empowered to influence them.[62]

There are a variety of principles which may govern the development of an institution. This dissertation will suggest a flexible theory relating to the institutionalizing of slavery within the American colonies. First, a group must have some relative agreement regarding a collection of beliefs and practices in life. These agreements are a product of sociocultural norms and also contribute to the concretizing of sociocultural norms. The varied agreements and norms within society are both products of human habits and a means of establishing them (*habitualization*).[63] Second, the sociocultural agreements and norms are usually derived from a flexible understanding of one's community relating to the existence of the collective-Other. The bodies of information that assist in understanding us and them can be referred to as *typification* or typologies. These typologies are the collection of generalized beliefs/stereotypes, associated languages/rhetoric, and designated roles within society as they relate to us and them.[64] Thus, it can be interpreted that an institution can develop in multiple ways. There can be cultural, legal, social, and religious institutions.

Slavery had to be progressively institutionalized within the settlement. Theoretically, this was a development whereby the established sociocultural customs of Europeans toward Africans had to be eventually concretized by government laws. The concept and practice of slavery existed prior to the arrival of those first African slaves because the concept of ethnic, racial, and national superiority was already embodied within the British settlers prior to their arrival on American soil. The process of concretizing slavery developed as the slaves arrived and were distributed within society (cultural and social). As the roles of masters and slaves were being developed, the government had merely created laws which were a product of the sociocultural customs. Slave laws were in part a means

62. Berger, *Invitation to Sociology*, 104–7, 128; Berger, *Sacred Canopy*, 9–10; Berger and Luckman, *Social Construction of Reality*, 55–58.

63. Berger and Luckman, *Social Construction of Reality*, 53.

64. Berger and Luckman, *Social Construction of Reality*, 31, 39, 43, 72.

of enforcing those sociocultural norms from a transcendent authority. Laws governed slavery and allowed the government to benefit economically from the sociocultural practice. The initial absence of concrete slave laws does not presuppose the absence of slavery on both a psychological and sociocultural level. The rejection of the gradualist perspective has some credence if one were to consider some historical events regarding the relationship between Black and White people within the settlements. It can be interpreted that certain sociocultural customs and new laws distinguished and defined the value of both Black and White humanity.

On September 17, 1630, a White indentured servant by the name of Hugh Davis was publicly flogged in Jamestown, Virginia, for having sexual relations with a Black woman.[65] A law was passed on January 6, 1639, which allowed all citizens (including native Indians), "except Negroes," to bear arms and acquire ammunition.[66] Additionally, in 1640, three indentured servants, two White men and a Black male named John Punch, had attempted to escape from their contracts of service. They were eventually caught and brought before a court of law. The two White men (Victor, a Dutchman, and James Gregory, a Scotchman) were punished by having three years added to their original length of service. However, John Punch was punished by being sentenced to a lifetime of servitude to his master.[67] With this in mind, the statement of historian George Williams seems plausible:

> The legal distinction between slaves and servants was, "slaves for life, and servants for a time." Slavery existed from 1619 until 1662, without any sanction in law. On the 14th of December, 1662, the foundations of the slave institution were laid in the old law maxim, "*Partus sequiter ventrum*,"—that the issue of slave mothers should follow their condition.[68]

To phrase Williams's statements another way: "That which is brought forth follows the womb." The status of the newborns must follow that of their mother. This law applied even to those biracial children with White biological fathers. For Williams, slavery existed since the initial

65. Hopkins, *Down, Up, and Over*, 19; G. Williams, *History of the Negro Race*, 165.

66. Hopkins, *Down, Up, and Over*, 19; G. Williams, *History of the Negro Race*, 165.

67. Jordan, *White over Black*, 75; Jordan, "Decisions of the General Court," 236; Quarles, *Negro in the Making*, 35.

68. G. Williams, *History of the Negro Race*, 166. See also Quarles, *Negro in the Making*, 36.

arrival of the twenty African slaves in 1619. However, it was only in 1662 that the government created a law which defined enslavement at birth.

My stance is that slavery was practiced in 1619 and was gradually institutionalized into society before the slave laws of the 1630s. Slavery began as a sociocultural institution and sociopsychological development which naturally developed into a legalized institution governed by the state. The early settlers of the British colonies were conscious of slavery as a practice and the ethnic, nationalistic, and proto-racist ideologies that were usually attached to it. Sir John Rolfe made it clear that during 1619 Governor Yeardley and Cape Merchant Abraham Peirsey bartered with Captain Jope and pilot Marmaduke, exchanging food and drink for twenty African *slaves*. Furthermore, according to historian Edmund Morgan, records from a census state that Yeardley and Peirsey owned fifteen of the twenty-three African slaves in 1625.[69] Oddly enough, historians have discovered that there were two additional arrivals of African slaves in 1621 and 1622. Thus, there were three separate arrivals of African slaves to have arrived at the British colony within four years. For some historians, their arrival is purely accidental and coincidental. However, I disagree. Slavery was not legalized within the colony. Therefore, the three separate arrivals of African slaves could be interpreted as evidence of the fact that slaves were *smuggled* within the colony without the full awareness of the British government. Evidence of this theory lies in the fact of vague and scant documents of the slaves' existence. Most slaves were merely given the title of *Negro* as an identity within these documents. Others are provided it as a surname, as was the case for Anthony Johnson (Antonio Negro). In the realm of politics within politics, we often see Whiteness turning against itself, as the sin of self-glorification and self-preservation causes the White-Self to elevate itself at the expense of the White-Other.

Additionally, it must be noted that during the early seventeenth century it was extremely difficult for England to import slaves into their British colonies. Why? As Wertenbaker has stated,

> It was impossible at this time for England to supply her plantation with this type of labor. The slave trade was in the hands of the Dutch, who had fortified themselves on the African coast and jealously excluded other nations. Thus while the demand for Negro slaves remained active in the colony, they increased in numbers slowly.[70]

69. Morgan, *American Slavery, American Freedom*, 105.

70. Wertenbaker, *Planters of Colonial Virginia*, 30–31.

England could not import any significant number of slaves into its colonies because of necessity, not from desire. This is why the cost of using indentured servants was cheaper during the early life of the Virginian colony. Furthermore, once the headright law is considered, the usage of indentured servants becomes more economically feasible. Indentured servants became an investment that could reap dual rewards by supplying the colony with European immigrants who functioned as a means of increasing the population and developing a social class of cheap labor. England did not begin to usurp the Dutch in the slave trade until roughly the middle to the late seventeenth century. It was during this period that the slave laws were being developed within the colonies. As England began to dominate the slave trade, the usage of indentured servants decreased, and the slave population increased.

Historians have emphasized the positive significance of freed Africans existing in the colonies before legalized slavery. For them, the existence of free and prosperous Africans and African Americans signifies that there was racial equality within the colonies. However, these same historians fail to mention that the elements I've mentioned throughout this discussion were also present during legalized slavery in America. There are testimonies to the fact of slaves buying their freedom from their masters. Other slaves were awarded their freedom upon their master's death, as stipulated within the master's will. Therefore, it must be questioned as to how legitimate the existence of free and prosperous slaves is to proving that racial equality was present from 1619 to the development of slave laws.

I am suggesting political corruption was more common in the colonies than we may realize. The acquiring of self-interest, at least for some European/European Americans, had priority over some romanticized political loyalty to their country. Many Africans and African Americans may have maintained some form of political relations with their former masters. The benefits they were to receive by this would have been greater than those received if they remained slaves and were free only to survive on their own. Mutual benefits between different races have often created concealed alliances, and these alliances create forms of politics that exist within politics. Furthermore, the quantity of freed Africans in comparison to enslaved Africans is considered to have been extremely small. To overemphasize freed slaves is to minimize or ignore the reality that:

> Neither the merchant nor the planters seem to have been conscious of any wrong in the seizure and sale of Negroes. They regarded the native Africans as hardly human, mere savages that were no more deserving of consideration than oxen or horses. And as it was right and proper to hitch the ox or the horse to the plow, so it was equally legitimate to put the Negroes to work in the fields of sugar cane or tobacco. Whatever hardships he had to endure upon the voyage to America or by reason of his enforced labor, they considered amply compensated by his conversation to Christianity.[71]

There are some scholars who have used the process of development to minimize and, at other times ignore, the *intentionality* of Europeans and American settlers in actively perfecting the institution of slavery. They locate a *legal* event in history, which allows them to create and attach an origins theory to it. Thus, it can be interpreted that slavery, for them, is primarily a legal issue that does not have any concrete beginnings culturally, psychologically, and socially apart from the state. This can be problematic if someone seeks to understand slavery beyond its legalized form. Otherwise, slavery will continue to be depicted as a government-sanctioned construct from a set of coincidental events with the involvement of agents who may or may not have any culpability in its creation.

The *legal* institutionalizing of slavery is not an initial stage of development. Rather, it is a mature and advanced stage along a complex spectrum of development. Legalized slavery, in most contexts, is the relationship between the sociocultural, socioeconomic, and sociopsychological self-interest of the qualitative and quantitative essence of a people group who seek to embody their ideologies of human superiority.

However, the difficult reality for us to digest is that morally and spiritually righteous people can exist and function within corrupt and dehumanizing institutions. It is especially difficult to discern the intent and heart of some people who practice, or benefit by extension, from institutions of oppression. Yet, I would argue that there was possibly a starting point within the mid seventeenth century whereby a small remnant of European Americans defended the sanctity of Black humanity against the dehumanization of American slavery.

71. Wertenbaker, *Planters of Colonial Virginia*, 129.

6

The Fragmentation of Colonial Whiteness

Antislavery Reform and Antislavery Christianity During the Seventeenth Century

THE BARBARISM OF BARBADOS

Colonialism was a period of religious contradiction, hypocrisy, and paradoxes that permeated throughout European and European American Christianity. The distinctive lines between sociopolitical theory and Christian theology became blurred. New forms of political theologies developed that justified and supported the enslavement of the non-European world. Thus, for some, the Christian church had wilfully embraced a variety of secular and even quasi-religious sociopolitical beliefs that advocated forms of imperialism and nationalism that contradicted the tenets of Christianity. For example, religious justification for the transatlantic slave trade was interpreted as the belief that the heathen would easily convert to Christianity. Furthermore, some people maintained that the African slaves would become civilized as they dwelled among Europe's advanced cultures. However, people eventually recognized these beliefs to be products of pseudo-religious sociopolitical propaganda to accumulate support for enslaving the non-European world. Various internal disagreements within Christendom surfaced which created debates on whether Christianity should be preached to the enslaved at all. Nevertheless, from roughly 1444 to 1700, Christianity was, in most contexts, intentionally withheld from African slaves.

Barbados influenced other British colonies in four ways. First, Barbadian colonists initially sought to define concretely the difference between servant and slave. This distinction developed through the usage of racial theory, which was gradually implemented in the colony's sociocultural customs and eventually established itself in Barbadian laws. Second, the Barbadian colonists utilized violence and other psychological forms of enslavement to create an efficient slave economy. Third, Barbados established a network with American mainland colonies. Many of the African slaves who arrived in mainland America were first conditioned for slave life within Barbados and the West Indies in general. Last, eventually Barbadian planters relocated to mainland America. They used their knowledge of slave production to create plantations within the American colonies. Referencing this, historians Daniel P. Mannix and Malcolm Cowley state, "With the growth of the slave trade, the plantation system began to spread through the South. Particularly in South Carolina its growth was encouraged by the arrival of colonists from Barbados."[1] Overall, Barbados supplied the British colonies with an established blueprint from which to create and sustain a slave-driven society. Mainland American colonies embraced this Barbadian blueprint and eventually superseded the Barbadian institution of slavery.

EARLY SLAVERY IN BARBADOS

Barbados was originally inhabited by a group of people known as the *Arawak*. However, during the sixteenth century, the Spaniards continually attacked and enslaved them. By the early seventeenth century, the island was relatively uninhabited because of enslavement and its apparent abandonment by a small remnant of people who survived their initial persecution. The English would eventually visit the island by 1625 through its rediscovery by Captain John Powell. In 1627, Charles I granted Scotsman James Hay, earl of Carlisle, an inordinate amount of power over the island. Carlisle, in turn, granted permission to a group of London merchants to

1. Mannix and Cowley, *Black Cargoes*, 65; see also Breen and Innes, *"Myne Owne Ground,"* 19, 70.

populate and cultivate the island. Captain Powell would return with these London merchants to establish Barbados as a permanent colony.[2]

Powell returned with some of the Arawaks from Guinea whom he stated came on their own accord. There were also ten African slaves along for the voyage.[3] However, there was some apparent miscommunication or usurpation of Powell's authority by the other English settlers as they enslaved the Arawaks once Powell left Barbados.[4] Historian Richard Dunn has stated, "Powell's promise of freedom to the Arawaks was soon violated by the settlers in their drive to exploit labour. The Arawaks on Barbados were enslaved and only freed in the 1650s, when Powell intervened on their behalf."[5] Powell's agreement with the Arawaks stipulated that they would travel back to Barbados to teach the English settlers how to cultivate the land properly. In return, a portion of land would be returned to them. This agreement was nullified by the English settlers who chose to enslave the Arawaks rather than learn from them. Evidently, the English settlers saw no apparent distinction between Africans and Arawak in terms of their value as slaves. Over twenty years would pass before the Arawak were emancipated.

British colonies seemed to have always arrived at a period when they embodied a set of contradictions, ironies, and paradoxes, all of which generally evolved around concepts of freedom and power. As colonies, they were naturally under the authority of England. This authority permeated throughout the realms of sociocultural, political, and religious governance. However, with geographical distance came a strong tension between the actual level of freedom and power embodied by the colony in relation to its attempts to develop as an independent authority.

The London merchants naturally established themselves as the planter-class elite of Barbados. Historian Simon P. Newman insists that the planter class exercised "nearly unrestrained political and judicial power, and they shaped the island to suit their interests."[6] It would be through this relative unrestrained power that concepts of Christianity,

2. Beckles, *Black Rebellion in Barbados*, 9; Amussen, *Caribbean Exchanges*, 24; Blackburn, *New World Slavery*, 225; Newman, *New World of Labour*, 54; Gerbner, "Ultimate Sin," 57.

3. Beckles, *Black Rebellion in Barbados*, 10; Jordan, *White over Black*, 64.

4. Dunn, *Sugar and Slaves*, 226–27.

5. Amussen, *Caribbean Exchanges*, 58.

6. Newman, *New World of Labour*, 59.

race, social hierarchy, and slavery created a dehumanized labor class within Barbados.

THE BARBADIAN LABOR CLASS

By 1629, there were 1,600 settlers residing in Barbados, which included the Arawaks and Africans who returned with Powell in 1627.[7] The Arawaks and Africans were present during the initial colonization of Barbados. However, Newman is adamant that "during the epochal first generation it was White Britons who dominated the bound work force, carrying out plantations from the forest and soil of the island, and powering a radical new system of labour informed by and yet dramatically from British precedents."[8] Newman has a rather romanticized emphasis on White labor in Barbados. This is considering the Barbadian elite did almost everything in their power to rely heavily, if not solely, upon the labor of the enslaved Arawaks and Africans in the colony.

Newman is correct that White indentured servants were *initially* the majority in the labor class of Barbados. Most were English settlers who were classified as criminals and disenfranchised by English society. Yet there were also present Irish and Scottish immigrants.[9] Naturally, the population of Barbados increased steadily within ten to twelve years of its initial colonization. Historian Robin Blackburn states that in 1638 there were 6,000 people on the island. Of the total population, roughly 2,000 were indentured servants and 200 were slaves.[10] This leaves around 3,800 people who formed the planter class and their families.

In 1638, England was still vying for a monopoly over the transatlantic slave trade. At this point, it would have been difficult and not economically feasible for Barbados to rely solely on African slave labor. This is probably why there was such a high quantity of White indentured servants on the island. British precedents had little to do with the ability to supply and sustain a slave labor class. As we shall see, according to some scholars, England would begin to establish itself as an elite slave-trading nation around 1660. However, even before becoming a proficient

7. Amussen, *Caribbean Exchanges*, 25.

8. Newman, *New World of Labour*, 54; see also 60, 68, 71, 189.

9. Jordan, *White over Black*, 63; Mannix and Cowley, *Black Cargoes*, 51.

10. Blackburn, *New World Slavery*, 235.

slaveholding nation, from 1627 to 1660, there was a noticeable increase in the slave labor class in Barbados.[11]

During this time, there were no records of a free class of Africans within Barbados. However, in 1636, "Governor Hawley announced that all Indians and African servants brought to the land, and their children, would be treated as chattel slaves unless they had a contract of service specifying otherwise."[12] A *chattel* slave was a person who served for their entire life. According to Newman, the presence and development of Barbadian slave laws is an important set of events. Barbadian slave laws "would provide the foundation for strikingly similar formulations in Jamaica, South Carolina, the Leeward Islands, and beyond."[13] Newman touches on a sensitive and important fact: Barbados influenced other British colonies in the creation of their own slave laws. Records show that Barbados influenced the colonies of Virginia, South Carolina, and Georgia. According to Donald R. Wright,

> The result in South Carolina and Georgia was the steady erosion of rights for blacks until they faced the strictest laws with the harshest punishments of anywhere in the English mainland colonies. The process took place first in South Carolina, where in the 1690s the Assembly began borrowing from the slave codes of its "parent" colony, Barbados.[14]

The development of slave laws was necessary since the slave population had increased as England continually gained control of the slave trade. The elite of Barbados were intentional in using Africans and Indians as slaves rather than Europeans. Historian Lester B. Scherer states, "In 1643 the governor of Barbados even refused to enslave fifty of the hated Portuguese who had been captured and offered for slave[ry] by a Dutch captain."[15] This may have been due to the European identification

11. I am discussing scholars who employ conflicting statistics regarding the number of slaves in Barbados throughout the seventeenth century. My aim is to provide a general understanding of the colony's progressive reliance upon African slave labor and how it coincided with the rise of England as an elite slave trading nation.

12. Blackburn, *New World Slavery*, 235; Beckles, *Black Rebellion in Barbados*, 11; Rugemer, "Development of Mastery," 433; Gregg, *Englishmen Transplanted*, 125; Jordan, *White over Black*, 64.

13. Newman, *New World of Labour*, 193.

14. D. Wright, *African Americans in the Colonial Era*, 81; Rugemer, "Development of Mastery," 429–33; Franklin and Moss, *From Slavery to Freedom*, 55; Quarles, *Negro in the Making*, 41.

15. Scherer, *Slavery and the Churches*, 25; Blackburn, *New World Slavery*, 236.

and pigmentation of the Portuguese. Nonetheless, according to historian Winthrop Jordan, these fifty captured Portuguese were set free.[16] In 1643 there were fewer than 3,000 African slaves in Barbados.[17] Yet, Amussen states that over 1,000 African slaves were believed to have been purchased in 1645 alone.[18] Nevertheless, Newman advocates that by the end of 1646, there were close to 25,000 slaves, and in 1654, there were close to 46,000.[19]

If these statistics are relatively close to the truth, they support the theory that there had always been a distinction between an indentured servant and a slave. However, a nation naturally needs political power to supply its colonies with the cheapest labor. The cheapest labor had always been an African slave above and beyond a European indentured servant. The distinction between servant and slave developed and became concretized through concepts of race. Each British colony exercised some form of political corruption that established a sociopolitical elite and a labor class. The labor class consisted of White indentured servants and Black slaves. However, as England grew in power, it supplied their colonies with the cheapest labor of Black slaves. Subsequently, the White labor class became minimalized and/or they were used to create a quasi-middle-class within society.

Racial theory was both an isolated ideological system and a form of justification for the institution of slavery. By 1680, England had complete control of the slave trade, and it actively supplied its colonies with a daunting quantity of slave labor. During this time, Barbados had a dwindling population in general, but an estimated 38,782 Black slaves and 2,317 White indentured servants were still present on the island.[20] Thus, according to Newman, the slave population decreased by roughly 7,218 between 1654 and 1680.

As the slave population increased, the White indentured class decreased and began to embody a more authoritarian role on the plantation. Amussen maintains that “in a system utilizing both indentured servants and slaves, English servants were increasingly necessary not

16. Jordan, *White over Black*, 64–65.

17. Jordan, *White over Black*, 190–91.

18. Amussen, *Caribbean Exchanges*, 29.

19. Newman, *New World of Labour*, 191.

20. Newman, *New World of Labour*, 193. The estimated 38,782 Black slaves around 1680 marks a 7,218 decrease of Black slaves from the roughly 46,000 who resided in Barbados in 1654.

for hard labor but for policing enslaved Africans."[21] Eventually, Barbados would be known as a wealthy British colony through its exportation of sugar. The colony would also be known for its exploitation and degradation of its slave labor class. The barbarism of Barbados's labor system would eventually awaken the once lethargic conscience of some European Christian leaders. Consequently, they would unknowingly assist in creating the traditions of European-American slavery reform and antislavery Christianity.

A central issue that separated proslavery, slavery reform, and antislavery Christians was their usage of essentialist/racialized binary reasoning that emphasized a qualitative and quantitative difference in servitude.

SERVITUDE: THE QUALITATIVE AND QUANTITATIVE DIFFERENCE

It is easy to entertain the misconception of universalizing almost every institution of slavery in recorded history. From this fallacious reasoning, slavery is slavery, and there may or may not be a qualitative and quantitative difference between each institution. The level of pain, suffering, and overall oppression experienced by the enslaved is relative. Furthermore, this line of reasoning displays a strong reluctance to examine the cultures and societies of the enslavers apart from their socioeconomic benefits. There is even the rejection that through oppression, the enslaver and enslaved are dehumanized in their own unique ways.

This perspective of universalizing slavery is rather troubling, and it avoids the distinctive character of each institution. Each institution is created within a culture and society. Slavery is contextualized in distinct ways according to the sociocultural, socioeconomic, and sociopsychological needs of the enslavers. An obsessive focus on generating wealth and establishing oneself as the elite in society were influential factors shaping the treatment of the labor class. Productivity and revenue were more valuable and generated more concern than the well-being of the servants and slaves. However, these elements are generally present within every institution of slavery. What elements made the Barbadian slave system distinct?

Generally, White indentured servants and Black slaves were never perceived as equals within most European nations. Indentured servitude

21. Amussen, *Caribbean Exchanges*, 129.

was a contractual agreement of labor for an allotted time. The individual chose to be a servant. However, a slave was forced into labor regardless of his or her desire and typically served their master until death. Both groups were deemed inferior and suffered abuse by the elite class.

British author Richard Ligon (1585–1662) lived in Barbados for three years (1647–50). He describes his experiences there in *A True and Exact History of the Island of Barbados*. Ligon provides some vivid accounts of servants experiencing abuse from their masters: "I have seen an Overseer beat a servant with a cane about the head, till the blood has followed, for a fault that is not worth the speaking of; and yet he must have patience, or worse will follow. Truly, I have seen such cruelty there done to servants, as I did not think one Christian could have done to another."[22] Ligon's account of Barbados is valuable; however, it is not void of the cultural elitism, proto-racism, and sexism of his era. On one occasion, he describes Africans "as near beasts as may be." For Ligon, the White indentured servants within the colony experienced more abuse than the Black slaves. However, there was always a qualitative and quantitative difference regarding their level of freedom experienced, servitude, and perception/treatment of one's humanity. The neglect and extreme violence toward the slave class is what initially made Barbados distinct from other institutions. As historian Richard S. Dunn explains, "From the beginning English West Indian slavery had a style of its own. It was physically more cruel and debilitating than Negro bondage in the English mainland settlements, yet psychologically perhaps less traumatic."[23] Cruelty was an influential element in the method of *breaking-in* or *seasoning* the African slaves.[24] These were slave terminologies referring to any systematic usage of physical and psychological violence toward the slaves. The intent was to establish paralyzing fear, insecurity, and subservience within the slave. European masters viewed African slaves not as humans who were equal to them. Rather, the slave was perceived as a brute without a conscience or an untamed animal. Violence, as the European masters embraced it, was an efficient means of deconstructing the slave's humanity.

Castration was one of the most horrific physical and psychological methods in breaking-in a slave. This affected not only the individual who was castrated but also the entire slave community that witnessed

22. Ligon, *True and Exact History*, 44.

23. Scherer, *Slavery and the Church*, 13; Dunn, *Sugar and Slaves*, 226.

24. D. Wright, *African Americans in the Colonial Era*, 24; Franklin and Moss, *From Slavery to Freedom*, 43–46.

the event or had secondary knowledge of the circumstance. African men were castrated to the extent that laws were created to govern the act.[25] It was an acceptable practice socio-politically and religiously for some within society. The practice of castrating African men, according to William G. McLoughlin and Jordan, had originated in Barbados, and other colonies such as South Carolina merely adopted the practice:

> In a few instances, particularly in the West Indies, individual planters emasculated their slaves, sometimes in outbursts of sadism involving hideous tortures which planter society deplored but did not effectively control until the latter part of the eighteenth century. Far more significant, castration was dignified by specific legislative sanction as a lawful punishment in Antigua, the Carolinas, Bermuda, Virginia, Pennsylvania, and New Jersey.[26]

McLoughlin and Jordan describe a conflict over the practice of castration. This conflict had developed in 1711 at a Baptist church within South Carolina. Apparently, the leadership of a slaveholding Baptist church had written to their governing board in England regarding the practice. In response, the governing board stated, "Now your law Seem[s] to be grounded on necessity; and the End of it (as your Selves inform us) to prevent Vagrancy, theft, robory, insurrections, and Outrages of your Slaves, and So Serves for the common good, preserving order and we cannot think (circums[tan]ses considered) that it is against God's word, but rather according to it."[27] Castration and violence toward the slaves were sanctioned socio-culturally and legally. They were a means of not only suppressing sin from the slaves, such as vagrancy, theft, robbery, and insurrection, but they were an effective form of social control. For the members of this governing body, and many other Christians throughout Barbados, violence toward the slave did not violate any Christian principles.[28]

Physical cruelty was sanctioned by a form of proslavery European Christianity, which utilized race, and concepts of human development, as quasi-philosophical and theological justification for slavery. Furthermore, it cannot be ignored that this same form of proslavery Christianity had

25. McLoughlin and Jordan, "Baptists Face the Barbarities," 495.

26. Jordan, *White over Black*, 154.

27. McLoughlin and Jordan, "Baptists Face the Barbarities," 498.

28. Newman, *New World of Labour*, 54–55, 192–93.

theologically justified attempts to withhold *salvation*, or the presentation of the Christian gospel message to the slaves. Thus, European economic self-interests (materialism) and a sociopsychological notion of superiority had greater value than any religious or spiritual self-interests of the African slaves. Barbados will undergo turmoil as proslavery Christians are confronted with the constructive theologies of the slavery reformers and antislavery Christians.

AN ACCOUNT OF SLAVERY REFORM AND ANTISLAVERY CHRISTIANITY: A QUAKER VIEW

Humanization and an Awakened Conscience

Originally, Barbadian Christianity was a Puritan form of proslavery Christianity. Many planters on the island between 1627 and 1655 identified as Puritan. The Religious Society of Friends, also known as the Quakers, developed in England after 1647, following the religious convictions of George Fox (1624–91). However, it was not until 1655 that the movement sent two missionaries to evangelize Barbados in the tenets of Quakerism. Anna Austin and Mary Fisher were the first Quaker missionaries who brought religious conflict and conviction, which assisted in initiating change to Barbadian Christianity.[29] Yet, their impact on Barbados should not be romanticized. As Herbert Aptheker remarks,

> There is a prevailing general impression that the Quakers represented, as a body, throughout their history a solid phalanx aligned against human enslavement. This is, however, fallacious. One finds upon examination of the facts that the development of antislavery feeling among the Society of Friends was a very slow process indeed, and that the group never, until just before the Civil War, really represented a solid, unified, genuinely articulate opposition to slavery.[30]

Aptheker is correct. Quakerism has the general stereotype of being the first Christian group to uniformly oppose slavery. This perception has elements of truth, but glosses over the reality that there were many Quakers who owned African slaves. Quakerism, like any other Christian group, had to undergo internal conflict and resolution regarding the

29. Vipont, *Story of Quakerism*, 50–51; Gerbner, "Ultimate Sin," 61.

30. Aptheker, "Quakers and Negro Slavery," 331.

practice of slavery. This internal conflict may have been present since the initial birth of the group. Brycchan Carey insists, "The first Quakers of the 1640s and 50s were not automatically opposed either to slavery or the slave trade, and some Friends remained active slaveholders and slave traders into the late eighteenth century."[31] Not only had Barbados inspired the development of mainland slave laws, but its form of proslavery Quakerism influenced the development of mainland proslavery Christianity.

The Quakers were generally known to be pacifists and denounced any *idolatrous* loyalty to an established government. This naturally created tension with the Puritans of Barbados. The Puritans were initially the sociopolitical elite of the island, and they actively used violence as a means of racial and social control. Planters still maintained an allegiance to the institution of slavery despite converting to Quakerism. Apparently, Barbadian Quakers had embraced violence and remained active in the slave trade to the extent that it created a troubling reputation throughout the world that had eventually reached George Fox in England.

George Fox's First Attempt: Timid Suggestions

In 1657, two years after the arrival of Austin and Fisher, George Fox published *To Friends Beyond The Sea, That Have Blacks and Indian Slaves*.[32] Fox's message is extremely brief and communicates the universal message of the gospel. The tone of Fox's writing is one of slight concern, and he appears hesitant to make any direct accusations, although slavery appears to be the underlying influence of the letter:

> Dear Friends, I was moved to write these things to you in all those plantations. God, that made the world, and all things therein, giveth life and breath to all, and they all have their life and moving, and their being in him, he is the God of the spirits of the flesh, and is no respecter of persons; but "whosoever fearth him and worketh righteousness, is accepted of him." And he hath made all nations of one blood to dwell upon the face of the earth, and his eyes are over all the works of his hands, and seeth every thing that is done under the whole of heaven; and "the earth is the Lord's and the fullness thereof." And he causeth

31. Carey, "'Power That Giveth Liberty,'" 27.

32. Aptheker, "Quakers and Negro Slavery," 332; Scherer, *Slavery and the Churches*, 40.

> the rain to fall upon the just and the unjust, and also he causeth the sine to shine upon the just and the unjust; and he commands to "love all men," for Christ loved all, so that he "died for sinners." And this is God's love for the world, in giving his son into the world; that "whosoever believeth in him should not perish." And he doth "enlighten every man that cometh into the world," that they might believe in the son. And the gospel is preached to every creature under heaven; which is the power that giveth liberty and freedom, and is glad tidings to every captivated creature under the whole heavens. And the word of God is in the heart and mouth, to obey and do it, and not for them to ascend or descend for it; and this is the word of faith which was and is preached. For Christ is given for a covenant to the people, and a light to the Gentiles, and to enlighten them, who is the glory of Israel, and God's "salvation to the ends of the earth." And so ye are to have the mind of Christ, and to be merciful, as your heavenly Father is merciful.[33]

There are important principles that can be gleaned from Fox's short letter. Its content negates and transcends the essentialist/racialized binary thinking that characterized European Christianity. First, Fox makes a persistent case for the sovereignty of God. God has created all life, and his love for humanity is epitomized by the gospel message. Fox's emphasis on an inclusive God and universal gospel are passively associated with the African slaves. He alludes to this by the statement that God "is no respecter of persons; but 'whosoever fearth him and worketh righteousness, is accepted of him.' And he hath made all nations of one blood to dwell upon the face of the earth." Fox cements this interpretation with a reference to John 3:16 (God loved the world), and the direct statement of Christ's love for humanity, which is connected to spiritual salvation via the gospel message. Fox describes the gospel as a source of power, liberty, and freedom to an audience of mostly proslavery Christians who openly participated in the transatlantic slave trade. He passively confronts Barbadian proslavery Christianity in ways that made his position regarding the relationship between Christianity and the slaves very clear to the casual reader.

For Fox, Christianity represented the religious ideals of freedom and equality. However, proslavery European Christians generally refused to allow Christianity to be interpreted and practiced similarly by the African slaves. Not only were some Barbadian Quakers benefiting from the

33. Fox, *To Friends Beyond the Sea.*

institution of slavery, but those residing in America were as well. Carey, referencing *To Friends Beyond The Sea, That Have Blacks and Indian Slaves*, argues that "Quakers were buying both African and Native American slaves from the outset of their settlement in America, and that Fox must have come to a rapid view of the practice once it had come to his attention."[34] Fox initiates a slavery reform constructive theology devoid of essentialist/racialized binary reasoning, that develops as he becomes increasingly aware of the sinful practices of Barbadian Quakers and the level of dehumanization Barbadian slaves experienced.

One of the greatest hypocrisies and sins of European Christianity was the manipulation of evangelism as adequate justification for the participation of the churches in slavery. Initially, during the fifteenth century, proslavery Christianity, in varied degrees, advocated that the African heathen already existed in physical and spiritual bondage. Therefore, through slavery, they would have the opportunity to hear the gospel of Christ and be civilized by European cultures. However, the convoluted nature of this religious perspective became more apparent as internal debates surfaced regarding the legitimacy of this claim. Debates regarding the conversion of slaves surfaced throughout the world during the sixteenth and seventeenth centuries. Yet, for the most part, scant attempts to evangelize the slaves had yet developed, as most European Christians had advocated an anti-evangelism stance.

Then 1660 marked a year of transition as England was on the brink of usurping the Dutch as the leader in the slave trade. During that year, Charles I and the Church of England asserted that all slaves should be converted to Christianity. Or, at the least, they would receive the opportunity to be taught the gospel message of Jesus Christ.[35] Barbados created two unique laws in 1661 governing servants and slaves in the colony. These laws were referred to as the "Masters and Slave Act" and the "Act for the Better Ordering and Governing of Negroes." They established concrete distinctions in the roles of a servant and a slave. Servants had begun to exercise more rights than previously. Yet, the laws regarding the slaves reduced them completely to property and were heavily racialized with stereotypes of inferiority.[36] In this same year, Barbados also passed

34. Carey, "'Power that Giveth Liberty,'" 31.

35. Jernegan, "Slavery and Conversion," 508–9; Gerbner, "Ultimate Sin," 61.

36. Amussen, *Caribbean Exchanges*, 129–31; Gregg, *Englishmen Transplanted*, 119; Newman, *New World of Labour*, 191–92; Dunn, *Sugar and Slaves*, 239; Blackburn, *New World Slavery*, 250–51.

a law of provision. All masters were to provide adequate clothing for their slaves.[37] Subsequently, Virginia created slave laws between 1660 and 1662. One law stipulated that any African or Black child born within the colony would assume the same status as his or her mother. Thus, a child could be born a slave. Other laws served to further punish anyone who engaged in interracial relationships.[38]

According to Katherine Gerbner, in 1661, the British Parliament instructed Lord Willoughby, the reinstated governor of Barbados, to legally enforce the conversion of the slaves. In 1663, Willoughby presented such a bill to the Council of Barbados; however, the ruling planter elites ignored it.[39] In short, the proslavery planters were fearful that Christian slaves would eventually seek to undermine the institution of slavery. During this period, there was growing tension between an antislavery minority and most proslavery planters in Barbados, among both Quakers and Puritans. The attempts of the British Parliament to encourage the evangelization of the slaves, and the presence of a small group of antislavery Christians on the colony, may have created a context whereby Fox's letter to local Quakers would have been warmly received by those who shared his convictions.

RADICAL OPPOSITION: GEORGE FOX'S VISIT TO BARBADOS

In 1671, George Fox visited Barbados as part of a global circuit which ended in America. Accompanying him was William Edmondson (1627–1712), the founder of Quakerism in Ireland, as well as fellow Quaker Elizabeth Hooton (1600–1672).[40] Hooton is considered the first woman to be ordained as a Quaker minister. She is believed to have been one of Fox's initial converts to the movement and one of his mentors. Hooton was accustomed to traveling across the world as a Quaker missionary. During 1665–66 she developed a reputation as a fiery preacher in her visit to New England and Rhode Island. Yet, Hooton never overtly spoke out against slavery. She focused on the responsibility of the slave masters.

37. Gregg, *English Transplanted*, 130.

38. D. Wright, *African Americans in the Colonial Era*, 68; Franklin and Moss, *From Slavery to Freedom*, 54; Jordan, *White over Black*, 79, 81.

39. Gerbner, "Ultimate Sin," 61.

40. Vipont, *Story of Quakerism*, 43–44, 108.

Apparently, Hooton was extremely concerned that the slaves in Barbados were known as thieves. Many of these slaves were from the wealthy plantations of the colony. Hooton viewed the slaves' thievery as sin but understood that they stole out of necessity. Their slave masters did not provide adequate clothing and food for them. Thus, Hooton reminded the wealthy planters of their responsibility to provide the basic provisions for their slaves. Tragically, Elizabeth Hooton would die in Jamaica of natural causes after leaving Barbados in 1672.[41]

Regarding Fox, fourteen years had passed since he had written his first letter to Barbadian Quakers. One can only imagine the reputation Barbados had developed throughout those years. During this period, institutionalized slavery developed, as did the form of proslavery Christianity which justified and sustained it. Fox was confronted by the overwhelming reality that many Quakers were active slave masters who abused their slaves and practiced gross immorality. This was not only an affront to his leadership but also a great violation to God's commandments. Fox and Edmondson were extremely disturbed by what they experienced in Barbados. Evidently, the reputations of island slaveholders for dehumanizing the slaves and for the staunch presence of proslavery Christianity were accurate.

Fox and Edmondson's actions within the colony were in total defiance of Barbadian Christianity and the colony's government. The two Quaker leaders actively sought to undermine both Barbadian institutions. Fox and Edmondson preached Christianity to the African slaves, held joint church services with them, and argued that the proslavery Quakers were to denounce their immoral lifestyles. Fox recorded his experiences and general thoughts in the 1672 publication *To the Ministers, Teachers, and Priests (So called, and so Stileing your-selves) in Barbados*. The biblical and theological content of this publication is extremely direct and radical and provides a strong rebuke against Barbadian proslavery Christianity, which is applicable to proslavery Christians in its entirety.

In *To the Ministers*, Fox levels another strong critique upon the overall authority structures of Barbados. His greater focus was on the proslavery Christians within the colony who justified the institution, withheld the gospel message to the slaves, and advocated the permissibility of violence to subjugate the slaves. The nature of African humanity is important to Fox. This is possibly because proslavery Christianity had

41. Manners, *Elizabeth Hooton*, 71–72; Weddle, *Walking in the Way of Peace*, 34, 100.

disputed its existence and/or relegated it to an inferior status to European humanity. Fox emphasizes that there is equality between both groups of people through his constant references to the gospel message and to the fact that Jesus Christ died for all of humanity. Thus, the principles of discipleship and evangelism undergird Fox's theological anthropology. The biblical doctrine of the *imago Dei* (humanity made in God's image) also influenced Fox.

Fox aggressively attacked the beliefs and practices of proslavery Barbadian Christianity. For him, these proslavery Christians completely rejected the Great Commission, to go and make disciples of all nations (Matt 28:16–20), and the commandments to love God and their neighbor (Luke 10:27). Fox continually displayed harsh sarcasm through his array of rhetorical questions toward the Barbadian elites. Regarding proslavery Christianity, the core Christian beliefs of the Great Commission and love commandments were racialized and subjected to a theoretical hierarchy of human development and superiority. Fox argued, "Now consider, Christ (I say) saith, *Go teach all nations*: Have you obeyed his commandment, or have you heard his voice (as was said before) or are you of those that have climed up another way? And what doth Christ call such?"[42] Fox engages the Barbadian proslavery Christians as if they were representatives of the Pharisees that Jesus confronted during his ministry. Fox can be interpreted as implying that slavery was an institution of destruction, murder, and thievery.

Fox seemed baffled as to how the Great Commission was relegated by the Barbadian elite exclusively to Europeans. He could not accept an ethnic, nationalistic, or racialized gospel, because his Christian faith determined that all humans were equal and deserved to hear the gospel message. Fox insisted,

> And if you be Ministers of Christ, are you not teachers of *Blacks* and *Taunies* (to wit, *Indians*) as well as of the *Whites*? For, is not the Gospel to be preached to all creatures? And are not they creatures? And did not Christ taste Death for every man? And are not they Men? And was not he a Propitiation for the Sins of the whole World, as well as for the Saints? And so consider, if the Gospel was to be preach[ed] unto all (according as Christ commanded) why do you not teach the *Blacks* and *Taunies* here?[43]

42. Fox, *To the Ministers, Teachers, and Priests*, 5.

43. Fox, *To the Ministers, Teachers, and Priests*, 5.

Fox attempts to reason with the proslavery Christians through a set of logical sequences based on texts in the bible. He first questions the literal and symbolic identity of the slaveholders as ministers of Christ. This identity assumes a set of divine responsibilities that are not negotiable—for example, the spiritual call to preach and teach the gospel to every person without discrimination. Hence, Fox's direct reference to Blacks, Taunies, and Indians being associated with Whites, all of whom are creations of God. Equality was also reinforced by Fox's statement that everyone was guilty of sin and required Christ's death for atonement. Fox understood Barbadian proslavery Christians advocated that non-White humanity was not worthy of spiritual *salvation.*

In his conclusion, Fox issues a strong rhetorical question that further reveals the proslavery Christians' deviation from basic Christian scripture. He suggests that, ironically, the self-righteousness of the planter elites had thrust them into a state of self-deception. They were not aware, or did not acknowledge, that the slaves were mimicking their immoral and sinful lifestyles:

> But it seems your *Blacks*, are taught to Swear, and to Curse, and to say, *God dam them*; and many of them do Swear almost at every word, which they have been taught and learned here among you called Christians (for they learn no such kind of Speech in their own country) and is not this sad, that Christians, who profess Christianity, should have such things amongst them?[44]

Fox continues to strip away the proslavery Christians' illusions of superiority over their slaves and over other Barbadian Christians who disavowed participation in slavery. He issues a strong moral condemnation of the Barbadian Christians that centers on the actions of their slaves. Again, we read Fox's reasoning through logical sequences. He mentions that the slaves have expressed excessive vulgar language that was not present in their homeland and could only be learned from their *Christian* masters. This is compounded by the fact that the Christian masters not only practiced vulgar language but permitted it among their slaves. Immorality was always depicted as the innate and compulsory state of the African slaves. African immorality was perceived as evidence of their inferiority and justification for their enslavement. However, within the greater context of colonialism, it was common for masters to indulge in sin and promote it within slave societies. In this context, conversion is

44. Fox, *To the Ministers, Teachers, and Priests*, 5.

equated to enslavement, not Christianity, and those individuals who are entrusted with divine responsibility disgrace themselves as well as insult YHWH by teaching their subordinates to practice immorality at a greater level than themselves.

Fox was perceived as an extreme threat by the elite class of Barbados. Evidently, there were harmful rumors spread about him throughout the colony. One such accusation was that he had brought an Englishwoman with him to Barbados as a sexual companion. Another rumor was that Fox had sexual relations with his sister.[45] Supposedly, Fox's sexual companion was believed to have been Elizabeth Hooton. However, he adamantly denied such things.

Fox interpreted the inverted gospel of proslavery Christianity as a perversion, and one that corrupted its advocates through forms of denial and self-deception. Fox continued to levy rhetorical sarcasm as he critiqued the fragmented morality of the Barbadian Christians:

> What faith the Prophet of the Lord in *Isa.*26.9? *When thy Judgments are on the Earth the inhabitants of the world will learn Righteousness*. But alas! Are you not rather worse then you were before, and hardened more then you were before (Pharaoh-like) as it is in the 10th verse, *Let Favour be shewn to the wicked, yet will he not learn righteousness, &c*. O! it is not the work of Christ's Ministers, to fall upon the Righteous, and persecute the Innocent, and let Swearers, Drunkards, Whore-Masters and Adulterers go free: And do you not pronounce the Blessing of God to be upon them, and Peace be unto them all, in the State and Condition wherein they remain unconverted?[46]

Fox probes the faith of the Barbadian proslavery Christians and does not associate them with the righteous, but with the unrighteous who reject the teachings of Christ, live immorally, and cannot understand the basic revelations of God. Fox refers to the Barbadian proslavery Christians as "Pharaoh-like" and once again questions their responsibility as ministers of God. This is complemented by his sarcasm toward questioning and describing the actions of the Barbadian proslavery Christians as the antithesis to godly living. For Fox, they not only participate in sin, and bless those that do also, but have deprived people from receiving salvation. Thus, the "innocent" of Barbadian society alludes to the slave

45. Fox, *To the Ministers, Teachers, and Priests*, 8.

46. Fox, *To the Ministers, Teachers, and Priests*, 10.

class as they experienced spiritual oppression along with their sociopolitical subjugation.

Fox passively opposed slavery through the immorality of the slave masters. I interpret Fox as a slavery reformer, as his views assumed that slavery could be practiced in humane ways that glorified God. Initially, Fox expressed rage against the gross immorality and debasement of the slave masters that he interpreted as a direct offense to God. For him, this was the primary reason that spurred the Barbadian Christians to neglect and abuse their slaves by teaching them to be immoral, as well as to refuse to evangelize them. His reasoning for seeking to undermine the institution, if it can be defined as that at all, was not from economic and sociopolitical self-interest, but rather from a spiritual concern for the planter and slave classes. European nations viewed slavery as a benefit to their economic, imperialistic, and general political agendas. They were not concerned with any beliefs and practices of altruism, as well as any modern concept of edifying the world community. Fox, perceiving himself as a minister of the gospel, sought to undermine the institution through biblical and theological reform. I interpret his 1672 pamphlet, *To the Ministers, Teachers, and Priests (So called, and so Stileing your-selves) in Barbados*, as contributing an initial template and as offering ongoing inspiration for European slavery reform Christianity.

Fox articulated a constructive theology of slavery reform that was devoid of essentialist/racialized binary reasoning and sought to humanize African slaves in a way that expressed their divine value and ability to comprehend the gospel of Jesus Christ. Fox's theology stimulated other European Christians to reflect upon opposing slavery, but also into developing aggressive ways to abolish the institution. During this moment, there was another symbolic ripple in the ocean initiated by an English Puritan named Richard Baxter.

PURITAN REFORM: THE EMERGENCE OF RICHARD BAXTER

The English Puritan Richard Baxter (1615–91) issued a stern rebuke against the proslavery Christianity in the West Indies in his 1673 publication, *A Christian Directory*.[47] This multivolume theological treatise dealt

47. Amussen, *Caribbean Exchanges*, 180; Gregg, *Englishmen Transplanted*, 161; Scherer, *Slavery and the Churches*, 27, 36–38; Jordan, *White over Black*, 200.

with the issue of slavery in a section titled "To those Masters in Foreign Plantations who Have Negros and other Slaves." Baxter's discourse on slavery is reminiscent to George Fox's *To the Ministers, Teachers, and Priests (So called, and so Stileing your-selves) in Barbados*. However, Baxter is more systematic in the presentation of his views. Although Fox's pamphlet was biblically centered, his message was more emotional and intense. Like Fox, Baxter insisted that slavery was permissible within specific situations. First, the institution could not create conflict with God's interest. For Baxter, God is sovereign and has structured life in a manner whereby humanity was the center of his attention. Baxter associated this to God's desire for every person to experience salvation, including everyone who was enslaved. Second, an individual could be enslaved as punishment for a crime and forced into manual labor, as each citizen was responsible for paying their debt to society. Baxter argued that even within this context the gospel should be preached, and a life of Christian morality was to be embodied regardless of a person's social status. Last, a person could wilfully hire themselves as indentured servants or sell themselves into slavery. Baxter was aware that many people experienced financial hardship and had no social mobility as they were considered the impoverished of society.[48]

Baxter displayed an extreme abhorrence for the dehumanization of the slaves and the thievery that created the transatlantic slave trade. For him, slavery that was immorally established was clearly a sin before God. Baxter argued,

> To go as pirates and catch up poor negroes or people of another land, that never forfeited life or liberty, and to make them slaves, and sell them, is one of the worst kinds of thievery in the world; and such person are to be taken for the common enemies of mankind; and they that buy them and use them as beasts, for their mere commodity, and betray, or destroy, or neglect their souls, are fitter to be called incarnate devils than Christians, though they be no Christians whom they so abuse.[49]

The freedom of the human will is a dominant theme in Baxter's interpretation of slavery. He emphasizes that people must "forfeit life or liberty" to participate in slavery. Moreover, Baxter appears incensed at individuals who dehumanize slaves through the treatment of them as mere

48. Baxter, *Christian Directory*, 216; Scherer, *Slavery and the Churches*, 36.

49. Baxter, *Christian Directory*, 217.

animals, entertainment, or property. Reminiscent of Fox, Baxter recognizes the importance of honoring the slave's humanity and constantly proclaiming their spiritual right to receive the gospel message. Baxter's views stressed an interpretation of theological ethics that structured the Christian life to glorify God despite a person's social standing. *Incarnate devils* were those self-righteous Christians, being self-deceived, who intentionally justified slavery to fulfill their sociopolitical self-interest. These proslavery Christians practiced immorality despite what they knew Christianity advocated to be a set of beliefs and lifestyles that were pleasing to their God.

The importance of nurturing the slave's humanity was a pressing issue for Baxter. He vehemently argued that no human should be treated as an animal. Furthermore, regardless of the events that made people slaves, Baxter continually reminded the Christian masters that everyone was spiritually equal. He maintained, "Remember that they have immortal souls, and are equally capable of salvation with yourselves. And therefore you have no power to do anything which shall hinder their salvation.[50]" This complements Baxter's emphasis on God's sovereignty that involves his self-interest in the salvation of every person on earth. Thus, human self-interest must submit to, as well as be guided by, the self-interests of God: "Therefore, God's interest is them and by them must be served first."[51] However, Barbadian Christianity, like other forms of proslavery Christianity, rejected most traditional biblical principles as being applicable to the African slaves. Proslavery Christianity had racialized Christianity, and it justified a qualitative judgment upon the nature of humanity that correlated to its supposed *worthiness* of the gospel message. Aware of this, Baxter issued a stern rebuke,

> Those therefore that keep their negroes and slaves from hearing God's Word, and from becoming Christians, because by the law they shall then be either made free, or they shall lose part of their service, do openly profess rebellion against God, and contempt of Christ the Redeemer of souls, and a contempt of the souls of men, and indeed they declare, that their worldly profit is their treasure and their God.[52]

50. Baxter, *Christian Directory*, 212.
51. Baxter, *Christian Directory*, 214.
52. Baxter, *Christian Directory*, 213.

Baxter was conscious of certain laws that stated conversion into Christianity produced sociopolitical freedom or severely limited the service of the enslaved. However, this was unimportant to him in relation to the Christian's responsibility to preach the gospel to everyone. Sociopolitical laws did not transcend God's will and word. Thus, anyone who prioritized their sociopolitical self-interest above God's self-interest was interpreted as being in rebellion against him. Baxter argued that proslavery Christians who withheld the gospel from their slaves were committing idolatry, in that materialism became their God and the principles of economics defined their morality.[53]

Yet, Baxter's stance regarding slavery should not be romanticized. He was a product of colonialism and displayed subtle contradictions in his beliefs about slavery. He did not completely condemn the institution. Baxter held Eurocentric notions and a paternalistic understanding of scripture. Nevertheless, he aggressively advocated for the acknowledgment, respect, and nurturing of the slaves' humanity, as well as their divine right to hear the gospel message of Jesus Christ. Historian Thomas Drake states, "Seventeenth-century Puritan thinking on slavery went no further than Richard Baxter carried it, and few Puritans paid any attention to his words."[54] Baxter's constructive theology of slavery reform demonstrates that other European Christians, besides Fox, opposed proslavery through similar theological principles.

However, the Quakers' struggle within Barbados did not end with Fox's initial visit and call for slavery reform. Fox's protégé, William Edmondson, would take a radical stance against slavery that influenced many people to critically reflect upon their practice of the institution.

53. Scherer, *Slavery and the Churches*, 37.

54. T. Drake, *Quakers and Slavery in America*, 3. Sadly, this was the same fate of George Fox's principles of slavery reform among the Quakers, and of the reception of John Wesley's (1703–91) rebuke of slavery within Methodism. Twenty-seven years would pass before another Puritan would confront the institution of slavery and issue a stern rebuke against its bedfellow, proslavery Christianity. Sewall (1652–1730), the famous Puritan Salem witch judge, initiated eighteenth-century antislavery Christian discourse with his pamphlet *The Selling of Joseph* (1700).

WILLIAM EDMONDSON'S SECOND TRIP TO BARBADOS: ANTISLAVERY FERVOR TO AMERICA

William Edmondson returned to Barbados in 1675.[55] Little had changed since his previous visit with Fox and Hooton. The authorities of Barbados remained apathetic toward Fox's rebuke of their immorality and the dehumanizing treatment of their slaves. A small number of Quakers that rebelled against the Barbadian authorities, and disavowed any participation into slavery, had to continually endure a relative degree of persecution. Edmondson, without hesitation, continued in the new Quaker tradition of protesting slavery. He preached the gospel to the slaves, held integrated/interracial church services, actively sought the humane treatment of the slaves, and encouraged their masters to repent for their immoral lifestyle.

The planter elites always expressed a sense of fear and paranoia regarding the potentiality of a slave rebellion. This influenced the development of a militia and the determination to maintain order by any means necessary. Yet, the presence of an armed force could not completely quell the fears of a slave revolt. These fears were intensified by the actions of the Quakers as they sought slavery reform, which eventually developed into an influential antislavery position within the colony. Antislavery Quakers stood in complete opposition to the Barbadian authorities and, as a result, garnered intense suspicion. Previously, George Fox had to defend the Quakers from slander as some became fearful that they were seeking to incite slave insurrections. Edmondson found himself in a similar situation.

Edmondson was accused of being a secret Irish Jesuit by a Barbadian priest named Ramsey. Ramsey had spread rumors that Edmondson wanted to create social disorder and instability within Barbados. He was depicted as punishing the slaves through his supposed heretical sermons of freedom and equality in Christ. Evidently, Ramsey was successful in preying on the fears of the colony. He convinced the governor of Barbados that Edmondson was encouraging the slaves to revolt. Upon hearing this, Edmondson sought to discuss these rumors with the governor:[56]

> He was informed that I was making the Negros Christians, and would make them rebel and cut their Throats. I told him, It was a good Work to bring them to Knowledge of God and Christ Jesus, and to believe in him that died for them, and for

55. T. Drake, *Quakers and Slavery in America*, 8.
56. Aptheker, "Quakers and Negro Slavery," 333.

> all Men, and that would keep them from rebelling or cutting any Man's Throat; but if they did rebel and cut their Throats, as he said, it would be through their own Doings, in keeping them in Ignorance, and under Oppression, giving them Liberty to be common with Women (like Beasts) and on the other Hand start them for want of Meat and Clothes convenient, so giving them Liberty in that which God restrained, and restraining them in that which God allowed and afforded to all Men, which was Meat and Clothes.[57]

For Edmondson, Ramsey was utterly misguided. A slave revolt would not occur through preaching the gospel message. Edmondson argued that Christian principles of freedom and equality would not incite anyone to violence. However, a revolt would occur from the masters dehumanizing and oppressing their slaves. Edmondson firmly believed the slaves were treated inhumanely. They were forced to endure periods of starvation and neglect of other necessary provisions. This was the same argument that Fox levied upon the proslavery Christians on their first visit to the colony.

Cautiousness, timidity, and uncertainty did not characterize Edmondson's disposition. Reminiscent of Fox, Edmondson leveled harsh critiques upon the religious and sociopolitical elites of Barbados. Apparently, Barbados practiced and endorsed so much immorality that he compared the colony to the biblical city of Sodom:

> The Lord God of Heaven and Earth is highly provoked to Anger and Wrath against this Island: For if ever the Sins of Sodom cried to the Lord, then no doubt but the Sins of Barbados cry aloud in his righteous Ears, who certainly will punish Wickedness. O that you Rulers would consider and put a Stop to these Things which undoubtedly kindle the Wrath of God, and will bring Judgments upon this Island before many may be aware of it.[58]

Edmondson's remarks were a complete affront to the religious and sociopolitical authorities. He further stated that sexual perversion was so common in Barbados that, "one Man having several Women, and one Woman having several Men, and none is sorry nor mourns for these Wickednesses committed against the Lord."[59] Edmondson only stayed

57. Besse, *Collection*, 305–6.

58. Besse, *Collection*, 306.

59. Besse, *Collection*, 306.

in Barbados for five months. He then traveled to America to continue with his missionary journey.

Edmondson's experience in Barbados shaped his views on slavery. In America, he proclaimed in 1676 that slavery was biblically and theologically a sin. This was a step his mentor, George Fox, had not taken. Edmondson also advocated that the masters of Maryland, New England, and Virginia should emancipate their slaves. This appeal had evangelistic assumptions, in the sense that he believed it would bring the slaves to Christ. In contrast, Fox had only suggested that the slaves be set free after a considerable amount of time. However, Edmondson maintained that the mere *possession* of a human was sinful and that any act of oppression was an affront to the gospel. Edmondson was a pioneer and radical leader in establishing what was an emergent European American antislavery discourse.[60] From Edmondson, we also witness a form of evangelism that contributes to the development of colonial African American Christianity.

60. T. Drake, *Quakers and Slavery*, 9, 14–15; Gregg, *English Transplanted*, 164; Scherer, *Slavery and the Churches*, 41–42.

7

The Fragmentation of Colonial Whiteness

Antislavery Reform and Antislavery Christianity During the Seventeenth Century, Part 2

FOX'S THIRD ATTEMPT: A SLIGHTLY DIFFERENT APPROACH

George Fox published his third discourse on slavery in 1676. It was a collection of thoughts and sermons he preached during his visit in 1671. The pamphlet, *Gospel Family-Order, Being a Short Discourse Concerning Ordering of Families, Both of Whites, Blacks and Indians*, continued where his 1672 diatribe had ended. Many of the same themes were present but with less emotion and intensity. The style of *Gospel Family-Order* is biblically centered in its approach. Fox still adheres to his personal religious convictions, which are expressed through three biblical principles. First, all Christian masters must acknowledge their sinful ways and understand the full spiritual consequences of neglecting their responsibility unto God. Second, this responsibility involves the spiritual salvation of everyone under their earthly authority, including the slaves. Third, any neglect of this responsibility brings them and their entire household under the wrath of God.

In *Gospel Family-Order*, Fox employed the narrative of Abraham to teach the spiritual responsibility of evangelizing the entire household, even the slaves. Fox stated that Abraham was a righteous man in God's eyes. Even in practicing slavery, Abraham submitted to God's commandments of bringing the entire household into his spiritual family and supplied proper provisions for everyone under his authority. To a certain extent, even this basic interpretation could be viewed as an Old Testament form of religious paternalism. Yet, Fox perceived the Barbadian Christian masters as living in complete disobedience to God. The Christian masters had neglected and rejected this testimony of scripture. Fox also used the figure of Abraham and the Old Testament principle of *circumcision* as precursors of the New Testament commandments of evangelism and salvation:

> Yea, all Sons and Daughters, Masters or Mistresses of Families must be circumcised *with the Spirit, that puts off the Body of Death*, the Sins of the Flesh with the Circumcision of the Spirit, *that is not made with Hands*; and also all that you have bought with Money, all *Strangers*, and all that are born in your Houses (of Strangers) which are not of your own Seed, must you not bring all these to the Circumcision of the Spirit? Else how are you the Friends of God, as Abraham was, who obeyed God; and therefore call upon all your Families, and your Servants whom you bought for Money, and those that were born of them in your families, and let them be circumcised, and endeavour to bring them to that which doth circumcise them.[1]

One of the important emphases in Fox's statement is the concern for the *stranger*. The stranger was interpreted as a non-Israelite who may or may not have been a slave. God's concern for the stranger transcended Abraham's self-interest in the institution of slavery. All strangers were to be treated as family if they were under a man's authority and/or accepted YHWH as their God. The biblical figure of Joshua was employed by Fox to reinforce the legitimacy of this interpretation. Facing an immoral community that surrounded him, Joshua made a strong religious statement in defiance of them, "But if serving the Lord seems undesirable to you, then choose for yourselves this day whom you will serve, whether the gods your ancestors served beyond the Euphrates, or the gods of the Amorites, in whose land you are living, But as for me and my household, we will serve the Lord" (Josh 24:15). Fox interprets Joshua as representative of a righteous person exercising their authority to determine the religious direction of their household. Thus, the supposed Christian masters

1. Fox, *Gospel Family-Order*, 4.

of Barbados were to make the same decision. They were to either remain in their immoral state of self-dehumanization and the dehumanization of their household, or to repent and treat their slaves not as beasts but as equals in the eyes of God. If anyone chose to remain in their sin, they were to fall under God's judgment.[2]

A surprising point in Fox's discourse is the *suggestion* that Christian masters emancipate their slaves after a considerable number of years. He referenced the Old Testament law regarding the Year of Jubilee (Lev 25:8–13).[3] Influenced by this, Fox states,

> And to close up all, let me tell you, it will doubtless be very acceptable to the Lord, if so be that Masters and Families here would deal so with their Servants, the Negroes and Blacks, whom they have bought with their Money, to let them go free after a considerable Term of Years, if they have served them faithfully, and when they go, and are made free, let them not go away empty-handed.[4]

However, it must be noted that Fox does not call for the end of slavery but merely advocates the biblical justification for emancipating slaves after an allotted time. He only seeks to introduce some reform regarding the humane treatment of the slaves, the gospel being preached to them, and the repentance of the slave masters whose sin was causing great disorder within society. Fox could be interpreted as advocating a passive transition from slavery to indentured servitude. The phrase "considerable Term of Years" is rather ambiguous.

Fox was a strong pioneer in seventeenth-century slavery reform discourse. He established a foundation upon which his peers and many others in the eighteenth century built. Fox's focus on slavery reform directly influenced Edmondson's call for an antislavery movement within Quakerism.

Barbados was a place where proslavery Christianity, and the seared conscience of its advocates, awakened the conscience of slavery reformers and antislavery proponents. Fox, Baxter, and Edmondson brought their advocacy for slavery reform from England to Barbados and America to preach against the institution in various ways. These ripples in the ocean continued to develop into noticeable waves as other influential Christians developed similar positions.

2. Fox, *Gospel Family-Order*, 8–13.
3. Fox, *Gospel Family-Order*, 16.
4. Fox, *Gospel Family-Order*, 15–16.

PATH TO AMERICA: MORGAN GODWYN, A MINISTER TO BARBADOS AND VIRGINIA

There were strong connections between Barbados and the American colonies. Plantation masters, overseers, and most slaves relocated from Barbados to colonies such as New England, Pennsylvania, South Carolina, and Virginia. Moreover, there were many evangelists, missionaries, and preachers who traveled similar paths. The Anglican minister Morgan Godwyn (1640–ca. 1690) was one of these people. In 1665, Godwyn arrived in Virginia, and after two years, he returned home to England. Roughly ten years would pass before he traveled once again to do ministry in Barbados.[5] It was in Barbados that Godwyn stumbled upon a Quaker antislavery pamphlet (possibly from Fox or Edmondson), and it impacted him to the extent that his views regarding the institution began to change.

Godwyn would eventually publish two pamphlets on slavery reform. *The Negro's and Indian Advocate, Suing for their Admission into the Church*, was published in 1680.[6] During 1681, Godwyn published a condensed version with fresher insight, entitled *A Supplement to the Negro's and Indian Advocate.*[7] Godwyn sought to establish three principles within his work. First, he argued that masters and slaves were equal in the context of an individual's natural rights to hear and practice religion. The slave should be able to exercise those rights, and "of which 'tis most unjust in any part to deprive them."[8] Second, he maintained that Christianity adamantly promoted religious and spiritual equality among all humans. Any objection to this was based primarily on human "inconvenience." Godwyn determined that an individual's inconvenience was defined by a set of self-interests. Therefore, he argued that an individual's self-interest did not have greater significance than God's self-interest for the slave. Any attempt to elevate a person's self-interest over God's desires is a renunciation of their Christian identity. Last, the inconvenience of the master was interpreted as unjustified upon examination. The rational thinking, humane behavior, and overall existence of the slaves were used

5. T. Drake, *Quakers and Slavery*, 2–3; Scherer, *Slavery and the Churches*, 31–33.

6. Godwyn, *Negro's and Indian Advocate.*

7. Godwyn, *Supplement*; Gregg, *Englishmen Transplanted*, 161–62, 164; Jernegan, "Slavery and Conversion," 509; Jordan, *White over Black*, 97, 229–31.

8. Godwyn, *Negro's and Indians*, 9.

by Godwyn to reveal the depths of their master's irrational beliefs.[9] Godwyn defiantly preached the gospel and baptized the slaves of Barbados as he constantly referenced their universal applicability.

Godwyn also sought to understand the masters' point of view in the context of their relationship with the slaves. In one sense, his pamphlets of reform were polemics against their proslavery beliefs based upon refuting the rationale of the slave masters. For example, Godwyn recounts a discussion with a Christian woman regarding a slave's baptism: "With no small passion and vehemancy, and that by a Religious person (for so in all things else she appeared), that I might as well Baptize a Puppy, as a certain young Negro."[10] We witness the extent of how proslavery advocates interpreted the humanity of Africans in relation to spiritual salvation and basic Christian tenets. It was common to associate or reduce African humanity to an animal. The Christian woman could not accept any notion of equality with a slave. Nor could she accept any religious and spiritual significance in baptizing a supposed inferior human. Godwyn added, "And another of the same sex, upon my baptizing a Male Negro of hers, of about thirty Years old, speaking English plainly, and earnestly beseeching it; caused this message to be delivered to me, That Baptism, I was to understand was to one of those no more beneficial, than to her Black Bitch."[11]

Godwyn showed that racism was present among both genders. Men and women expressed the same beliefs and emotions regarding inequality with the slaves. He was adamant in showing the extent to which the Barbadian elites were self-deceived. Generally, slaves were depicted as being so ignorant that it would be relatively impossible to teach them the English language. For Godwyn, this was absurd. The slave whom he baptized was "speaking English plainly." Despite this, the master believed it was pointless to baptize her slave. Godwyn seemed continually dumbfounded toward anyone who held this perspective. For him, no sensible person abused an animal that they valued. Yet, regarding the Christian masters, Godwyn argued that the masters were ultimately "treating their slaves with far less Humanity than they do their Cattle."[12]

9. Godwyn, *Negro's and Indians*, 7.

10. Godwyn, *Negro's and Indians*, 38.

11. Godwyn, *Negro's and Indians*, 38.

12. Godwyn, *Negro's and Indians*, 40; see also Gregg, *Englishmen Transplanted*, 161–62, 164.

Godwyn also accused the Christian masters of manipulating their slaves, advocating that they would not accept Christianity as their religion. Supposedly, the slaves were innately hostile toward "sophisticated" religion. However, Godwyn adamantly disagreed and argued that any slave who rejected Christianity had possibly done so through the influence of their master. The slaves had to endure countless acts of abuse in the name of Christianity. Furthermore, their masters had outright denied them the opportunity to hear anything about the religion and made Sunday a mandatory workday, which stopped them from attending church services. Godwyn maintained that the slaves were deeply religious. He held that many had theistic beliefs. Thus, converting them was a matter of the master's desires rather than the slave's inclinations to reject Christianity.[13]

The emphasis on the humanity of the slaves was a consistent issue during colonialism. For the slave masters, the ability and desire to *season* or *break-in* the slaves were crucial to managing a slave economy, as well as to developing a system of human subjugation. Godwyn was aware of this and sought to provide an alternative perspective that explained the masters' reluctance to Christianize their slaves. He did not view it as a matter of economics. Rather, he considered the reluctance of slave owners to be centered on a refusal to acknowledge the slaves' humanity as equal to their own:

> One thing more there remains to be added, of which, tho they may be most afraid, yet they carefully keep it to themselves, and that is the possibility of their Slaves Expectation, not of Freedom, but of more merciful Usage from them. (which is but reason they should have, whether made Christians or not,) As, That their frequent Emasculatings, Amputations of Legs, cropping off of Ears (and of Heads too), feant allowance for Food and Cloaths, and (often) no less marking, than starving them to Death, and their unmerciful Correction of them, will not be so commendably practices upon them, when (nor now by) Christians, as they are thought safe and allowable in their present State of Brutality and Gentilism.[14]

Godwyn describes a disturbing list of abuses which the slaves had to endure. The male slaves had undergone emotional, physical, and psychological trauma throughout their subjugation. Sadly, Godwyn implies

13. Godwyn, *Negro's and Indians*, 106–7.

14. Godwyn, *Negro's and Indians*, 41.

that some slaves only desired to be treated humanely, and this was rejected by their masters who felt dehumanization was a central means to remaining empowered. Godwyn keenly reveals the irrationality of the masters' perspective, which is centered on the incomprehensibility of senselessly abusing and often destroying the primary source of their labor.

Godwyn was one of a few Christian leaders who argued for the humane religious reform for the slaves to an inhumane quasi-religious institution that was partially sustained by the Christian church.[15] During colonialism, his prophetic voice bore similarity to Baxter, Edmondson, Fox, and others who maintained proslavery Christianity was not a biblically centered contextual expression. Rather, it was a skewed quasi-religious belief system which redefined not only morality and sin but the essence of what it meant to be a human. His experiences in Barbados and Virginia subjected him to the sinful lives of proslavery Christians, and the consequences of their sins, which distorted their perception as well as care for the slaves' humanity. According to Godwyn, this brought proslavery Christians into God's judgment, not his mercy.

Society had generally ignored Godwyn's constructive theology of slavery reform as they did those before him. He provided testimony to the struggle some Anglicans experienced as they fought against proslavery Christianity in Barbados and America. His ministry signifies that Whiteness was never fully corrupt, and it represents a remnant of European Christians who did not become captivated by conceptions of power or socioeconomic self-interests. Godwyn's constructive theology should be recognized as contributing to the development of the European American antislavery discourse. In America, rather than witnessing individual

15. The English merchant Thomas Tryon (1634–1703) was also one of these individuals. He was an English Dissenter who converted from Anabaptism to a more mystical Christian faith. Tryon lived in Barbados for several years during the 1660s. However, it was not until 1684 that he published three tracts on dietary, religious, and slavery reform. *Friendly Advice to the Gentlemen Planters of the East and West Indies* was his first tract that advocated new dietary concerns for the British colonist. Tryon's next two tracts dealt primarily with religious and slavery reform. *The Negro's Complaint of their hard Servitude, and the Cruelties Practiced upon them by divers of their masters professing Christianity in the West Indian Plantations*, according to Amussen, "was written in the voice of a slave objecting to his treatment." Tryon's third tract was titled *A Discourse, in Way of Dialogue, Between an Ethiopian or Negro Slave and a Christian, that was his Master in America*. This tract was written in a way that "offered a slave the opportunity to question his master about the principles of Christianity and then use those principles to question the basis of slavery." Amussen, *Caribbean Exchanges*, 180–81.

voices standing in defiance of systemic slavery, an entire community is united against the inhumane institution.

THE GERMANTOWN PROTEST OF 1688: "WE ARE AGAINST THE TRAFFICK OF MEN-BODY"

William Penn (1644–1718) was a fellow Quaker who was responsible for populating the territory known as Pennsylvania. The territory had a history of practicing slavery well before Penn was awarded it.[16] He could have inherited a small slave economy once the former Dutch territory was under English control. Despite his knowledge of William Edmondson and George Fox's rebuke of proslavery Christianity and calls for reform, Penn saw no contradiction with a Christian participating in the institution. It was only toward the end of his life that he started to question the legitimacy of slavery. Yet, historian Allen Clapp Thomas states, "Penn himself at one time held slaves, and through no fault of his own, appears to have died owning two or three old slaves whom he intended to have set free some years before."[17] Slavery was an accepted institution by many Quakers throughout the surrounding territories. Many successful Quaker businessmen understood the benefits of the institution, and the means of acquiring the necessary slaves to work on their plantations: "The wealthy Quaker merchant James Claypoole, soon after he decided to move his family and business from London to Philadelphia, urgently wrote to his brother Edward in Barbados to request four black slaves."[18] This testifies to the efficiency and notoriety of the Barbadian slave institution and the Christians who supported it.

Penn invited a group of Dutch and German immigrants to America in 1683. They were believed to have been mostly Dutch who fled Holland to Germany from economic and religious persecution. However, there were many Germans among the group as well.[19] Regarding religion, they were former Mennonites converted to Quakerism. Through the leadership of Francis Daniel Pastorius, these immigrants eventually settled in Pennsylvania and founded a place referred to as Germantown.

16. Nash and Soderlund, *Freedom by Degrees*, 9.

17. Thomas, "Attitude of the Society," 266.

18. Nash and Soderlund, *Freedom by Degrees*, 9–10.

19. Pennypacker, "Settlement of Germantown," 18; Fretz, "Germantown Anti-Slavery Petition," 42–59.

Germantown, Pennsylvania, is recognized by many scholars as the location of the first written American antislavery document.[20]

Evidently, a business associate of Penn from Amsterdam by the name of Benjamin Furly requested that Penn refrain from allowing slaves to enter his territory: "Furly's letter to Penn is of particular interest because his clients included the four signers of the 1688 protest," and furthermore "his letter was written in 1683, when Pastorius and the future Germantowners were in contact with him in Rotterdam. It suggests that the Germantowners may have been concerned about slavery in America even before their emigration."[21] Thus, we witness a remnant of antislavery Christians in Europe before their arrival in America. This was a legitimate concern of the Dutch and German immigrants, because of the reputation that many Quakers had as slave-owners in America. In December of 1684, 150 slaves arrived in Philadelphia, Pennsylvania.[22] They were purchased from a known slave ship by the name of *Isabella.* Many of these slaves had possibly come from Barbados.

What became known as the Germantown Protest took place at a Quaker monthly meeting on February 18, 1688. The document was signed by four leaders within the Germantown Quaker community, Pastorius being one of them. The intentions of the group were not only to make a direct stance against slavery, but also to bring their views to the attention of their religious superiors during their Quaker yearly meeting. Thus, the act of defiance within Germantown was not only a personal communal stance, but an evangelistic posture geared toward influencing Quakers around the world. The document itself is concise and clearly displays the beliefs of the Germantown community. The Germantowners adhered to the biblical principles of the Golden Rule, rejected racism, proclaimed care for the slaves' humanity, rebuked the sins of the masters, and believed slavery was an institution of thievery. These principles were originally presented with the discourses of George Fox and William Edmondson.

20. Carey, *From Peace to Freedom*, 72–73; Fisher, "Friends of Humanity," 188. The full document of the Germantown Protest of 1688 can be read in Hughs, *Version of Blackness*, 368–70.

21. Gerbner, "'We Are Against the Traffik of Men-Body,'" 157; Gerbner, "Antislavery in Print," 552–75; Aptheker, "Quakers and Negro Slavery," 334–35.

22. Nash and Soderlund, *Freedom by Degrees*, 10; Jackson, *Let This Voice Be Heard*, 11; Nash, "Slaves and Slaveowners," 226.

A MINUTE AGAINST SLAVERY, ADDRESSED TO GERMANTOWN MONTHLY MEETING, 1688

> This is to ye Monthly Meeting held at Richard Worrell's.
> These are the reasons why we are against the traffick of men-body, as foloweth. Is there any that would be done or handled at this manner? Vis., to be sold or made a slave for all the time of his life? How fearful and faint-hearted are many on sea, when they see a strange vessel, being afraid it should be a Turk, and they should be taken, and sold for slaves into Turkey. Now what is this better done, as Turks doe? Yea, rather it is worse for them, which say they are Christians; for we hear that ye most part of such negers are brought hither against their will and consent, and that many of them are stolen. Now, tho they are black, we can not conceive there is more liberty to have them slaves, as it is to have other white ones. There is a saying that we shall doe to all men like as we will be done ourselves; make no difference of what generation, descent or colour they are. And those who steal or robb men, and those who buy or purchase them, are they not all alike?[23]

The Germantowners sought to establish empathy within the consciences of the Quaker masters. There is a subtle emphasis in their argument on one's natural rights and the theological doctrine of human freewill. This is seen in the reference to violating the slaves' "will and consent." Racist beliefs were also rejected. African slaves were not perceived as inferior based upon his or her skin color, nor did this justify perpetual enslavement. For the Germantowners, slavery was a sinful institution of thievery which violated one's natural will. To buy stolen *goods* makes the purchaser culpable to the original sin of thievery, and it forces them to embody the consequential sin of thievery regarding false ownership of what is not rightfully theirs:

> Here is liberty of conscience wch is right and reasonable; here ought to be liberty of ye body, except of evil-doers, wch is an other case. But to bring men hither, or to rob and sell them against their will, we stand against. In Europe there are many oppressed for conscience sake; and here there are those oppressed who are of a black colour. And we who know than men must not comitt adultery, some do commit adultery, in separating

23. The following quotes are from Society of Friends, "Germantown Friends' Protest."

> wives from their husbands and giving them to others; and some sell the children of these poor creatures to other men. Ah! Doe consider will this thing, you who doe it, if you would be done at this manner?

The Germantowners sought to employ forms of empathetic reasoning that revealed the contradiction and hypocrisy that occasionally develops when the oppressed community gain their freedom, become empowered, and then began to oppress other communities. The Germantowners understood what it meant to be the oppressed of society within Europe, considering they fled Europe because of political and religious persecution. The Germantown community referenced the Christian sin of adultery and the consequential culpability in its practice by destroying one's family structure. They were aware that African mothers and fathers were habitually separated from their families. None were spared from the financial self-interests of their masters.

Despite these sinful practices, many White Christian masters were adamant that Black slaves were immoral brutes, even though they were primarily responsible for creating and benefiting from this supposed immorality:

> And if it is done according to Christianity? You surpass Holland and Germany in this thing. This makes an ill report in all those countries of Europe, where they hear of, that ye Quakers doe here handel men as they handel there ye cattle. And for that reason some have no mind or inclination to come hither. And who shall maintain this your cause, or pleid for it. Truly we can not do so, except you shall inform us better hereof, viz., that Christians have liberty to practise these things. Pray, what thing in the world can be done worse towards us, than if men should rob or steal us away, and sell us for slaves to strange countries; separating husbands from their wives and children. Being now that this is not done in the manner we would be done at therefore we contradict and are against this traffic of men-body. And we who profess that it is not lawful to steal, must, likewise, avoid to purchase such things as are stolen, but rather help to stop this robbing and stealing if possible. And such men ought to be delivered out of ye hands of ye robbers, and set free as well as in Europe. Then is Pennsylvania to have a good report, instead it hath now a bad one for this sake in other countries. Especially whereas ye Europeans are desirious to know in what manner ye Quakers doe rule in their province; and most of them doe look

> upon us with an envious eye. But if this is done well, what shall we say is done evil?

The Germantown Quakers were astonished that slavery could be practiced in the name of Christianity. For them, the amount of oppression created by American slavery had usurped the oppression they experienced in Holland and Germany. Reminiscent of Barbados, Pennsylvania had developed a repulsive reputation which deterred some Europeans from relocating there. For the Germantowners, this stemmed from the fact "that ye Quakers doe here handel men as they handel there ye cattle." Through subtle sarcasm the Germantown Quakers questioned the supposed Christian liberty to oppress or dehumanize another human. The freedom of an individual did not create the moral right to reduce or deny the freedom of another person. The Germantowners sought to install empathy within the proslavery Quaker masters, as they challenged them to reflect upon their lives if they too were enslaved and separated from their families.

> If once these slaves (wch they say are so wicked and stubborn men) should join themselves,—fight for their freedom,—and handel their masters and mastrisses as they did handel them before; will these masters and mastrisses take the sword at hand and war against these poor slaves, licke, we are able to believe, some will not refuse to doe; or have these negers not so much right to fight for their freedom, as you have to keep them slaves?
>
> Now consider will this thing, if it is good or bad? And in case you find it to be good to handle these blacks at that manner, we desire and require you hereby lovingly, that you may inform us herein, which at this time never was done, viz., that Christians have such a liberty to do so. To the end we shall be be satisfied in this point, and satisfie likewise our good friends and acquaintances in our natif country, to whose it is a terror, or fairful thing, that men should be handeld so in Pennsylvania.
>
> This is from our meeting at Germantown, held ye 18 of the 2 month, 1688, to be delivered to the Monthly Meeting at Richard Worrel's.
>
> Garret henderich
> Derick up de graeff
> Francis daniell Pastorius
> Abraham up Den Graef

The Germantowners separated themselves from the wider proslavery Quaker communities. For them, proslavery Quakerism had regressed into a form of Christianity that rejected traditional Quaker convictions. An example of this regression would be the use of violence as a means of enslaving another human. This touched the consciousness of the Germantowners because of their strict adherence to pacifism. Freedom, as the Germantowners perceived it, was based upon human equality, and all humans were equal in God's eyes. Therefore, to enslave another person was more than a violation of their natural rights, but a violation of a divine edict. The enslavement of another person created a variety of incalculable consequences that negatively affected the enslaver and enslaved. An example is the skewed and irrational logic that justifies the dehumanizing enslavement of another human. The Germantowners established a logical sequence of critical reflection that associated the Turkish enslavement of Europeans with the European enslavement of Africans. If Europeans used violence to remain free, or achieve emancipation from Turkish slavery, then violence was permissible for the slaves to use for their goal of liberation. To phrase it another way, pertaining to another context, if violence was used as a means of creating injustice, it could also be used in a just manner to restore equality. Thus, for the Germantowners, there was always the possibility and legitimacy of the enslaved using violence as a means of restoring their freedom.

The Germantowners were a religious people primarily focused on worshiping God and establishing a new life in America apart from the dehumanizing oppression they experienced in Europe. Furthermore, they were not interested in the enslavement of people to achieve any economic and sociopolitical self-interest. For them, to do so would have created a similar form of oppression that they fled from in Europe. Additionally, they never expressed any infatuation with romanticized ideologies of cultural or human superiority. They were a community of integrated Dutch and German immigrants who shared a religious heritage in Anabaptism. These immigrants relocated to Pennsylvania to enjoy economic, political, and religious freedom that was withheld from them in Europe.

However, the Germantown Protest was eventually subjected to the same treatment as previous antislavery discourses: it was ignored. The Germantowners had their request granted. Their petition was brought before the committee of the Philadelphia quarterly meeting. The committee determined to postpone a review of the document until the yearly meeting, citing that the topic was too *weighty* to be discussed at that present time. During the yearly meeting, it was postponed again until the next year. There are no records indicating that the Germantown petition was ever formally discussed in a Quaker meeting. The document had mysteriously disappeared, only to resurface roughly ninety years later.[24] It was not a coincidence that the Germantown petition was dismissed. Quakerism during that period was not distinct from the rest of Christendom. Throughout colonialism, Christians within relatively every denomination had overwhelmingly embraced racism and slavery.

The Germantowners had situated themselves within a suppressed legacy of European American antislavery Christian discourse. Their petition is recognized as the first to be written in America. Yet, this document would go on to influence the second American antislavery document, written by a controversial Quaker by the name of George Keith.

GEORGE KEITH: THE REBELLIOUS ANTISLAVERY ADVOCATE

The controversial George Keith (1638–1716) was a Scottish missionary born in Peterhead, Aberdeenshire, Scotland. He was educated at Marischal College in Aberdeen, Scotland. Keith converted from Presbyterianism to Quakerism during the 1660s. Like many before him, Keith had traveled to Barbados, preaching Quakerism and experiencing the barbarity of Barbadian slavery. In 1680, Keith had relocated to East Jersey as a surveyor-general. He would later move to Pennsylvania in 1688, the same year as the Germantown Protest.[25] Keith became a controversial figure because of his political and religious disagreements regarding the direction of the movement. Growing increasingly frustrated, he decided to present many of his concerns as well as political and religious beliefs during Quaker monthly meetings. However, on each occasion, Keith was met with intense dismay and opposition. For example, during a yearly meeting, Keith presented his beliefs regarding church polity:

> Included were proposals for a confession of faith to be required of those seeking admission to the Society, for the election of elders and deacons within each meeting, and for the silencing of persons "raw and unseasoned" or unsure in their beliefs. In

24. Gerbner, "Antislavery in Print," 562–63; Carey, *From Peace to Freedom*, 72–73; D. B. Davis, *Problem of Slavery*, 337–38; T. Drake, *Quakers and Slavery*, 12–13.

25. Nash, *Quakers and Politics*, 145; D. B. Davis, *Problems of Slavery*, 338–39.

> addition, Keith stressed the need to place more emphasis upon the Bible as a fountain of spiritual growth and less on hidden sources—"the light within" which Quakers taught was residual in every individual.[26]

As a passionate Quaker, Keith had continued his radical calls for reform well into the following year. Politically, he believed that Quakerism lacked adequate organizational structure. For him, this allowed people such as fellow Quaker Thomas Lloyd the opportunity to satisfy their political self-interest. Doctrinal disagreements between the Quaker elite and Keith had centered in part on his Christology. For Gerbner, "Keith believed that Philadelphia Quakers had downplayed the relevance of the scriptures and that the Ministerial Assembly had acquired too much power."[27] Eventually, fellow Quaker William Stockdale had delivered a charge of heresy against Keith. This created more tension between him and the Quaker elite. Keith was later disowned at the Philadelphia monthly and quarterly meetings during 1692, as well as the London yearly meeting in 1695.[28] Through his religious fervor, Keith had established his own sect referred to by Quakers as the "Keithians," or as Keith named them, the "Christian Quakers."

Keith is recognized as creating the second written antislavery document on American soil. *An Exhortation and Caution to Friends Concerning buying and keeping of Negroes* was published in 1693, five years after the Germantown Protest. The two documents share similar themes and may have possibly been influenced by the same group of people. Gerbner suggests that Keith was present during the signing of the Germantown Protest. His attendance indicates that he may have had close relations with the Germantowners, and that they shared similar religious convictions regarding the institution of slavery. Gerbner maintains,

> The philosophical similarity between the *Exhortation* and the "Germantown Protest"—and the appearance of the Exhortation in the first place—is not a coincidence. At least twelve of the Keith's Christian Quakers were residents of Germantown, and one of Keith's strongest supporters, Abraham op den Graeff, signed the 1688 protest.[29]

26. Nash, *Quakers and Politics*, 146.
27. Gerbner, "Antislavery in Print," 567; Nash, *Quakers and Politics*, 147.
28. T. Drake, *Quakers and Slavery*, 14; Vipont, *Story of Quakerism*, 137.
29. Gerbner, "Antislavery in Print," 568; Carey, *From Peace to Freedom*, 85–86.

Gerbner continues to suggest that Keith's *Exhortation* was merely a linguistically polished and expanded version of the Germantown Protest. Furthermore, she implies that Keith did not write the pamphlet alone. Rather, the *Exhortation* was a collective effort of Keith and the community he had identified with. Gerbner's views are compelling. This is considering that Keith moved to Pennsylvania in 1688, developed close relationships with the Germantowners, and shared similar convictions regarding slavery. Keith was indeed a radical thinker, and every attempt at reform he sought to enact was ardently opposed. Quakers who sympathized with him may have feared disownment or other forms of rebuke for their identification with Keith. During this period, most Quakers were slave owners. Antislavery Quakers, who were the minority, were either ignored or disowned. This can be seen in the general reactions to George Fox, William Edmondson, and the Germantowners. It is very likely that Gerbner is correct. The first two antislavery documents in America may have, in part, come from the same communities.

AN EXHORTATION AND CAUTION TO FRIENDS CONCERNING BUYING OR KEEPING OF NEGROES

> Seeing our Lord Jesus Christ hath tasted Death for every Man, and given himself a Ransom for all, to be testified in due time, and that his Gospel of Peace, Liberty and Redemption from Sin, Bondage and all Oppression, is free'y to be preached unto all, without Exception, and that Negroes, Blacks and Taunies are a real part of Mankind, for whom Christ hath shed his precions Blood, and are capable of Salvation, as well as White Men.[30]

Keith, being influenced by Fox, had emphasized the universal nature of the gospel, and referenced that the Negroes as well as Taunies were worthy to hear its message. The gospel was not only for everyone, but it was also designed to liberate everyone from *all oppression*; it was not a means to oppress others. Furthermore, Keith reaffirms the humanity of the enslaved, which was aggressively denied by proslavery Christians: "Negroes, Blacks, and Taunies are a real part of Mankind." European Christianity had created and imposed a qualitative standard upon non-European humanity. They judged the non-European world as an inferior existence and, therefore, unworthy of hearing the gospel message. Keith

30. Keith, *Exhortation and Caution*, 1.

merely reasserted that all humans were equal and shared a non-exclusive right to experience communion with God:

> Therefore we judge it necessary that all faithful Friends should discover themselves to be true Christians by having the Fruits of the Spirit of Christ, which are Love, Mercy, Goodness, and Compassion towards all in Misery, and that suffer Oppression and severe Usage, so far as in them is possible to care and relieve them, and let them free of their hard Bondage, whereby it may be hoped, that many of them will be gained by their beholding these good Works of sincere Christians, and prepared thereby, through the Preaching the Gospel of Christ, to imbrace the true Faith of Christ.[31]

For Keith and his community, only those who are *true believers* in Christ can bear his image, and they will embody these biblical truths through the fruit of the Spirit (Gal 5:22–23). The fruit of the Spirit was emphasized as a means of creating empathy toward the slaves. Keith identified the slaves as all who experienced misery, oppression, and extreme labor. Thus, for him, any person who claimed to be a *true Christian* had to treat the slaves in a humane manner. This ultimately implied the eventual emancipation of the slaves. Emancipating the slaves was representative of a loving act of evangelism that could influence the slaves to convert to Christianity.

The reference to *true Christians* may be a subtle questioning of the proslavery Christians' claim of communion with God. The insinuation leads to the critique that proslavery Christians may not have had an authentic Christian faith at all. This line of reasoning was originally employed by Fox as he sarcastically questioned the Barbadian proslavery Christians' identities as ministers of God. Nevertheless, Keith continued to argue:

> Therefore, in true Christian Love, we earnestly recommend it to all our Friends and Brethren, Not to buy any Negros, unless it were on purpose to let them free, and that such who have bought any, and have them at present, after some reasonable time of moderate Service they have had of them, or may have of them, that may reasonably answer to the Charge of what they have laid out, especially in keeping Negroes Children born in their House, or—house, when under Age, that after a reasonable time of service to answer that Charge, they may let them at

31. Keith, *Exhortation and Caution*, 2.

> Liberty, and during the time they have them, to teach them to read, and give them a Christian Education.[32]

The influence of George Fox can be seen in Keith's view of emancipation. Fox originally advocated the necessity of educating the slaves. It was also Fox who initially discussed a limited term of service for the slaves. He disagreed with the notion of lifetime servitude and recommended a term of seven years. Yet, subtle controversy developed after Fox's death when revisions were made to his pamphlets. The seven-year suggestion was ambiguously revised as "a considerable term of service."

Keith advocates refraining from participating in slavery just as William Edmondson and the Germantowners did previously. In part, radical Keithian reform developed by stating that a slave should only be bought for the sole purpose of emancipating them. It may be argued that an antislavery Quaker tradition advocated the eventual liberation and educational empowerment of the slaves. Keithian reform could be interpreted as a revivalism of Fox and Edmondson's views. Keith maintained that Fox established principles that the movement steadily rejected. Gradually, Quakerism became corrupted by various obsessions regarding its leaders' sociopolitical self-interests and the rejection of practicing orthodox Quaker doctrines.

There were four principles that structured the Keithian antislavery discourse. First, Keith continued to advocate that slavery was an institution of thievery. Since slavery was a sin, any Christian who practiced slavery was to come under God's wrath, as stated in Exod 21:16. "He who kidnaps a man, whether he sells him or he is found in his possession, shall surely be put to death." Thus, for Keith, ignorance was not justification for participating in slavery. Anyone who was in possession of stolen goods must seek adequate restoration of that property. Since all humans are the possession of God, restoration in this context is the emancipation of the slave and the hope that they would convert to Christianity. Second, the Quaker emphasis on the Golden Rule is discussed. The Golden Rule functions as the spiritually transcendent principle that negates any cultural, racial, and sociopolitical notion of human superiority.[33] This was originally emphasized by the Germantowners.

The third Keithian antislavery principle stems from Deut 23:15–16, "You shall not hand over to his master a slave who has escaped from

32. Keith, *Exhortation and Caution*, 3.

33. Keith, *Exhortation and Caution*, 2.

his master to you. He shall live with you in your midst, in the place which he shall choose in one of your towns where it pleases him; you shall not mistreat him." This is one of the most radical scriptures used in antislavery discourse. It transcends any attempt at empathetic reasoning and establishes a conception of mutual identification. Emancipation and restoration are embodied in the relationship between the believer and the enslaved. The believer is called to rebel against any sociopolitical custom or law of slavery. The slave is emancipated in community with the believer and is given the option of dwelling among them in a place of their choosing. Furthermore, the slave's reintroduction into bondage, which was very common, was prohibited as it was not permissible to enslave them within the community of believers. This principle stands in opposition to the New Testament Epistle to Philemon. In it, the apostle Paul was sought by a non-Christian slave by the name of Onesimus. Onesimus fled his abusive Christian master, Philemon. Onesimus converts to Christianity, and Paul sends him back to his master as an equal within Christendom. However, their sociopolitical relationship as master and slave had not changed. Fourth, no Christian could oppress the slave in any way (Deut 24:14–15):

> You shall not oppress a hired servant who is poor and needy, whether he is one of our countrymen or one of your aliens who is in your land in your towns. You shall give him his wages on his day before the sun sets, for he is poor and sets his heart on it; so that he will not cry against you to the Lord and it become sin in you.

The apex of dehumanizing the slaves had developed from the belief that they were less human than their masters. Consequently, this belief in a qualitative difference in humanity influenced the masters to treat their slaves as animals. One of the staggering realities was that masters habitually withheld adequate provisions for their slaves. Many slaves experienced insufficient clothing and food throughout the year to the extent of starvation. Keith was aware of this as he had visited Barbados, and experienced similar situations in America. He maintained,

> And many that buy them do exceedingly afflict them and oppress them, not only by continual hard Labour, but by cruel Whippings; and other cruel Punishments, and by short allowances of Food, some Planters in Barbados and Jamaica, 'tis said, keeping one hundred of them, and some more, and some less,

> and giving them hardly any thing more than they rasie on a little piece of Ground appointed them, on which they work for themselves the seventh dayes of the Week in the after-noon, and on the firss days, to raise their own Provisions.[34]

Keith asserts the irrationality of the slaves' labor throughout the week. Slaves were generally forced to work six to six and a half days on their masters' crops. They were only allowed one day, or the afternoon of that seventh day, to attend to their own small piece of land. This schedule made it relatively impossible for them to attend church services on the seventh day, considered Sunday.

Last, Keith believed that the judgment of God would fall upon all who practiced slavery. For him, Europe was representative of the famous corrupt nation within the Bible, Babylon. Keith argued that the wrath of God would come, "Because Slave and Souls of men are some of the Merchandise of Babylon by which the Merchants of the Earth are made Rich; but those Riches which they heaped together, through the cruel Oppression of these miserable Creatures, will be a means to draw Gods judgment upon them."[35] Keith's *Exhortation* was eventually ignored by the greater Quaker community. Defeated and possibly full of bitterness, he returned to England in 1694. In 1695 the Quaker yearly meeting had completely severed ties with him. In 1699 Keith converted to Anglicanism. He began working for the Society for the Promotion of Knowledge and returned to Pennsylvania as a missionary in 1702. For roughly two years Keith voiced his anti-Quaker concerns throughout the American colonies.

Keith's antislavery and reform stances were not entirely new to Quakerism. In many ways, he merely continued in the traditions established by George Fox and William Edmondson. Yet, Keith's attack upon corrupt Quaker politics, underdeveloped organizational structure, and doctrinal comprehension and his call to end slavery had indeed influenced American Quakerism. His aggressive ministry had undoubtedly pricked the callous conscience of proslavery Quakers. For others, Keith merely provided them with the courage to stand for their convictions.

34. Keith, *Exhortation and Caution*, 5.
35. Keith, *Exhortation and Caution*, 6.

GROWING DISDAIN: THE SPREADING OF QUAKER ANTISLAVERY AND REFORM DISCOURSE

In 1696, there was an increase in Quaker concern regarding the practice of slavery. Two prominent Quakers by the names of Cadwalader Morgan of Merion and William Southeby of Philadelphia had their papers discussed during the Philadelphia yearly meeting of that year. Each had articulated concerns regarding the importation of slaves into Pennsylvania and educating any slave that remained within the territory.[36] Morgan and Southeby's outcry had influenced the Philadelphia yearly meeting to suggest, "It's the advice of this meeting that Friends be careful not to encourage the bringing in of any more Negroes."[37] Southeby was disturbed by this, interpreting the Philadelphia yearly meeting as taking a passive stance against slavery. The Quaker elite appeared more concerned with their safety and self-interest. The slave population was continually growing in Pennsylvania. With this came the normative increase in fear of a potential slave insurrection. Undeterred, Southeby would intensify his antislavery discourse.

In 1698, another influential Quaker by the name of Robert Pyle from Chester County, Pennsylvania, had rejected participation in slavery. He articulated his views in a paper presented during a Quaker meeting.[38] Pyle had considered purchasing a slave for lifetime service, because his White indentured servants were working sufficient hours and had families to attend to. He decided to consult the Lord for guidance before acquiring a slave. He recounts a prophetic dream regarding a ladder that extended to heaven. Alongside it lay a black pot. He attempted to ascend the ladder while holding the black pot but was frustratingly unsuccessful. Pyle soon realized that it was impossible to bring the black pot with him to heaven. Awakened from the dream, he interpreted it as conveying a message from the Lord that he should refrain from participating in slavery. Pyle advocated that slavery had negated the Golden Rule, needed violence to maintain the institution, created wars in Africa, and hindered any attempt to evangelize the slaves. Regarding Pyle's antislavery discourse, historian Drake suggests,

36. T. Drake, *Quakers and Slavery*, 19–20; Soderlund, *Quakers and Slavery*, 19.

37. Cadbury, "Another Early Quaker," 211; T. Drake, *Quakers and Slavery*, 20.

38. Robert Pyle's short paper is reprinted in an article by Cadbury. See Cadbury, "Early Quaker Anti-Slavery Statement," 492–93.

> His unique contribution was the suggestion that quarterly meetings ought to assure responsibility for arranging with Quaker slaveholders a definite date for liberating their Negroes; and, further, that meetings should require a settlement between Friends and their ex-slaves to compensate the Negroes for their labor while they had been in bondage.[39]

Additionally, on October 30, 1698, the Philadelphia quarterly meeting made a decision that could be interpreted as one of bold confrontation or extreme desperation. The community, of whom Southeby was a part, had sent a letter to Barbados requesting that they cease importing slaves into Pennsylvania. Yet, there are no records indicating that the Barbadian elite had ever acknowledged its reception.[40] Eventually, during the early eighteenth century Southeby was excommunicated by the Quaker elite because of his antislavery discourse.

The 1690s marked a transition within Quakerism and what is generally referred to as American Christianity. At this point the antislavery and reform theologies were gradually developing, and an increasing number of Christians were seeking to practice these beliefs socio-politically within society. George Fox, Richard Baxter, William Edmondson, Morgan Godwyn, the Germantowners, and George Keith were the primary figures that established forms of Christian antislavery and reform discourses that maintained a strong presence throughout the world. Their religious convictions and practices created noticeable defiance toward all corrupt religious and sociopolitical authorities. The collective effort of Fox, Baxter, Edmondson, Godwyn, the Germantowners, and Keith contributed to the origins of European American Christian antislavery and slavery reform discourse during the seventeenth century. These movements also established the foundation upon which the European American abolitionism movement was built.

39. T. Drake, *Quakers and Slavery*, 20–21.

40. Cadbury, "Another Early Quaker," 211–12; T. Drake, *Quakers and Slavery*, 21–22, 28; Soderlund, *Quakers and Slavery*, 20.

Conclusion

Continual Introspection and a Precursor to the Gospel According to Jupiter Hammon

African American culture and scholarship, at least aspects of them, appear trapped, confined within cycles of stagnation. There could be numerous reasons why, as I don't presume to know an extensive list. I'm only focusing on some key issues that concern me, and what I believe we have control over but appear to relinquish to Whiteness. If we don't relinquish our responsibilities and initiatives to action, we construct the illusion of confrontation and oppression, to conceal the prioritizing of our self-centeredness that creates certain self-interest, which causes the diminishment of the greater Black community. Hence, my continual questioning of our identities, solidarity, genuine religious beliefs, and thoughts on Black caricatures and Black mannequins.

This current project, *Introspection*, can be read as the precursor to my previous work, *An Introduction to Colonial African American Evangelical Theology*. *Introspection* provides more clarity on my views on essentialist/racialized binary reasoning and their effects on aspects of African American culture, religion, and scholarship. *Introspection* also questions the compromises established within African American studies that creates a distinct set of problems by African American scholars, not Whiteness. For example, I'm continuously perplexed by some Black Christians who seemingly ignore their right and responsibility to contribute to traditional Christian scholarship. Yet perhaps I'm projecting a foreign *faith* and *calling* upon them. Again, *Introspection* is not an attack on African American scholars and scholarship. Nor is it an attempt to evangelize people with differing views. *Introspection* is presented in the spirit of inquiry and the Spirit of Truth. This work also lays the groundwork for other theological projects, one of which is a theological reading of Jupiter Hammon.

As an African American Christian, I find it peculiar that some African Americans are willing to set aside their Christian beliefs for the sake of a particular Black solidarity and a liberated Black consciousness. I'm emphasizing the word *particular*. I'm not rejecting Black solidarity and a liberated Black consciousness. I'm only questioning how it's constructed, its limitations, and who is invited to contribute to its creation.

African American culture and scholarship, at least in some areas, have become intentionally ambiguous in ways that are deceptive and unedifying. Hence, my critique of Black religion and, by extension, African American theology. They are frustratingly broad constructs of overgeneralizing that ironically create a distorted hermeneutic of equality and are subsequently created by said hermeneutic. For example, some colonial African American Christians are reimagined/reinterpreted in ways that conceal their genuine Christian faith under the generic banner of "spiritual" or "Black spirituality." This coincides with the absence of mentioning identity specific markers: Jesus Christ, gospel, evangelical, Holy Spirit, and other orthodox Christian theological categories.

We can also view this through interpretations of Hammon's work. Scholars tend to approach him with certain *disciplinary* and *sociopolitical biases*. Hammon's literature is exposed to concepts of an Ideal-Blackness that is defined by levels of militancy toward, and separation from, *Whiteness*. For example, when an African American slave does not aggressively confront, distance themselves from, and recreate a new Black identity apart from Whiteness, they are consequently ignored, dismissed, or interpreted in a demeaning manner. Stated previously, these methodologies appear designed and utilized to *de-Christianize* or *secularize* certain Christian slaves and their texts. Occasionally, scholars will discuss the unavoidable Christian overtones but excessively emphasize the writer's use of a secret or *coded* discourse through Christianity as a sociopolitical tool for their Liberationist beliefs. At times this approach is excessive, as such scholars continuously question and deny the individual's conversion to Christianity. The Christian identity of the individual and text(s) are minimized to the extent that scholars can reinterpret them to correspond with their sociopolitical agenda. Aside from this, many people are unaware of Hammon and his contribution to African American Christianity.

A BRIEF DISCUSSION OF HAMMON

Jupiter Hammon was an African American Christian slave who lived from roughly 1711 to 1806. He is recognized as the first African American to publish a poem and a body of literature.[1] Hammon was a conservative Christian who possessed a fundamental understanding of Pauline New Testament theology. He was also a talented poet who lacked formal training in Western poetry or a seminary education in the tenets of Christianity. Hammon displayed a deep passion for studying scripture and for articulating his beliefs through poetry. Alongside Hammon's grasp of New Testament theology, as I view him, was the influence of Hebrew wisdom literature which helped shape his poetic theology.[2] Thus, I refer to Hammon as the first known African American Christian *poetic theologian*. Yet, I am not alone in interpreting Hammon as a slave theologian. Sondra A. O'Neale observes that Hammon's writing "includes the first, and most comprehensive, statement of Black theology as well as the earliest antislavery protests by a Black writer in all of American literature."[3] I view Hammon as an evangelical Christian, because his writings appear to be heavily influenced by, and point the reader to, the gospel of Christ Jesus.

As a poetic theologian, Hammon articulated a strong Christology and presented a well-defined view of the gospel. His Christology was nuanced with an eschatological focus that glorified Jesus Christ, but minimized much of the traditional Christological and eschatological

1. Lucy Terry (1724/25/32?–1821) was born in Africa and sold into American slavery through Bristol, Rhode Island. She was purchased and brought to New England at five years old. In 1746, Terry wrote a poem called "Bars Fight," which was inspired from a 1746 Indian attack upon two local White families of Deerfield, Massachusetts. The area of this attack was named "the Bars." Terry received local popularity from the poem. Residents of Deerfield preserved the poem orally until it was published in the *Springfield Republican* (1854), and Josiah Gilbert Holland's *History of Western Massachusetts* (1855). See Kaplan, *Black Presence*, 209–11; Jarrett, *Wiley Blackwell Anthology*, 7–8. In 1760, an African American named Briton Hammon had published his narrative, *Narrative of the Uncommon Sufferings and Surprizing Deliverance of Briton Hammon, a Negro Man*. Hammon is considered by most as the first African American to publish a narrative. Very little is known about Hammon apart from his narrative. For example, scholars are uncertain if he was born in Africa or America, as the narrative begins with his life in America. Nor can anyone determine his birthdate and year of death. Surprisingly, scholars have written much about Briton Hammon. See Jarrett, *Wiley Blackwell Anthology*, 10–14.

2. Hebrew wisdom literature consists of Ecclesiastes, Job, Psalms, Proverbs, Ecclesiastes, and the Song of Solomon.

3. O'Neale, *Jupiter Hammon*, 1.

apocalyptic overtones. Hammon's poetic theology emphasized God's grace, repentance, sanctification, and salvation in our present context.

Hammon was a slave of the prominent Lloyd family, who were manual landlords and merchants of Long Island. Scholars maintain that Hammon served the Lloyd family for three generations, which spanned his entire life. Thus, Hammon, like many other slaves, died in bondage. However, he lived a progressive life as a slave. The Lloyd family provided Hammon with adequate education, greatly encouraged his desire to study the Bible, and helped cultivate his *calling* as a Christian evangelist/preacher to African/African American slaves.[4] Scholars have discovered that Hammon was a trusted slave to the extent that he had open access to Henry Lloyd's (patriarch of the family) personal library, and as an adult worked alongside his master.[5] These privileges were rare for slaves.

Hammon published his work during this period, a collection of nine different poems and prose, with one poem yet to be rediscovered. His collection consists of "An Evening Thought. Salvation by Christ, with Penetential Cries: Composed by Jupiter Hammon, a Negro belonging to Mr Lloyd, of Queen's Village, on Long Island, the 25 of December, 1760"; "An Address to Miss Phillis Wheatly, Ethiopian Poetess, in Boston, who came from Africa at eight years of age, and soon became acquainted with the gospel of Jesus Christ" (1778); "An Essay on Ten Virgins" (1779);[6] "A Poem for Children on Death" (1782); "A Dialogue Entitled the King Master and the Dutiful Servant" (1782), which was published as part of a prose titled "An Evening Improvement. Shewing, the Necessity of beholding the Lamb of God" (1782); "A Winter Piece: Being a Serious Exhortation, With a Call to the Unconverted: And a Short Contemplation on the Death of Jesus Christ" (1782); and a particular work published for the members of the African Society in New York, "An Address to the Negroes of the State of New York" (1786). Last, there is the newly

4. Ransom et al., *America's First Negro Poet*, 11–41; Franklin and Moss, *From Slavery to Freedom*, 87; Kaplan, *Black Presence*, 171; Davis et al., *New Cavalcade*, 18.

5. Sidney Kaplan provides an example of this by stating, "He [Hammon] refers to the English divines, Burkitt and Beveridge, whose works were in Henry Lloyd's library." Kaplan, *Black Presence*, 171; see also Jarrett, *Wiley Blackwell Anthology*, 31.

6. A copy of "An Essay on Ten Virgins" (1779) has yet to be recovered. However, scholars have shown that it indeed existed based on an advertisement in the *Connecticut Courant*, on December 14, 1779. See Kaplan, *Black Presence*, 173; Davis et al., *New Cavalcade*, 18.

discovered unpublished poem titled "An Essay on Slavery, with Justification to Divine Providence" (1786).[7]

To some extent, scholars have struggled to articulate Hammon's theology with much specificity. Most interpretations of Hammon's Christian theology are ambiguous. The methodology most historians use is centered on a religio-cultural analysis of Long Island society and the greater British colonies of the eighteenth century. Rather than concentrating directly upon his literature, scholars seek to interpret Hammon's Christianity through an understanding of the people, beliefs, and religious movements that may or may not have influenced him. Some scholars develop vague eighteenth-century interpretations of the Anglican, Methodist, and Puritan hymnists, preachers, and theologians that lack an obvious connection to Hammon. Or they simply do not dedicate an effort to demonstrate those possible connections. There is also the presence of cursory and demeaning generalizations of Hammon's discourse. The importance and necessity of providing a detailed *exegesis*, or interpretation, of Hammon's work appears to evade them. However, Sondra A. O'Neale is an exception. O'Neale's work establishes a basic biblical interpretation of Hammon's theology. Surprisingly, this type of interpretation was not attempted until 1993 and since then has gone relatively ignored by some contemporary scholars, especially Black liberation theologians. Nonetheless, the issue remains that since there have not been consistent biblical and theological interpretations of Hammon's work, scholars have broadly defined his Christian beliefs as the mere *parroting* of White Christianity. Hammon's literature has an important place within African American literature, and it's time he received more attention placed upon his genuine Christian faith and theology.

7. J. M. Washington, *Conversations with God*, 3–5; Berry, *From Bondage to Liberation*, 51–55; Wegelin, *Jupiter Hammon*; Starling, *Slave Narrative*, 55–57; Jarrett, *Wiley Blackwell Anthology*, 32–33; May and McCown, "Essay on Slavery," 457–71.

Bibliography

Aceto, Donna, and Matt Tracy. "LGBTQ Activists Protest Police Killing of Tyre Nichols." *GayCityNews*, Jan. 31, 2023. www.gaycitynews.com/lgbtq-activists-protest-police-killing-tyre-nichols/.

Allen, Richard. *The Life, Experience, and Gospel Labours of the Rt. Rev. Richard Allen.* Philadelphia: Martin & Boden, 1833.

Amussen, Susan Dwyer. *Caribbean Exchanges: Slavery and the Transformation of English Society, 1640–1700.* Chapel Hill: University of North Carolina Press, 2007.

American History Central Staff. "The Headright System in Colonial America: 1618–1779." American History Central. https://www.americanhistorycentral.com/entries/headright-system-in-colonial-america/.

Anderson, Victor. *Beyond Ontological Blackness: An Essay on African American Religious and Cultural Criticism.* New York: Continuum, 1995.

Andrews, Dale P. *Practical Theology for Black Churches: Bridging Black Theology and African American Folk Religion.* Louisville: Westminster John Knox, 2002.

Andrews, William L. *Classic African American Women's Narratives.* Oxford: Oxford University Press, 2003.

———. *Sisters of the Spirit: Three Black Women's Autobiographies of the Nineteenth Century.* Bloomington: Indiana University Press, 1986.

———. *To Tell a Free Story: The First Century of Afro-American Autobiography, 1760–1865.* Chicago: University of Illinois Press, 1986.

Ansbro, John J. *Martin Luther King, Jr.: Nonviolent Strategies and Tactics for Social Change.* Lanham, MD: Madison, 2000.

Aptheker, Herbert. "The Quakers and Negro Slavery." *Journal of Negro History* 25 (1940) 331–62.

Aquilina, Mike. "The Martyrdom of Polycarp." In *The Fathers of the Church: An Introduction to the First Christian Teachers*, 69–73. 3rd ed. Huntington: Our Sunday Visitor, 2013.

Ater, Renée. "In Memoriam: I Can't Breathe." *Renée Ater* (blog), May 2020. www.reneeater.com/on-monuments-blog-ag/list+of+unarmed+black+people+killed+by+police.

Austin, Michael W. *American Christian Nationalism: Neither American nor Christian.* Grand Rapids: Eerdmans, 2024.

Barbour, Floyd B., et al., eds. *The Black Power Revolt.* Boston: Extending Horizons, 1968.

Barrett, Lindon. "African-American Slave Narratives: Literacy, the Body, Authority." *American Literary History* 7 (1995) 415–42.

Baxter, Richard. *A Christian directory, or, A summ of practical theologie and cases of conscience directing Christians how to use their knowledge and faith, how to improve all helps and means, and to perform all duties, how to overcome temptations, and to escape or mortifie every sin: in four parts.* London: Robert White for Nevill Simmons, 1673.

Beckles, Hilary. *Black Rebellion in Barbados: The Struggle Against Slavery, 1627–1838.* Bridgetown, Barbados: Crib Research and Publications, 1987.

Bennett, Lerone, Jr. *Before the Mayflower: A History of Black America.* 8th ed. Chicago: Johnson, 2007.

———. *The Shaping of Black America: The Struggles and Triumphs of African-Americans, 1619 to the 1990s.* New York: Penguin, 1993.

Ben-Zvi, Yael. "Equiano's Nativity: Negative Birthright, Indigenous Ethic, and Universal Human Rights." *Early American Literature* 48 (2013) 339–423.

Berger, Peter. *Invitation to Sociology: A Humanist Perspective.* Middlesex: Penguin, 1986.

———. *The Sacred Canopy: Elements of a Sociological Theory of Religion.* 2nd ed. New York: Anchor, 1990.

Berger, Peter, and Thomas Luckman. *The Social Construction of Reality: A Treatise in the Sociology of Knowledge.* New York: Anchor, 1967.

Berlin, Ira. *Generations of Captivity: A History of African-American Slaves.* Cambridge, MA: Harvard University Press, 2003.

———. *Many Thousands Gone: The First Two Centuries of Slavery in North America.* Cambridge, MA: Harvard University Press, 1998.

Berry, Faith, ed. *From Bondage to Liberation: Writings by and About Afro-Americans from 1700 to 1918.* New York: Continuum, 2006.

Besse, Joseph. *A Collection of the Sufferings of the People Called Quakers: For the Testimony of a Good Conscience, from the Time of their being first distinguished by that Name in the Year 1650, to the Time of the Act, commonly called the Act of Toleration, granted to Protestant Dissenters in the first Year of the Reign of King William the Third and Queen Mary, in the year 1689.* Vol 1. London: Luke Hinde, 1753.

Bevans, Stephen B. *Models of Contextual Theology.* Maryknoll, NY: Orbis, 2008.

Bibb, Henry. *Narrative of the Life and Adventures of Henry Bibb, an American Slave. Written by Himself.* New York, 1815.

Blackburn, Robin. *The Making of New World Slavery: From the Baroque to the Modern, 1492–1800.* London: Verso, 1997.

Bland, Sterling Lecater, Jr., ed. *African-American Slave Narratives: An Anthology.* Vol. 1. Westport, CT: Greenwood, 2001.

Blassingame, John W. *The Slave Community: Plantation Life in the Ante-Bellum South.* New York: Oxford University Press, 1972.

———. *Slave Testimony: Two Centuries of Letters, Speeches, Interviews, and Autobiographies.* Baton Rouge: Louisiana State University Press, 1977.

Bodie, John Bennett. "Edward Bennett of London and Virginia." *The William and Mary Quarterly*, 2nd ser., 13 (1993) 117–30.

Bradley, Anthony B. *Liberating Black Theology: The Bible and the Black Experience in America.* Wheaton, IL: Crossway, 2010.

Breen, T. H., and Stephen Innes. *"Myne Owne Ground": Race and Freedom on Virginia's Eastern Shore, 1640–1676*. Oxford: Oxford University Press, 1980.

Brenner, Robert. *Merchants and Revolution: Commercial Change, Political Conflict, and London's Overseas Traders, 1550–53*. Cambridge: Cambridge University Press, 1993.

Brewer, James H. "Negro Property Owners in Seventeenth-Century Virginia." *The William and Mary Quarterly*, 3rd ser., 12 (1955) 575–80.

Brown, Kathleen M. *Good Wives, Nasty Wenches and Anxious Patriarchs: Gender, Race, and Power in Colonial Virginia*. Chapel Hill: University of North Carolina Press, 1996.

Bruce, Dickson D. "Politics and Political Philosophy in the Slave Narratives." In *The Cambridge Companion to the African American Slave Narrative*, edited by Audrey Fisch, 28–43. Cambridge: Cambridge University Press, 2007.

Bruce, Philip Alexander. *Institutional History of Virginia in the Seventeenth Century: An Inquiry into the Religious, Moral, Educational, Legal, Military, and Political Condition of the People Based on Original and Contemporaneous Records*. Vol. 2. Gloucester: Pete Smith, 1964.

Brunner, Emil. *Man in Revolt: A Christian Anthropology*. Philadelphia: Westminster, 1939.

———. "Nature and Grace." In *Natural Theology*, by Emil Brunner and Karl Barth, 15–64. Eugene, OR: Wipf & Stock, 2002.

Burrow, Rufus, Jr. "Who Teaches Black Theology?" *Journal of Religious Thought* 43 (1986) 7–18.

Butterfield, Stephen T. "The Use of Language in the Slave Narratives." *Negro American Literature Forum* 6 (1972) 72–78.

Cadbury, Henry J. "An Early Quaker Anti-Slavery Statement." *The Journal of Negro History* 22 (1937) 488–93.

———. "Another Early Quaker Anti-Slavery Document." *Journal of Negro History* 27 (1942) 210–15.

Carey, Brycchan. *From Peace to Freedom: Quaker Rhetoric and the Birth of American Antislavery, 1657–1761*. New Haven, CT: Yale University Press, 2012.

———. "'The Power That Giveth Liberty and Freedom': The Barbadian Origins of Quaker Antislavery Rhetoric, 1657–76." *Ariel: A Review of International English Literature* 38 (2007) 27–47.

Carmichael, Stokely. "Power and Racism." In *The Black Power Revolt*, edited by Floyd B. Barbour et al., 61–71. Boston: Extending Horizons, 1968.

Carmichael, Stokely, and Charles V. Hamilton. *Black Power: The Politics of Liberation in America*. Middlesex: Penguin, 1967.

Carretta, Vincent. *Equiano, the African: Biography of a Self-Made Man*. New York: Penguin, 2005.

———. "Olaudah Equiano or Gustavus Vassa? New Light on an Eighteenth-Century Question of Identity." *Slavery and Abolition: A Journal of Slave and Post-Slave Studies* 20 (1999) 96–105.

Carrigan, Anthony. "Negotiating Personal Identity and Cultural Memory in Olaudah Equiano's Interesting Narrative." *Wasafiri* 21 (2006) 42–47.

Carson, Clayborne, and Kris Shepard, eds. *A Call to Conscience: The Landmark Speeches of Dr. Martin Luther King, Jr.* London: Little, Brown, 2001.

Carter, J. Kameron. *Race: A Theological Account*. Oxford: Oxford University Press, 2008.

Casmier-Paz, Lynn A. "Slave Narratives and the Rhetoric of Author Portraiture." *New Literary History* 34 (2003) 91–116.

Clay, Elonda. "A Black Theology of Liberation or Legitimation? A Postcolonial Response to Cone's Black Theology and Black Power at Forty." *Black Theology* 8 (2010) 307–26.

Cleage, Albert B., Jr. *The Black Messiah*. New York: Sheed and Ward, 1968.

———. *Black Nationalism: New Directions for the Black Church*. New York: Morrow, 1972.

Cone, Cecil Wayne. *The Identity Crisis in Black Theology*. Nashville: AMEC, 1975.

Cone, James H. "America: A Dream or a Nightmare." *Journal of the Interdenominational Theological Center* 1 (1986) 263–78.

———. "Black Consciousness and the Black Church: A Historical-Theological Interpretation." In "The Sixties: Radical Change in American Religion." Special issue, *Annals of the American Academy of Political and Social Science* 387 (1970) 49–55.

———. "Black Power, Black Theology, and the Study of Theology and Ethics." *Theological Education* 6 (1970) 202–15.

———. *Black Theology and Black Power*. 14th ed. Maryknoll, NY: Orbis, 2012.

———. *A Black Theology of Liberation*. 40th anniv. ed. Maryknoll, NY: Orbis, 2010.

———. "Christian Faith and Political Praxis." *Encounter* 43 (1982) 132.

———. *The Cross and the Lynching Tree*. Maryknoll, NY: Orbis, 2013.

———. "Demystifying Martin and Malcolm." *Theology Today* 51 (1994) 27–37.

———. *For My People: Black Theology and the Black Church*. Maryknoll, NY: Orbis, 1984.

———. "God and Black Suffering: Calling the Oppressors to Account." *Anglican Theological Review* 90 (2008) 701–9.

———. *God of the Oppressed*. 9th ed. Maryknoll, NY: Orbis, 2006.

———. *Martin and Malcolm and America: A Dream or a Nightmare*. Maryknoll, NY: Orbis, 1991.

———. "Martin Luther King, Jr., and the Third World." *Journal of American History* 74 (1987) 455–67.

———. "Martin Luther King, Jr., Black Theology, Black Church." *Theology Today* 40 (1984) 409–20.

———. *My Soul Looks Back*. Maryknoll, NY: Orbis, 1986.

———. *Risks of Faith: The Emergence of a Black Theology of Liberation, 1968–1998*. Boston: Beacon, 1999.

———. *Speaking the Truth: Ecumenism, Liberation, and Black Theology*. Maryknoll, NY: Orbis, 1986.

———. "The Theology of Martin Luther King, Jr." *Union Seminary Quarterly Review* 40 (1986) 21–39.

———. "Theology's Great Sin: Silence in the Face of White Supremacy." *Black Theology* 2 (2004) 139–52.

Cone, James H., and Gayraud S. Wilmore, eds. *Black Theology: A Documentary History, 1966–1979*. Maryknoll, NY: Orbis, 1979.

Cooper, Valerie C. *Word, Like Fire: Maria Stewart, the Bible, and the Rights of African Americans*. Charlottesville: University of Virginia Press, 2011.

Cornelius, Janet Duitsman. "'We Slipped and Learned to Read': Slave Accounts of the Literacy Process, 1830–1865." *Phylon* 44 (1983) 171–86.

———. *When I Can Read My Title Clear: Literacy, Slavery, and Religion in the Antebellum South*. Columbia: University of South Carolina Press, 1991.

Craven, Wesley Frank. *The Southern Colonies in the Seventeenth Century, 1607–1689*. Vol. 1: *A History of the South*. 4th ed. Baton Rouge: Louisiana State University Press, 2015.

Crummell, Alexander. *Destiny and Race: Selected Writings, 1840–1898*. Edited by Wilson Jeremiah Moses. Amherst: University of Massachusetts Press, 1992.

Cumming, Ryan P. "Contrasts and Fragments: An Exploration of James Cone's Theological Methodology." *Anglican Theological Review* 91 (2009) 395–416.

D'Ambrosio, Marcellino. "The Martyrdom of Polycarp." In *When the Church Was Young: Voices of the Early Fathers*, 29–37. Cincinnati: Franciscan Media, 2014.

Davis, Arthur P., et al. *The New Cavalcade: African American Writing from 1760 to the Present*. Vol. 1. Washington, DC: Howard University Press, 1991.

Davis, Darren W., and Ronald E. Brown. "The Antipathy of Black Nationalism: Behavioral and Attitudinal Implications of an African American Ideology." *American Journal of Political Science* 46 (2002) 239–52.

Davis, David Brion. *The Problem of Slavery in Western Culture*. Ithaca, NY: Cornell University Press, 1966.

Douglas, Kelly Brown. *The Black Christ*. Maryknoll, NY: Orbis, 1994.

Douglass, Frederick. *The Narrative of the Life of Frederick Douglass, an American Slave. Written by Himself.* Boston, 1845.

Drake, St. Clair. *The Redemption of Africa and Black Religion*. Chicago: Third World Press, 1970.

Drake, Thomas E. *Quakers and Slavery in America*. New Haven, CT: Yale University Press, 1950.

Dunn, Richard S. *Sugar and Slaves: The Rise of the Planters Class in the English West Indies, 1624–1713*. Chapel Hill: University of North Carolina Press, 1972.

Eliade, Mircea. *The Sacred and the Profane*. Orlando: Harcourt Brace Jovanovich, 1987.

Equiano, Olaudah. *The Interesting Narrative of the Life of Olaudah Equiano, or Gustavus Vassa, the African. Written by Himself.* Vol 1. London, 1789. Docsouth.unc.edu/neh/equiano1/equiano1.html.

Erskine, Noel Leo. "Black Theology: Retrospect and Prospect." *Theology Today* 36 (1979) 176–85.

———. *Plantation Church: How African American Religion Was Born in Caribbean Slavery*. Oxford: Oxford University Press, 2014.

Evans, Curtis J. *The Burden of Black Religion*. Oxford: Oxford University Press, 2008.

Evans, James H., Jr. *We Have Been Believers: An African American Systematic Theology*. Minneapolis: Fortress, 1992.

Eze, Emmanuel Chukwudi, ed. *Race and the Enlightenment: A Reader*. Oxford: Wiley-Blackwell, 1997.

Fairclough, Adam. *Martin Luther King, Jr.* Athens: University of Georgia Press, 1995.

Fausset, Richard. "What We Know About the Shooting Death of Ahmaud Arbery." *New York Times*, Aug. 8, 2022. www.nytimes.com/article/ahmaud-arbery-shooting-georgia.html.

Fields, Bruce L. *Introducing Black Theology: Three Crucial Questions for the Evangelical Church*. Grand Rapids: Baker Academic, 2001.

Finton, Lucas. "3 Memphis Fire Department Personnel Fired for Not Providing Aid to Tyre Nichols." *USA Today*, Jan. 30, 2023. www.usatoday.com/story/news/nation/2023/30/memphis-fire-employees-fired-tyre-nichols/11151451002/.

Fisher, Miles Mark. "Friends of Humanity: A Quaker Anti-Slavery Influence." *Church History: Studies in Christianity and Culture* 4 (1935) 187–202.

Floyd-Thomas, Stacey, et al. *Black Church Studies: An Introduction*. Nashville: Abingdon, 2007.

Foster, Frances Smith. *Witnessing Slavery: The Development of Ante-Bellum Slave Narratives*. Madison: University of Wisconsin Press, 1974.

Fox, George. *Gospel Family-Order, Being a Short Discourse Concerning the Ordering of Families, Both of Whites, Blacks and Indians*. N.p., 1676.

———. *To Friends Beyond the Sea, That Have Blacks and Indian Slaves*. N.p., 1657.

———. *To the Ministers, Teachers, and Priests (So called, and so Stileing your-selves) in Barbados*. N.p., 1672.

Fox News. "'The Five': Release of 'Horrifying, Disgusting' Footage Has Cities Preparing for Unrest." YouTube video, Jan. 27, 2023. https://www.youtube.com/watch?v=ZuSFAE9G-3c.

———. "Tucker: This Is a Highly Aggressive Propaganda Campaign." YouTube video, Jan. 27, 2023. https://www.youtube.com/watch?v=oLZbBEMprU4.

Franklin, John Hope, and Alfred A. Moss Jr. *From Slavery to Freedom: A History of Negro Americans*. 6th ed. New York: McGraw-Hill, 1988.

Frazier, E. Franklin, and C. Eric Lincoln. *The Negro Church in America* and *The Black Church Since Frazier*. New York: Schocken, 1974.

Fretz, J. Herbert. "The Germantown Anti-Slavery Petition of 1688." *Mennonite Quarterly Review* 33 (1959) 42–59.

Frey, Sylvia R., and Betty Wood. *Come Shouting to Zion: African American in the American South and British Caribbean to 1830*. Chapel Hill: University of North Carolina Press, 1998.

Garnet, Henry Highland. *An Address to the Slaves of the United States of America*. New York, 1848.

———. *A Memorial Discourse: Delivered in the Hall of the House of Representatives*. Philadelphia, 1865.

Garvey, Marcus. *Philosophy and Opinions of Marcus Garvey*. Vol. 1. Mansfield Centre, CT: Martino, 2014.

Gerbner, Katherine. "Antislavery in Print: The Germantown Protest, the 'Exhortation,' and the Seventeenth-Century Quaker Debate on Slavery." *Early American Studies: An Interdisciplinary Journal* 9 (2011) 552–75.

———. "The Ultimate Sin: Christianising Slaves in Barbados in the Seventeenth Century." *Slavery and Abolition: A Journal of Slave and Post-Slave Studies* 31 (2010) 57–73.

———. "'We Are Against the Traffik of Men-Body': The Germantown Quaker Protest of 1688 and the Origins of American Abolitionism." *Pennsylvania History: A Journal of Mid-Atlantic Studies* 74 (2007) 149–72.

Glasson, Travis. *Mastering Christianity: Missionary Anglicanism and Slavery in the Atlantic World*. Oxford: Oxford University Press, 2010.

Glaude, Eddie S., Jr. *African American Religion: A Very Short Introduction*. Oxford: Oxford University Press, 2014.

Godwyn, Morgan. *The Negro's and Indian Advocate, Suing for their Admission into the Church Or a Persuasive to the Instructing and Baptizing of the Negro's and Indians in our Plantations. Shewing That as the Compliance therewith can prejudice no Mans just Interest; So the wilful Neglecting and Opposing of it, is no less than a manifest Apostacy from the Christian Faith*. London, 1680.

———. *A Supplement to the Negro's and Indian's Advocate: Or, Some further Considerations and Proposals for the effectual and speedy carrying on of the Negro's Christianity in our Plantations (Notwithstanding the late pretended Impossibilities) without any prejudice to their Owners.* London, 1681.

Goodman, Amy, and Amber Sherman. "Memphis BLM Activist: Tyre Nichols' Killing Is Part of Police Brutality Crisis Facing Black Residents." *Democracy Now*, Jan. 27, 2023. www.democracynow.org/2023/1/27/tyre_nichols_police_beating_murder_charges.

Gossett, Thomas F. *Race: The History of an Idea in America.* Dallas: Southern Methodist University Press, 1963.

Grant, Jacqueline. "Black Christology: Interpreting Aspects of the Apostolic Faith." *Mid-Stream* 24 (1985) 366–75.

Gregg, Larry. *Englishmen Transplanted: The English Colonization of Barbados, 1627–1660.* Oxford: Oxford University Press, 2003.

Gronniosaw, James Albert Ukawsaw. *A Narrative of the Most Remarkable Particulars in the Life of James Albert Ukawsaw Gronniosaw, an African Prince, as Related by Himself.* Bath, 1772.

Guasco, Michael. *Slaves and Englishmen: Human Bondage in the Early Modern Atlantic World.* Philadelphia: University of Pennsylvania Press, 2014.

Haley, Alex, and Malcolm X. *The Autobiography of Malcolm X.* New York: Grove, 1966.

Hammon, Briton. *Narrative of the Most Uncommon Sufferings and Surprizing Deliverance of Briton Hammon, a Negro Man.* Boston, 1760. http://docsouth.unc.edu/neh/hammon/menu.html.

Hammon, Jupiter. "An Address to Miss Phillis Wheatly, Ethiopian Poetess, in Boston, who came from Africa at eight years of age, and soon became acquainted with the gospel of Jesus Christ." 1778. In *Jupiter Hammon and the Biblical Beginnings of African-American Literature*, by Sondra A. O'Neale, 66–82. Metuchen: Scarecrow, 1993.

———. "An Address to the Negroes of the State of New York and An Essay on Slavery, with Justification to Divine Providence." 1786. In *Jupiter Hammon and the Biblical Beginnings of African-American Literature*, by Sondra A. O'Neale, 212–52. Metuchen: Scarecrow, 1993.

———. "Dear Hutchinson Is Dead and Gone." 1770. New York Heritage Digital Collections. https://nyheritage.contentdm.oclc.org/digital/collection/p16124coll1/id/32885/.

———. "A Dialogue Entitled the King Master and the Dutiful Servant." 1782 In *Jupiter Hammon and the Biblical Beginnings of African-American Literature*, by Sondra A. O'Neale, 191–211. Metuchen: Scarecrow, 1993.

———. "An Essay on Ten Virgins." N.p., 1779.

———. "An Evening Improvement. Shewing, The Necessity of beholding the Lamb of God." 1782. In *Jupiter Hammon and the Biblical Beginnings of African-American Literature*, by Sondra A. O'Neale, 148–90. Metuchen: Scarecrow, 1993.

———. "An Evening Thought. Salvation by Christ, with Penitential Cries: Composed by Jupiter Hammon, a Negro belonging to Mr Lloyd, of Queen's Village, on Long Island, the 25 of December, 1760." 1760. In *Jupiter Hammon and the Biblical Beginnings of African-American Literature*, by Sondra A. O'Neale, 41–65. Metuchen: Scarecrow, 1993.

———. "A Poem for Children on Death." 1782. In *Jupiter Hammon and the Biblical Beginnings of African-American Literature*, by Sondra A. O'Neale, 134–47. Metuchen: Scarecrow, 1993.

———. "A Winter Piece: Being a Serious Exhortation, With a Call to the Unconverted: And a Short Contemplation on the Death of Jesus Christ." 1782. In *Jupiter Hammon and the Biblical Beginnings of African-American Literature*, by Sondra A. O'Neale, 83–133. Metuchen: Scarecrow, 1993.

Hanch, Kate. *Storied Witness: The Theology of Black Women Preachers in 19th-Century America.* Minneapolis: Fortress, 2022.

Hanna, Jason, and Travis Caldwell. "Jury Finds Ahmaud Arbery's Killers Were Racially Motivated in Chasing Him." CNN, Feb. 23, 2022. www.cnn.com/2022/02/22/us/ahmaud-arbery-hate-crime-trial-tuesday/index.html.

Harden, Mark Gawain. "Toward a Practical Black Theology and Liberation Ethic: An Alternative African-American Perspective." *Black Theology* 9 (2011) 35–55.

Harding, Vincent. "Black Power and the American Christ." In *The Black Power Revolt*, edited by Floyd B. Barbour et al., 85–93. Boston: Extending Horizons, 1968.

———. "The Religion of Black Power." In *African American Religious Thought: An Anthology*, edited by Cornel West and Eddie S. Glaude Jr., 715–45. Louisville: Westminster John Knox, 2003.

———. *There Is a River: The Black Struggle for Freedom in America.* New York: Vintage, 1983.

Haykin, Michael A. G. *Rediscovering the Church Fathers: Who They Were and How They Shaped the Church* Wheaton, IL: Crossway, 2001.

Haynes, Lemuel. "The Character and Work of a Spiritual Watchman Described." 1792. In *The Faithful Preacher: Recapturing the Vision of Three Pioneering African-American Pastors*, by Thabiti M. Anyabwile, 25–36. Wheaton, IL: Crossway, 2007.

———. The Important Concerns of Ministers and the People of Their Charge. 1797.In *The Faithful Preacher: Recapturing the Vision of Three Pioneering African-American Pastors*, by Thabiti M. Anyabwile, 37–46. Wheaton, IL: Crossway, 2007.

———. "The Sufferings, Support, and Reverend of Faithful Ministers, Illustrated." 1820. In *The Faithful Preacher: Recapturing the Vision of Three Pioneering African-American Pastors*, by Thabiti M. Anyabwile, 47–74. Wheaton, IL: Crossway, 2007.

———. *Universal Salvation: A Very Eminent Doctrine; with some Account of the Life and Character of Its Author. A Sermon Delivered at Rutland, West Parish, in the Year 1805*. Madison, 1805.

Herskovits, Melville J. *The Myth of the Negro Past.* Boston: Beacon, 1958.

Heyward, Giulia. "Mostly Peaceful Protest Held Across the U.S. After Release of Tyre Nichols Footage." NPR, Jan. 28, 2023. www.npr.org/2023/01/27/1152255708/memphis-police-killing-tyre-nichols-protest.

Hopkins, Dwight N. *Down, Up, and Over: Slave Religion and Black Theology.* Minneapolis: Fortress, 2000.

———. *Introducing Black Theology of Liberation.* Maryknoll, NY: Orbis, 1999.

———. *Shoes That Fit Our Feet: Sources for a Constructive Black Theology*. Maryknoll, NY: Orbis, 1993.

Hopkins, Dwight N., and George Cummings. *Cut Loose Your Stammering Tongue: Black Theology in the Slave Narratives.* Maryknoll, NY: Orbis, 1991.

Hughs, Derek. *Version of Blackness: Key Texts on Slavery from the Seventeenth Century.* Cambridge: Cambridge University Press, 2007.

Iati, Marisa, et al. "Nearly 250 Women Have Been Fatally Shot by Police Since 2015." *Washington Post*, Sept. 2020. www.washingtonpost.com/graphics/2020/investigations/police-shootings-women/.

Imasogie, Osadolor. "African Traditional Religion and the Christian Faith." *Review and Expositor* 70 (Summer 1973) 283–93.

Isaac, Benjamin. *The Invention of Racism in Classical Antiquity*. Princeton, NJ: Princeton University Press, 2004.

Jackson, Maurice. *Let This Voice Be Heard: Anthony Benezet, Father of Atlantic Abolitionism*. Philadelphia: University of Pennsylvania Press, 2010.

Jacobs, Harriet A. *Incidents in the Life of a Slave Girl (Harriet A. Jacobs). Written by Herself*. Boston, 1861.

James, Robison B. "A Tillichian Analysis of James Cone's Black Theology." *Prospectives in Religious Studies* 1 (1974) 16–30.

Jarrett, Gene Andrew, ed. *The Wiley Blackwell Anthology of African American Literature*. Vol. 1: *1746–1920*. Hoboken, NJ: Wiley-Blackwell, 2014.

Jennings, Willie James. *The Christian Imagination: Theology and the Origins of Race*. New Haven, CT: Yale University Press, 2010.

Jernegan, Marcus W. "Slavery and Conversion in the American Colonies." *American Historical Review* 21 (1916) 504–27.

Johnson, Andre E. "The Prophetic Persona of James Cone and the Rhetorical Theology of Black Theology." *Black Theology* 8 (2010) 266–85.

Jones, LeRoi. "The Need for a Cultural Base to Civil Rites and Power Moments." In *The Black Power Revolt*, edited by Floyd B. Barbour et al., 119–26. Boston: Extending Horizons, 1968.

Jones, William. "Theodicy and Methodology in Black Theology: A Critique of Washington, Cone and Cleage." *Harvard Theological Review* 64 (1971) 541–57.

Jordan, Winthrop D. "Decisions of the General Court." *Virginia Magazine of History and Biography* 5 (1898) 236–87.

———. *White over Black: American Attitudes Toward the Negro, 1550–1812*. Chapel Hill: University of North Carolina Press, 1968.

Justice News. "Federal Judge Sentences Three Men Convicted of Racially Motivated Hate Crimes in Connection with the Killing of Ahmaud Arbery in Georgia." Department of Justice, Aug. 8, 2022. www.justice.gov/opa/pr/federal-judge-sentences-three-men-convicted-racially-motivated-hate-crimes-connection-killing.

Kaplan, Sidney. *The Black Presence in the Era of the American Revolution: 1770–1800*. Norwalk, CT: New York Graphic Society, 1973.

Keith, George. *An Exhortation and Caution to Friends Concerning buying or keeping of Negroes*. New York, 1693.

King, Corretta Scott. *My Life With Martin Luther King, Jr.* London: Hodder and Stoughton, 1969.

King, Martin Luther, Jr. *The Autobiography of Martin Luther King, Jr.* Edited by Clayborne Carson. London: Little, Brown, 1999.

———. "Black Power." In *The Autobiography of Martin Luther King, Jr.*, edited by Clayborne Carson, 314–32. London: Little, Brown, 1999.

———. "Black Power." In *Where Do We Go from Here: Chaos or Community?*, 23–69. Boston: Beacon, 2010.

———. "Malcolm X." In *The Autobiography of Martin Luther King, Jr.*, edited by Clayborne Carson, 265–69. London: Little, Brown, 1999.

———. *Strength to Love*. Minneapolis: Fortress, 2010.

———. *A Testament of Hope: The Essential Writings and Speeches of Martin Luther King, Jr.* Edited by James M. Washington. New York: HarperOne, 1986.

———. *Where Do We Go from Here: Chaos or Community?* Boston: Beacon, 2010.

———. *Why We Can't Wait*. New York: Signet Classics, 2000.

Kolchin, Peter. *American Slavery, 1619–1877*. New York: Hill and Wang, 1993.

Kruger, E. T. "Negro Religious Expression." *American Journal of Sociology* 38 (1932) 22–31.

Kubic, Micah W. "Between Malcolm and Martin: James Cone's Black Theology as Pragmatic Ideological Alternative." *Souls: A Critical Journal of Black Politics, Culture, and Society* 11 (2009) 448–67.

La Peyrere, Isaac. *A Theological System upon That Presupposition, That Men Were Before Adam*. Book 2. London, 1655.

Laslett, Peter. "John Locke, the Great Recoinage, and the Origins of the Board of Trade: 1695–1698." *The William and Mary Quarterly*, 3rd ser., 14 (1957) 370–402.

Lee, Jarena. *A Brand Plucked from the Fire: An Autobiographical Sketch*. Cleveland: W. F. Schneider, 1879.

Levine, Lawrence W. *Black Culture and Black Consciousness: Afro-American Folk Thought from Slavery to Freedom*. Oxford: Oxford University Press, 2007.

Library of Virginia. "About the Virginia Land Office Patents and Grants/Northern Neck Grant and Surveys." http://www.lva.virginia.gov/public/guides/opac/lonnabout.htm.

Liftin, Bryan M. *Getting to Know the Church Fathers: An Evangelical Introduction*. Grand Rapids: Baker Academic, 2016.

Ligon, Richard. *A True and Exact History of the Island of Barbados*. London: Peter Parker, 1673. https://archive.org/details/mobot31753000818390.

Lincoln, C. Eric. *The Black Experience in Religion*. New York: Anchor, 1974.

Lovin, Robin W. *Reinhold Niebuhr and Christian Realism*. Cambridge: Cambridge University Press, 2004.

MacDonald, A. P. "Black Power." *Journal of Negro Education* 44 (1975) 547–54.

Malcolm X. *By Any Means Necessary: Malcolm X Speeches and Writings*. Atlanta: Pathfinder, 1992.

Manners, Emily. *Elizabeth Hooton: First Quaker Woman Preacher, 1600–1672*. London: Headley, 1914.

Mannix, Daniel P., and Malcolm Cowley. *Black Cargoes: A History of the Atlantic Slave Trade 1518–1865*. London: Penguin, 1962.

Marrant, John. "A Funeral Sermon Preached by the Desire of the Deceased, John Lock; The Text Chosen by Himself, from the Epistle of St. Paul to the Philippians, Chap. i., Ver. 21. And Was Preached According to Promise, before His Father and Mother, Brothers and Sisters, and All the Inhabitants round the Neighbouring Village, by the Rev. John Marrant." 1790. In *"Face Zion Forward": First Writers of the Black Atlantic, 1785–1798*, edited by Joanna Brooks and John Saillant, 161–90. Boston: Northeastern University Press, 2002.

———. "A Journal of the Rev. John Marrant, from August the 18th, 1785, to the 16th of March, 1790." 1790. In *"Face Zion Forward": First Writers of the Black Atlantic, 1785–1798*, edited by Joanna Brooks and John Saillant, 93–160. Boston: Northeastern University Press, 2002.

———. "A Narrative of the Lord's wonderful Dealings with John Marrant, a Black (Now Going to Preach the Gospel in Nova-Scotia) Born in New-York, in North-America. Taken Down from His Own Relation, Arranged, Corrected, and Published by the Rev. Mr. Aldridge. The 4th ed., Enlarged by Mr. Marrant, and Printed (with Permission) for His Sole Benefit, with Notes Explanatory." 1785. In *"Face Zion Forward": First Writers of the Black Atlantic, 1785–1798*, edited by Joanna Brooks and John Saillant, 47–75. Boston: Northeastern University Press, 2002.

———. "A Sermon Preached on the 24th Day of June 1789, Being the Festival of St. John the Baptist, at the Request of the Right Worshipful the Grand Master Prince Hall, and the Rest of the Brethren of the African Lodge of the Honorable Society of Free and Accepted Masons in Boston." 1789. In *"Face Zion Forward": First Writers of the Black Atlantic, 1785–1798*, edited by Joanna Brooks and John Saillant, 77–92. Boston: Northeastern University Press, 2002.

May, Cedrick, and Julie McCown. "'An Essay on Slavery': An Unpublished Poem by Jupiter Hammon." *Early American Literature* 48 (2013) 457–71.

McCarthy, Thomas. *Race, Empire, and the Idea of Human Development.* Cambridge: Cambridge University Press, 2009.

McColley, Robert. *Slavery and Jeffersonian Virginia.* 2nd ed. Urbana: University of Illinois Press, 1973.

McCormack, Donald J. "Stokely Carmichael and Pan-Africanism: Back to Black Power." *Journal of Politics* 35 (1973) 386–409.

McCoy, Beth A. "Race and the (Para)Textual Condition." *PMLA* 121 (2006) 156–69.

McKinney, Richard I. "Reflections on the Concept of 'Black Theology.'" *Journal of Religious Thought* 26 (1969) 10–14.

McLoughlin, William G., and Winthrop D. Jordan. "Baptists Face the Barbarities of Slavery in 1710." *The Journal of Southern History* 29 (1963) 495–501.

Mitchell, Henry H. *Black Church Beginnings: The Long-Hidden Realities of the First Years.* Grand Rapids: Eerdmans, 2004.

Moody, Joycelyn. *Sentimental Confessions: Spiritual Narratives of Nineteenth-Century African American Women.* Athens: University of Georgia Press, 2001.

Morgan, Edmund S. *American Slavery, American Freedom: The Ordeal of Colonial Virginia.* New York: Norton, 1975.

Moses, Wilson Jeremiah, ed. *Classical Black Nationalism: From the American Revolution to Marcus Garvey.* New York University Press: New York, 1996.

———. *The Golden Age of Black Nationalism, 1850–1925.* New York: Oxford University Press, 1978.

Muhammad, Elijah. *History of the Nation of Islam.* Phoenix: Secretarius MEMPS Publication, 2008.

Murphy, Larry. "African American Christian Perspectives on Christology and Incarnation." *Ex Auditu* 8 (1993) 73–82.

Nash, Gary B. *Quakers and Politics: Pennsylvania, 1681–1726.* Princeton, NJ: Princeton University Press, 1968.

———. "Slaves and Slaveowners in Colonial Philadelphia." *The William and Mary Quarterly*, 3rd ser., 30 (1973) 223–56.

Nash, Gary B., and Jean R. Soderlund. *Freedom by Degrees: Emancipation in Pennsylvania and Its Aftermath.* Oxford: Oxford University Press, 1991.

Nelson, Hart M., et al. *The Black Church in America.* New York: Basic Books, 1971.

Newman, Simon P. *A New World of Labour: The Development of Plantation Slavery in the British Atlantic*. Philadelphia: University of Pennsylvania Press, 2013.

Nichols, Charles H. *Many Thousands Gone: The Ex-Slaves' Account of Their Bondage and Freedom*. Bloomington: Indiana University Press, 1969.

Niebuhr, H. Richard. *Christ and Culture*. 50th anniv. ed. New York: HarperOne, 2001.

———. *Radical Monotheism and Western Culture with Supplementary Essays*. New York: Harper Torchbooks, 1960.

Niebuhr, Reinhold. *Christian Realism and Political Problems*. London: Faber & Faber, 1954.

———. *Pious and Secular America*. New York: Scribner's, 1958.

———. *The Self and the Dramas of History*. London: Faber & Faber, 1956.

Norman, Greg. "Tyre Nichols' Mother Urges Peaceful Protest: 'I Don't Want Us Burning Up Our Cities.'" *Fox News*, Jan. 27, 2023. www.foxnews.com/us/tyre-nichols-mother-urges-peaceful-protest-I-dont-want-us-burning-up-our-cities.

Olney, James. "'I Was Born': Slave Narratives. Their Status as Autobiography and as Literature." *Callaloo* 20 (1984) 46–73.

O'Neale, Sondra A. *Jupiter Hammon and the Biblical Beginnings of African-American Literature*. Metuchen: Scarecrow, 1993.

Otto, Rudolf. *The Idea of the Holy*. Oxford: Oxford University Press, 1958.

Parent, Anthony S., Jr. *Foul Means: The Formation of a Slave Society in Virginia, 1660–1740*. Chapel Hill: University of North Carolina Press, 2003.

Paul, Ronald. "'I Whitened My Face, That They Might Not Know Me': Race and Identity in Olaudah Equiano's Slave Narrative." *Journal of Black Studies* 20 (2009) 848–64.

Pennypacker, Samuel W. "The Settlement of Germantown, and the Causes Which Led to It." *Pennsylvania Magazine of History and Biography* 4 (1880) 1–41.

Peterson, Carla L. *Doers of the Word: African American Women Speakers in the North, 1830–1880*. New Brunswick, NJ: Rutgers University Press, 1995.

Pinkney, Alphonso. *Red, Black, and Green: Black Nationalism in the United States*. Cambridge: Cambridge University Press, 1976.

Poussaint, Alvin F. "The Negro American: His Self-Image and Integration." In *The Black Power Revolt*, edited by Floyd B. Barbour et al., 100–101. Boston: Extending Horizons, 1968.

Quarles, Benjamin. *The Negro in the Making of America*. New York: Collier, 1965.

Raboteau, Albert J. *Canaan Land: A Religious History of African Americans*. Oxford: Oxford University Press, 2001.

———. *A Fire in the Bones: Reflections on African-American Religious History*. Boston: Beacon, 1995.

———. *Slave Religion: The "Invisible Institution" in the Antebellum South*. Oxford: Oxford University Press, 2004.

Ransom, Stanley Austin, Jr., et al. *America's First Negro Poet: The Complete Works of Jupiter Hammon of Long Island*. Port Washington, NY: Kennikat, 1970.

Rawick, George P. *The American Slave: A Composite Autobiography*. Vol. 1: *From Sundown to Sunup: The Making of the Black Community*. Westport, CT: Greenwood, 1972.

Richie, Cristina S. "The Racial and Economic Theories of James Cone and Martin Luther King Jr. Illuminated by 'The Sermon on the Mount.'" *Black Theology* 8 (2010) 86–106.

Roberts, J. Deotis. *A Black Political Theology*. Louisville: Westminster John Knox, 1975.

———. *Black Religion, Black Theology: The Collected Essays of J. Deotis Roberts.* Edited by David Emmanuel Goatley. Harrisburg, PA: Trinity Press International, 2003.

Robinson, Dean E. *Black Nationalism in American Politics and Thought.* Cambridge: Cambridge University Press, 2001.

Rojas, Rick, and Jessica Jaglois. "Five Officers Charged with Murder in Memphis Police Killing." *New York Times*, updated Feb. 1, 2023. www.nytimes.com/2023/01/26/us/tyre-nichols-memphis-police.html.

Ruether, Rosemary Radford. "Black Theology and Black Church." *Religious Education* 64 (1969) 347–51.

Rugemer, Edward B. "The Development of Mastery and Race in the Comprehensive Slave Codes of the Greater Caribbean During the Seventeenth Century." *William and Mary Quarterly*, 3rd ser., 70 (2013) 429–58.

Russell, John H. *The Free Negro in Virginia, 1619–1865.* New York: Negro Universities Press, 1913.

Sainz, Adrian. "5 Memphis Police Officers Plead Not Guilty for Murder of Tyre Nichols." Associated Press, Feb. 17, 2023. www.pbs/newshour/nation/5-memphis-police-officers-plead-not-guilty-for-murder-of-tyre-nichols.

Sarson, Steven. *British America, 1500–1800: Creating Colonies, Imagining an Empire.* London: Hodder Arnold, 2005.

Scherer, Lester B. *Slavery and the Churches in Early America, 1619–1819.* Grand Rapids: Eerdmans, 1975.

Schreiter, Robert J. *Constructing Local Theologies.* Maryknoll, NY: Orbis, 2008.

Seale, Bobby, and Stephen Shames. *Power to the People: The World of the Black Panthers.* New York: Abrams, 2016.

Sekora, John. "Black Message/White Envelope: Genre, Authenticity, and Authority in the Antebellum Slave Narrative." *Callaloo* 53 (1987) 482–515.

Sewall, Samuel. *The Selling of Joseph.* Boston, 1700.

Smallwoood, Stephanie E. *Saltwater Slavery: A Middle Passage from Africa to American Diaspora.* Cambridge, MA: Harvard University Press, 2007.

Smith, Jean. "I Learned to Feel Black." In *The Black Power Revolt*, edited by Floyd B. Barbour et al., 207–18. Boston: Extending Horizons, 1968.

Smith, Luther E. "Black Theology and Religious Experience." *Journal of the Interdenominational Theological Center* 8 (1980) 59–72.

Society of Friends. "Germantown Friends' Protest Against Slavery 1688." Library of Congress. https://www.loc.gov/resource/rbpe.14000200/?st=text.

Soderlund, Jean R. *Quakers and Slavery: A Divided Spirit.* Princeton, NJ: Princeton University Press, 1985.

Sontag, Frederick. "Coconut Theology: Is James Cone the 'Uncle Tom' of Black Theology." *Journal of Religious Thought* 36 (1979) 5–12.

Starling, Marion Wilson. *The Slave Narratives: Its Place in American History.* Washington, DC: Howard University Press, 1988.

Stepto, Robert B. "I Rose and Found My Voice: Narration, Authentication, and Authorial Control in Four Slave Narratives." In *From Behind the Veil: A Study of Afro-American Narrative*, 3–31. Urbana: University of Illinois Press, 1979.

Stuckey, Sterling. *Slave Culture: Nationalist Theory and the Foundation of Black America.* Oxford: Oxford University Press, 2013.

Sweet, James H. *Recreating Africa: Culture, Kinship, and Religion in the African-Portuguese World, 1441–1770.* Chapel Hill: University of North Carolina Press, 2009.

Thomas, Allen Clapp. "The Attitude of the Society of Friends Towards Slavery in the Seventeenth and Eighteenth Centuries, Particularly in Relation to Its Own Members." *Papers of the American Society of Church History* 8 (1896) 263–99.

Thornton, John. *Africa and Africans in the Making of the Atlantic World, 1400–1800*. 2nd ed. Cambridge: Cambridge University Press, 1998.

Unknown. *The Martyrdom of Polycarp*. Translated by Alexander Roberts and James Donaldson. In *Ante-Nicene Fathers*, vol. 1. Edited by Alexander Roberts et al. Buffalo, NY: Christian Literature, 1885. Rev. and ed. by Kevin Knight. https://www.newadvent.org/fathers/0102.htm.

Van Deburg, William L. *Modern Black Nationalism: From Marcus Garvey to Louis Farrakhan*. New York: New York University Press, 1996.

Van Horne, Winston A. "The Concept of Black Power: Its Continued Relevance." *Journal of Black Studies* 37 (2007) 365–89.

Vaughn, Alden T. "Blacks in Virginia: A Note on the First Decade." *The William and Mary Quarterly*, 3rd ser., 29 (1972) 469–78.

Vipont, Elfrida. *The Story of Quakerism: 1652–1952*. London: Bannisdale, 1954.

Walker, David. *Walker's Appeal, in Four Articles; Together with a Preamble, to the Coloured Citizens of the World, but in Particular, and Very Expressly, to Those of the United States of America*. Boston, 1830. docsouth.unc.edu/nc/walker/menu.html.

Ware, Frederick L. *Methodologies of Black Theology*. Eugene, OR: Wipf & Stock, 2002.

Warner, Laceye C. *Saving Women: Retrieving Evangelistic Theology and Practice*. Waco, TX: Baylor University Press, 2007.

Warnock, Raphael G. *The Divided Mind of the Black Church: Theology, Piety and Public Witness*. New York: New York University Press, 2014.

Washington, James Melvin. *Conversations with God: Two Centuries of Prayers by African Americans*. New York: Harper, 1994.

Washington, Joseph R., Jr. *Black and White Power Subreption*. Boston: Beacon, 1969.

———. *Black Religion: The Negro and Christianity in the United States*. Boston: Beacon, 1966.

———. *The Politics of God*. Boston: Beacon, 1967.

Waters, Kristin. *Maria W. Stewart and the Roots of Black Political Thought*. Jackson: University Press of Mississippi, 2022.

Webber, Thomas L. *Deep Like the Rivers: Education in the Slave Quarter Community, 1831–1865*. New York: Norton, 1978.

Weddle, Meredith Baldwin. *Walking in the Way of Peace: Quaker Pacifism in the Seventeenth Century*. Oxford: Oxford University Press, 2001.

Wegelin, Oscar. *Jupiter Hammon: American Negro Poet. Selections from His Writings and a Bibliography*. Freeport: Books for Libraries, 1970.

Weisiger, Minor T. "The Virginia Land Office." Library of Virginia, Research Notes number 20. https://old.lva.virginia.gov/public/guides/Research_Notes_20.pdf.

Wendt, Simon. "Protection or Path Toward Revolution? Black Power and Self-Defense." *Souls: A Critical Journal of Black Politics, Culture, and Society* 9 (2007) 320–32.

Wertenbaker, Thomas J. *The Planters of Colonial Virginia*. New York: Russell & Russell, 1959.

West, Cornel. "The Four Traditions of Response." In *Prophesy Deliverance! An Afro-American Revolutionary Christianity*, 69–91. Philadelphia: Westminster, 1982.

———. *Prophesy Deliverance! An Afro-American Revolutionary Christianity* Philadelphia: Westminster, 1982.

Wheatley, Phillis. "Poems on Various Subjects, Religious and Moral by Phillis Wheatley, Negro Servant to Mr. John Wheatley, of Boston, in New England." 1773. In *The Collected Works of Phillis Wheatley*, edited by John Shields, 1–124. Oxford: Oxford University Press, 1988.

Whitlock, Jason. "The Tyre Nichols Tragedy Is a Result of Baby-Mama Culture Says Jason Whitlock." Youtube video, Jan. 27, 2023. https://www.youtube.com/watch?v=Mg6yWPAJ7oI.

Williams, George W. *History of the Negro Race in America From 1619 to 1880*. Vol. 1: *Negroes as Slaves, as Soldiers, and as Citizens*. North Charleston, NC: CreateSpace, 2014.

Williams, Preston N. "The Ethical Aspects of the 'Black Church/Black Theology' Phenomenon." *Journal of Religious Thought* 26 (1969) 34–45.

———. "James Cone and the Problem of a Black Ethic." *Harvard Theological Review* 65 (1972) 483–94.

Williams, Robert F. "From Negroes with Guns." In *The Black Power Revolt*, edited by Floyd B. Barbour et al., 149–61. Boston: Extending Horizons, 1968.

Wilmore, Gayraud S. *Black Religion and Black Radicalism: An Interpretation of the Religious History of African Americans*. Maryknoll, NY: Orbis, 1998.

———. *Pragmatic Spirituality: The Christian Faith Through an Afrocentric Lens*. New York: New York University Press, 2004.

Witvliet, Theo. "In Search of Black Christology: The Dialectic of Cross and Resurrection." *Cross Currents* 37 (1987) 17–32.

Woodson, Carter Godwin. *The Education of the Negro Prior to 1861: A History of the Education of the Colored People of the United States from the Beginning of Slavery to the Civil War*. London: Forgotten Books, 2012.

Wright, Donald R. *African Americans in the Colonial Era: From African Origins Through the American Revolution*. 2nd ed. Wheeling, IL: Harlan Davidson, 2000.

Wright, Jeremiah A., Jr. "Doing Black Theology in the Black Church." In *Living Stones in the Household of God: The Legacy and Future of Black Theology*, edited by Linda E. Thomas, 13–23. Minneapolis: Fortress, 2004.

Wright, Nathan, Jr. *Black Power and Urban Unrest*. New York: Hawthorn, 1967.

www.ingramcontent.com/pod-product-compliance
Lightning Source LLC
LaVergne TN
LVHW050618100826
845148LV00011B/1642

* 9 7 9 8 3 8 5 2 5 5 3 6 8 *